THE OBERON ANTHOLOGY OF CONTEMPORARY
AMERICAN PLAYS VOLUME TWO

THE OBERON ANTHOLOGY OF
CONTEMPORARY AMERICAN PLAYS

VOLUME TWO

Edited by Mark Subias

WHAT ONCE WE FELT by Ann Marie Healy

THE COWARD by Nick Jones

THE BOOK OF GRACE by Suzan-Lori Parks

THE EDGE OF OUR BODIES by Adam Rapp

OBERON BOOKS
LONDON

WWW.OBERONBOOKS.COM

This collection first published in 2018 by Oberon Books Ltd
521 Caledonian Road, London N7 9RH
Tel: +44 (0) 20 7607 3637 / Fax: +44 (0) 20 7607 3629
e-mail: info@oberonbooks.com
www.oberonbooks.com

Reprinted in 2019.

Cover photograph by Atisha Paulson

Visit www.oberonbooks.com to read more about all our books and to buy them. You will
also find features, author interviews and news of any author events, and you can sign up for
e-newsletters so that you're always first to hear about our new releases.

CONTENTS

WHAT ONCE WE FELT

Ann Marie Healy

Ann Marie Healy's play *What Once We Felt* was a finalist for the 2009 Susan Smith Blackburn Prize and a finalist for the Jane Chambers Playwriting Award. It was produced at Lincoln Center's LCT3 in 2009, directed by Ken Rus Schmoll, before receiving its Chicago premiere at About Face. Her play *The Legend of Minnie Willet* was developed at the National Playwrights' Conference (Eugene O'Neill Theater Center) in July 2008. *Have You Seen Steve Steven* was developed at the Sundance Theater Institute in the summer of 2007 and subsequently produced by 13P, the OBIE-Award-winning collective, directed by Anne Kauffman (Time Out NY and Flavor Pill picks). *The Night That Roger Went to Visit the Parents of His Old High School Girlfriend* premiered in the 2006 EST Marathon of One-Acts plays (directed by Andrew McCarthy). *Now That's What I Call a Storm* was the recipient of a development fellowship with MCC Theater (directed by Jo Bonney), and produced by Edge Theater Company in 2004, directed by Carolyn Cantor and featuring Marylouise Burke (Time Out NY picks). *Dearest Eugenia Haggis* was developed at LAByrinth Theater's 2004 summer intensive and The Cape Cod Theater Project and published in the anthology: *Funny, Strange, Provocative: Seven Plays* by Clubbed Thumb.

Ann Marie's plays are published through Samuel French, Smith & Kraus, Playscripts, PLAY: A Journal of Plays, and The Kenyon Review. She is an affiliated artist with the OBIE award-winning theatre company Clubbed Thumb, with whom she has often collaborated over the last ten years, including productions and workshops of her plays *Beach* and *Somewhere Someplace Else*. She is also a member of MCC's Playwrights' Coalition, a member of 13P, a former member of the Soho Rep Writer/Director Lab, a former member of EST's Youngblood, and a writing fellow at New River Dramatists.

Ann Marie was awarded a 2006/07 Sloan Commission for her new play exploring the life and work of evolutionary biologist Robert Trivers. She is currently working on commissioned plays for Clubbed Thumb/NYSCA, Yale Rep, and Playwrights Horizons. She completed her MFA with Paula Vogel and Bonnie Metzgar at Brown University (through the Lucille Lortel Fellowship.)

Introduction

During my last two years at Brown, I shared a table with Ann Marie Healy in our graduate workshop.

Ann Marie always received the writing of her peers with an open heart. Her plays revealed the revolutionary side of Ann Marie. Subversive beneath a veneer which cracked open quickly, her plays opened the envelope of possibilities for all of us in the room.

To enter into a Healy play is to fall into another world. She creates universes, with a sensation of mapping an off-stage world as we travel, vistas that go on and on. Her worlds are peopled with more than tidily written characters who fit into the equation of acting methods. We approach her work with the same thrill of discovery offered by authors such as Friedrich Durrenmatt, George Orwell, or Tolkien, following her plots as one might follow breadcrumbs into an unknown territory. But oftentimes, with a yawning forest before us, the crumbs cease to be a comforting map.

I love her work because it causes a thrill of terror married to a comic unease. With the same sly humor of Rod Sterling, she nudges us, giggling, past our resistance until there's an 'uh-oh' in our gullet: here we go. In Healy's *That's What I Call A Storm*, *Minnie Willet*, and *The Gentleman Caller*, the landscape is also familiar in the same instant that we lose our way: as familiar as the dream that has rearranged yesterday's reality in our sleep.

What Once We Felt created an immediate unified head swivel in the room, a collective hair raised on the back of our necks. We all felt the play immediately on its first reading, felt it viscerally as we read aloud from the printed page. Brilliantly unifying the policing of reproduction with the end of publishing and the printed page, Ann Marie ushers us into a parallel world that seems all too familiar In this world there are two races: the workers, now called tradepacks, riddled with genetic illness, and the keepers, the elite, genetically sequenced rulers of this world. The enormous gap between these two classes seems more than parallel with our current economic world. A world of post-apocalyptic Walmarts and fast food workers on a minimum wage is far removed from a small cosmos of the smart people, the people who attend and buy their way into the right school. How surreal is it for us to imagine an oligarchy that steps past the bodies of the poor on its way to trendy lunches at fashionable bistros?

Ironically, although I am aware of its classification as "dystopic", Ann Marie Healy's *What Once We Felt* analyzes the current war on culture and the individual voice, and the war on the working class with a surgical precision. Every now and then a play comes down the road that makes me feel alarm and an attention to present and prescient danger. *What Once We Felt* is one of those rare plays.

Paula Vogel

Production history

World Premiere at Lincoln Center Theater/LCT3 on November 9, 2009
under the direction of Ken Rus Schmoll

Scenic Designer: Kris Stone
Costume Designer: Linda Cho
Lighting Designer: Japhy Weideman
Sound Designer: Leah Gelpe
Stage Manager: Jane Pole

Presented by Lincoln Center Theater
Artistic Director, André Bishop; Executive Director Bernard Gersten;
LCT3 Artistic Director, Paige Evans

Cast

FEMALE SERVER/CLAIRE/JOAN:	Opal Alladin
MACY:	Mia Barron
FRANNY/LAURA/BORDER GUARD:	Marsha Stephanie Blake
CHERYL/BENITA/PAULINA PETROVSKY:	Lynn Hawley
VIOLET:	Ronete Levenson
ASTRID/YARROW:	Ellen Parker

Characters

VIOLET	A woman of indiscriminate age
MACY	30 or so
CHERYL	Doubles with BENITA/VOICE of PAULINA PETROVSKY
CLAIRE	Doubles with THE FEMALE SERVER/JOAN**
ASTRID	Doubles with YARROW
LAURA	Doubles with FRANNY/BORDER GUARD**

THE RECORDED VOICES of INSPECTOR OVID and THE SNOUT

**It is also possible to double cast CLAIRE with FRANNY and the BORDER GUARD & LAURA with THE FEMALE SERVER and JOAN

TIME
Long beyond the seven million two hundred sixty-sixth thousandth DNA micro array sequencing scan

LOCATION
A city by the river

The slash
//
Indicates a point of interruption

ACT ONE

We see the shadows and light of an early morning dawn in a city. As we watch this subtle transition occur, we hear the following radio voices in the dusty darkness. They sound tinny and scratched, like the memory of an old radio show.

INSPECTOR OVID: The thing is Snout, there's just no telling what surprises are in store. Look at the two of us for example: when we first met, I never would have imagined that we would be talking to each other.

THE SNOUT: There were plenty of other owners before you and some of them were pretty smart fellows. The difference is that none of them *believed*. None of them *believed* that I could really talk.

INSPECTOR OVID: So you're saying I'm more gullible?

THE SNOUT: I'm saying you have a better imagination Inspector Ovid. If you can't allow for it in your imagination then you'll never see it come true in reality.

INSPECTOR OVID: If we only just believe, we can make anything come true. Do you believe Snout?

THE SNOUT: I believe Inspector Ovid! I believe!

INSPECTOR OVID: Close your eyes and tell me you believe!

THE SNOUT: *(A cartoon whisper.)* I believe Inspector Ovid. I really believe.

INSPECTOR OVID: If we all believe in The Transition, we can change the world!

(The radio voices fade out or get cut off. By the time this aural section ends, we see CHERYL sitting behind a booth. Somewhere, far off in the distance, there is a giant, animated billboard. It displays a goofy looking INSPECTOR OVID and his cartoon dog. Only the glowing text is visible from so far away. It reads: "Number One on the Bestseller List EIGHTEEN YEARS in a Row!".)

SCENE ONE:
MACY AND CHERYL

CHERYL: Next

> *(MACY comes forward in patchwork attempts at stylish garb, carrying a large leather bag.)*

MACY: Hello I –

CHERYL: You're not next
I said // next

MACY: I know what you said
But you're speaking to the line
I am not really in // the line

CHERYL: I don't care where you are Miss
I want you to come forward when you are next
Not *Now* but *Next* //
(Calling out to an unseen person at the head of a line.)
NEXT!

MACY: You don't understand –
That line is for –
(She lowers her voice.)
(I'm a Keeper.)

> *(Pause.)*

CHERYL: You're a Keeper

MACY: I was going to take a cab across the bridge but then –
I thought it might be nice to walk

CHERYL: Why didn't you just scan your card at the machine?

MACY: It was out of order

CHERYL: Give me your scan card
(Calling out to an impatient person in the line.)
I'll be with you in a minute!

> *(MACY is searching in the depths of her cavernous leather bag for her scan card.)*

MACY: *(The following is no more than an imperceptible mumble.)*
(It's in here somewhere because I just had it and then I popped it in and it's like why do they make these damn bags so big it's like a limitless pool down there and any old thing can just fall in and – .)
(She produces a clear, slim "card" from her bag.)
Here it is!

> *(CHERYL "scans" MACY's card in an unseen machine. MACY speaks simply to pass the time.)*

MACY: They say these *(Another vague gesture towards the machine.)*
These bioinfowhatzit machines
Are getting more sophisticated –
Or sensitive –
Or both or –
Whatever –
You know what I mean –
At their readings?
So that makes them
(Vague gesture.)
Read better I guess.

CHERYL: Who says that?

MACY: I don't know
They do
Someone did or does
I've just heard that from friends, I guess
Have you heard that?

CHERYL: I'm a Tradepack so –
No.

MACY: Oh
Sorry of course I'm so sorry
(Another small pause.)

MACY: *(Looking at the machine.)* It's only supposed to take five seconds

CHERYL: It takes as long as it takes

MACY: !But it's been so much longer than five seconds!
I'm sorry
I know none of this is your fault

And I totally see how difficult and boring it must be
Having someone like me going off
In such a boring way
I must seem like "that woman"
"That woman" who goes off in "that way"
Do I seem like that?
Well I'm not –
I swear –
I'm really more –
I mean I'm the woman who makes fun of "that woman"
Do you know what I mean?
I'm "that woman"
So
So
Okay the truth is:
I'm going to a very important dinner
And I wanted to walk across the bridge just to calm my nerves
It's the kind of dinner
(Looking at the machine.)
!UNBELIEVABLE!
(Sorry.)
Still going?

CHERYL: It takes as long as it takes

MACY: It's the kind of dinner that just might
Change my life
In its way
And it's at Panet and everyone always says it's impossible
To even get a table at Panet these days
And it would be lovely
Don't you think
To just show up on time for once
No one ever shows up on time anymore
Have you noticed

      (CHERYL stares at her.)

CHERYL: What's Panet?

MACY: Panet?

Panet
It's a It's a
Bistro?
They serve carpaccio?
Urgh! Sorry
I meant
I meant
Panet
It's a bistro
On the river
On the other side of the bridge

CHERYL: It takes as long as it takes

MACY: *(Taking note of the machine.)*
Oh look!
It read me –
See –
Look –
It's done so –
Can I go?
Can I?
(CHERYL stops to fiddle with the unseen machine.)
This city –
Honestly this city is such a mess –
And I know it's not your fault
And I'm sorry to bore you but honestly
This whole place is headed for the shitter –
And now I'm late I'm late I'm late
So can I go now can I?

(The smallest of pauses.)

CHERYL: You can go.

MACY: Thank you Oh thank you so much
You've been a gem you know that
(She stops for a moment to take in CHERYL.)
I'm not usually such a wretch
Please believe me

It's just this dinner
It really might change my life
You know how that is
Oh! Late late late
Ta ta!

> *(MACY is off and gone. CHERYL watches her for a moment.)*

CHERYL: *(Under her breath.)*
Ta ta

> *(CHERYL looks out to the rest of the line waiting for her. She returns to work.)*

CHERYL: Next

SCENE TWO:
MACY & ASTRID
CHERYL & FRANNY

When the lights come up, we see the back scaffolding and electrical wiring of the giant, animated billboard. The outline of the goofy Inspector head casts a slight shadow over the scene and it moves back and forth in stilted animated motion. The silhouette of the cartoon dog tail moves back and forth mechanically in time with the head. The whole billboard is ever so slightly closer as we are oriented in an entirely different direction in the city now.

A cool light from the river water is cast over the outdoor dining at Panet. MACY is sitting with ASTRID, her literary agent, at a discreet table on the patio. Though there are no other tables in sight, it is clear that the two women are conscious of being overheard.

Perhaps we see a part of CHERYL and FRANNY's home in silhouette?

A FEMALE SERVER stands by ASTRID and MACY's table, ready to take their order.

ASTRID: Yes – I'll have your Duck Confit
(Reading the "small print" on the menu with some skepticism.)
(Now grazed with little sprigs of thyme
And accompanied by a Peach Melba Dust.)

Peach Melba…Dust?
What happened to my favorite Duck Confit dish?
This is a bistro
This is not a chemistry lab
I don't want *Dust* in my *Duck Confit*
(The FEMALE SERVER is about to speak but ASTRID runs over her.)
Honestly
Nothing of quality lasts in this world
Tsk tsk
(Motioning to MACY.) She will have the Short Ribs and
Don't tell me there is dust on those too…
And
And
(A final moment to inspect the menu with no thought of asking MACY.)
No no
That's all
C'est tout!

FEMALE SERVER: Yes M'am

ASTRID: Wait!
Wait!
One more of these
Right?
(Motioning to the drinks.)
One more of these these
(Vague hand gesture towards the giant fruity drinks.)
Pink Things
Bring this first
Before the food

FEMALE SERVER: Yes M'am

> *(The FEMALE SERVER goes. They watch her quietly. When she is safely out of distance, they continue to talk.)*

MACY: Okay
So // So?

ASTRID: So they read it
And they really love it

MACY: What does that *mean?*

ASTRID: They really love it means
They really love it
They want to publish it
You know
If if if //
Always if

MACY: If what?
They *want* to publish it or they *will?*

ASTRID: They *want to* //
If they want to badly enough
They *will*

MACY: There's a big difference
You know in intention
I've seen this sort of
Thing
Well you know that last //
Time

ASTRID: Of course I know that last time
We all know that last time //
Macy all of us ALL OF US
(Have heard about that last time.)

MACY: Oh god did I talk about that
Too much?
I should shut up about that last time
But they // you know they

ASTRID: I know I know
But *this* time is not like *that* time
They love *this*

MACY: And I'm willing to do some rewrites
I know I've left things somewhat ambiguous
So I'm open to discussing //
The ambiguity
(Not discussing the origin of it
But discussing the idea of the origin of it –
Or the idea of –
Whatever.)

ASTRID: Oh sure sure
　　No no that wasn't up –
　　Dear don't talk to yourself
　　You sound insane
　　When you do that don't do that Macy please
　　Now the rewrites weren't up for debate //
　　They just said

MACY: Was something else up for debate?
　　Astrid?
　　Astrid?

ASTRID: No no
　　They love it //
　　They love it

MACY: They *want* to publish it
　　Or they *will?* //
　　Astrid?

ASTRID: They want to
　　And they will
　　There is a different item //
　　Up for debate but it's
　　Negli –

MACY: So they want to
　　But we don't know if they will
　　(Just like last time.)

ASTRID: It's just a small thing
　　And we don't need to talk about it now
　　For now let's celebrate
　　We'll have that duck peach melba
　　Dusty Whatever Dish
　　And I will get good and drunk //
　　And tell you far too many juicy tales of –

MACY: I don't want to celebrate
　　No no Astrid
　　I want you to tell me –

　　　　(The FEMALE SERVER walks over and distributes ASTRID's drink.
　　　　They are silent in her presence. She leaves.)

ASTRID: Look at this
    Fruity spiky thing //
    In my drink

MACY: What is the item up for debate?

ASTRID: Did you see this
    Did you see this thing? //
    Is this a kumquat?

MACY: What is the item up for debate
    Tell me

ASTRID: They have a favor
    That's all
    It's not the //
    It's not

MACY: A favor!
    I wrote a novel!
    Why don't they do me a –

ASTRID: I offered them something in exchange
    For publishing your novel //
    It's not a big deal

MACY: !I thought that in exchange for *publishing my novel*
    !They got to read my novel in its *published form*
    !Exchange!?
    !Exchange!?

> *(ASTRID inspects her for a moment and takes a sip of her drink. It is possible, from the look on ASTRID's face, that some of the other Panet patrons have overheard MACY's outburst.)*

ASTRID: My dear
    You may think it is all the rage to express
    Ta passion
    But the rest of us –
    Your elders –
    We are not impressed.
    You might do well to tuck that temperament away
    Not the Bright Young Thing you once were
    Are you?

MACY: Typical

This is totally typical

!I give up then!

!The End!

!I am not in the business of bartering for my book!

ASTRID: You want to know what *really* happened last time?

This is what happened last time:

(Gesturing towards MACY's passionate display of emotion.)

This

We were minutes away from signing the deal and then they saw you –

(Vague gesture for MACY's temper.)

And then we lost –

(Vague gesture for "the whole deal".)

And now we're what?

What are we now?

MACY: !Now we're –

!We're –

!We're –

ASTRID: *(Displays of patience and a scan around the room.)*

Now we're not anything my dear

Now we are *reserved*

We are friendly to all

But we are *reserved.*

The refined reserve Macy

Is the "little black dress" of publishing.

It is always appropriate.

It is always en vogue.

A refined reserve

Will placate all

And

It will compliment my flamboyance perfectly!

(Motioning to her drink and taking a big gulp.)

Yes! It is indeed a kumquat!

(Slight Pause.)

Comprends ma cherie?

MACY: Yes

I understand.

A refined reserve

I get it.
(A little pause to start the conversation again.)
What what is the item up for debate?

ASTRID: The publisher
Claire Monsoon
You remember // her?

MACY: !Oh no *Claire Monsoon*?!
!Terrible taste!
!In books! In life! //
!Claire! Oh god a favor *for her*?!

ASTRID: Shhhhhhhhhh
Just listen
SHT!

MACY: I'm listening
Sorry
Refined reserve //
Listening

ASTRID: Because you don't even want kids
Anyway //
You said so yourself

MACY: Kids?
What do kids have to //
Do with this?

ASTRID: She
Claire
You know
She likes the novel
But it's *literary* and
You know how they are about *literary* these days
But they like it //
They said so

MACY: You said they loved it
Not liked it but loved it

ASTRID: She does love it
But Claire takes convincing

I have to serve up my secret Astrid sauce –
You know she just wants
Trash
She wants oh
You know
She wants all self-help
All the time
She wants fast and cheap digital downloads
Or else she wants Inspector Ovid
And his stupid talking dog
Oh my god will they ever stop pushing that inane Inspector Ovid on us?
So I just
You know
I threw something more enticing into the mix

MACY: More enticing than the actual novel?
Enticing as in?
(MACY tries to restrain herself.)
Enticing as in what?

ASTRID: Enticing as in –

> *(The FEMALE SERVER reappears with the food. They watch her silently. She goes and they begin to speak openly again.)*

ASTRID: *(Inspecting her food.)*
Enticing as in –
Well without me throwing a little extra into the mix –
Let's face it Macy:
The most you might have hoped for was was was
A few hundred digital downloads on some godforsaken hard drive who knows where
No *pizzazz*
No *olde thyme glamour*
Lord knows we all hoped that a novel of crystalline detail,
An old fashioned novel of "biting satire and dystopian leanings"
A novel that both pushed the form forward and yet referred back in time
To the Classics
To the Western Canon
A novel like that might somehow –

(ASTRID grabs at an air dream with her hands and then sets it free, sadly.)
But it seems that your –
Well it's –
This –
Quite frankly Macy, the book is just not enticing enough
On its own
To to to –

MACY: Not enticing enough to what?

ASTRID: Not enticing enough to make anyone want to read it.

>   *(Pause.)*

MACY: Oh
Not enticing enough to do that

>   *(Pause: fork on plate food back and forth back and forth and then set down without a single bite.)*

MACY: Well then
I guess this dinner is over

ASTRID: Macy
You haven't even touched –
Look at this food:
This is beautiful food!
You never get to eat at Panet
This food will change your life //
Enjoy enjoy my dear

MACY: *Change your life*
Do you know
I
On the way here
I
I wanted to walk across the bridge and the machines were broken
So some dreary clerk gave me a reading
And I had to wait for the results with all the Tradepacks
At the border crossing on the bridge
And her face
This Tradepack clerk
The way she looked at me

I told her I was going to a very important dinner at Panet
And she said
She said
"What's Panet"
What's Panet
This world is so –
(She looks up at ASTRID.)
Sorry
Never mind

ASTRID: *(Pulling a kumquat out and eating it with her fingers.)*
You really should try one
They're stuffed full of liquor
Like sucking a shot from a wet sock!

MACY: What did you offer Claire to *entice* her?

ASTRID: I shouldn't have
It was ahem
A very unconventional contingency //
I shouldn't have even tried

MACY: What did you offer her?

        (Pause.)

ASTRID: Claire mentioned to me that she –
She's in a bit of a sticky situation with the RSS –
That is –
Well she would like to download a baby but –
She can't, you see
She just –
She can't

MACY: I don't understand
Why can't she?

ASTRID: Because she –
Well –
It –
You know –
She doesn't have the right scan card

MACY: !Wait!
!Wait!
!Claire Monsoon is a!
A…
!Tradepack!?

ASTRID: *(Looking around Panet to see if anyone heard that.)*
Would you *please* keep your voice down *Please*

MACY: *(Lowered voice.)*
Claire Monsoon is a (Tradepack.)?

ASTRID: I don't know
She didn't say as much to me but –
Yes: It seems that Claire Monsoon is a *(Whisper.)* Tradepack
People used to be able to slip through the RSS
In the very early stages of The Transition
It used to be much more common
Wealthy people –
Powerful –
Someone like Claire Monsoon –
She probably paid off some bureaucrat at RSS
To keep it quiet
I've heard some people do that
So –

MACY: Claire Monsoon is a
Wow
Wow
I never would have
Wow

ASTRID: When The Transition started
You probably barely remember
They didn't have us all sequenced and added to the system
Not like now
It was totally chaotic back // then

MACY: Wow
So
So wait
So what was the item up for debate?
Astrid?

ASTRID: I wanted to entice her to do one last great novel in print
  Before they shut down all the presses
  And toss out all the pulp
  Not just some Self-Help Lipstick Stomach Staple Who Ha
  But a real gesture towards literature!
  A very special work of "biting satire and dystopian leanings"
  An exquisite, gold-embossed trim, first edition, print published novel
  that goes by the name of:

ASTRID and MACY: *Terror's Peon*

ASTRID: *(She tries to breeze through this next section.)*
  So I told her if she would publish *Terror's Peon* in print
  You might *(Vague gesture for "loan".)* her your scan card
  Just for a few months

MACY: I might *what?*

ASTRID: She wants to use your Keeper card
  To download a baby
  She can't download with a Tradepack card, of course //
  So

MACY: Wait
  !I might *what?!*

ASTRID: Loan her
  You might loan her your scan // card

MACY: *Loan her?!*
  Loan her!
  What?
  That's not not not
  She shouldn't even
  And what did she say?
  What could she possibly say // to that offer?

ASTRID: Yes

MACY: What?
  What did she say?

ASTRID: Yes
  She said yes

She said she would publish it
In print
Full slot
The last print published novel
Ever
Terror's Peon
Over 500,000 copies in the initial printing
But that's just the first run
She wants to make it look like one last farewell to fiction
Grand fanfare all that
Every airport on the planet will carry you
The big shakes before you know
She goes back to her Inspector Ovid and the talking dog trash
If you would
Just your card
No one will ever even know it's you
No one will ever know anything at all
They'll all think she's having her baby
Just like any other Keeper
(*ASTRID takes in MACY's face.*)
I'm sorry
It was wrong of me
I know you young ladies only get one download
But you said you didn't care for children
I didn't think it would matter
If you gave your download to //
To To To

MACY: I don't care about my download
!My download?
That's the last –
I care about –
My life –
My life *outside* of incarceration –
My
My
They execute women for this
That's what I've heard
The RSS has

In the North
In those weird little mountain towns
With the fucked up goats
They do
I've heard stories
If I went up for trial
In the North
I could be executed in some weird little mountain town
With a line of fucked up goats
Looking me in the eyes while I died
Alone
I would die
Alone
With the goats
Or
Or
This is the RSS
This is not your grandmother baking soda bread and handing you a
long tall glass of milk
This is the R-S-S
These women are MOTHERFUCKERS –

ASTRID: *(Clucking.)*
Is this just you or is this –

MACY: What?

ASTRID: Is this just you or is this generational?
This this behavior.
First of all, keep your voice down please.
Do I need to remind you:
We are in a public place Macy.
Not just a public place but *the* public place:
Panet
You do not shout out *(A whisper.) motherfucker* at
Panet
Honestly
Who raised you girls?
You young girls were raised in a school of barracudas
What happened to manners and
Tsk tsk

Sit up straight
Posture please my dear
Sit up straight
Using knives and forks and small sips
Swish the water in your mouth
Don't gulp
Mastication please mastication
All right
Let's discuss the issue at hand
Like *ladies*
Yes?
Okay?

MACY: Yes
Okay

ASTRID: Okay
Ladies?

MACY: Ladies yes
Ladies

ASTRID: Now
This is not about mountain goats
This is not even about the RSS
This is about your book:
Who will read your book
If your book is never published
Eh?
This is a simple contractual arrangement
You won't go to trial
You won't be put in prison
You are simply
This is simply
A business proposal

MACY: Loaning Claire Monsoon
My scan card
Has nothing to do with the business
Or the craft
Or the whatever
Of writing a novel

ASTRID: So you say
  Duly noted
  (ASTRID takes a moment to chomp on her kumquat drink.)
  She's just one woman Macy
  She's just one woman and she wants to download a baby
  Perhaps her DNA is less than perfect
  According to the RSS
  Perhaps
  But
  (A gesture for "is this so bad?".)
  At my age, I find perfection overrated
  (She waves her arms in a vague gesture.)
  Let's eat and
  Just forget the whole thing
  Eat eat!
  Those short ribs are positively sweating with delicious shivers!
  You must eat!

        (Pause. They eat in silence.)

MACY: The last print published novel
  Ever

ASTRID: Ever yes ever
  Farewell to Fiction!
  No more
  I hope you like Inspector Ovid
  They put his talking dog to sleep in Series Seven
  And then a canine angel comes to save the day

MACY: Right well

ASTRID: Eat eat
  Oh look there's Vivien LeFray
  She's working with Claire on that DNA diet scheme
  One of those Digi-Direct Downloads
  (A wave and then a sigh.)
  Seven secrets to something something

        (They both eat quietly.)

MACY: That clerk //
  I keep thinking of her face

ASTRID: What clerk

MACY: That woman
That Tradepack
You know who she reminded me of?
The Tradepack character in my novel
Just the way I imagined her face
Just the way I imagined her
Attitude
It was like I knew her
It was like we should have had some kind of *(Vague gesture for "connection".)*
But all I could do was ramble on and on about this dinner
(The FEMALE SERVER comes through to clear some dishes.)
Change your life
(MACY watches her leave the table and speaks to herself.)
Never mind

ASTRID: Hmmmmmmm
I think our waitress might be a Keeper
Don't you?
Did you see her hands?
So long and lean
Total Keeper hands
They must be running out of Tradepacks
For the service sector
Did you hear that?
Didn't someone say that?
Macy?

MACY: What?

ASTRID: I lost you for a moment

MACY: How can I be sure that no one would ever find out?

ASTRID: Oh! Well!
This is Claire Monsoon we're talking about here
Claire Monsoon has her ducks in a row

MACY: Yes
Okay yes
Sure
Yes

ASTRID: Yes
    She has her ducks in a row?

MACY: Yes
    I said
    Yes
    She can use my scan card
    Yes

        (Pause.)

ASTRID: All right
    Well then
    Congratulations

MACY: *(MACY pulls out the scan card and slides it to ASTRID.)*
    Take it
    Just take it and put it away and
    And let's
    I want one of those
    With the kumquat
    Get me one of those //
    Immediately

ASTRID: Absolutely
    Oh and
    This goes without saying
    I trust you will utilize
    That refined reserve
    When you go in to speak with them
    No one can
    You realize
    No one can ever know
    Any of the details.

MACY: Are you kidding me?
    Of course I'll be reserved
    I'll be impenetrable

ASTRID: Well then
    (She raises her pink drink in a cheer.)
    Cheers to you Macy

MACY: Look at my ridiculously useless life
   The only thing that makes any of it worthwhile
   Is getting people to read that book
   If I can just get people to read it

ASTRID: Not just read it dear
   Love it!
   They'll love it!

MACY: Just so long as they read it
   I will be refined
   I will be reserved
   I will be the cipher of Perseus Publishing

SCENE THREE:
CHERYL & FRANNY
MACY & ASTRID

MACY and ASTRID continue to eat and drink at PANET but we shift our focus to FRANNY's garret apartment. Almost the entire room is subsumed by darkness as it sits under the shadow of Inspector Ovid's head on the billboard.

CHERYL enters wearing her clerk uniform. She goes about her business, taking off work clothing and changing into a housedress. She turns on a bare light bulb or lights a lantern, casting more shadows. She kisses FRANNY perfunctorily and adjusts her blankets. FRANNY does not respond. CHERYL sits next to her and pulls out knitting. She knits and knits quietly next to FRANNY.

The knitting needles click against each other. Knitting and knitting until it seems that the scene might really be about CHERYL knitting. She holds up the pattern against FRANNY's body: it is a shawl. She counts off the numbers under her breath, quietly. And then, finally, she speaks.

CHERYL: A
   Keeper
   Came through my line
   You should have seen her
   Mom
   You should have seen her
   Attitude

Back in the day
Before The Transition
She wouldn't have dared
She said
When she left
Do you know what she said?
Mom?

(No response. Knitting knitting. Knitting knitting.)

She said Ta Ta
She said *Ta Ta* and
She told me about
Some bistro or some
Some some dinner that would change her life
Something
She said she was going to a dinner that would change her life
And I said
Fine you can go
Something something

(Pause. Knitting Knitting. Knitting Knitting.)

Change your life
Change your life
I didn't even know bistros
Still existed
I didn't know
You could just go to a dinner
A bistro
And change your life

(FRANNY *quietly moans in pain. She is essentially unconscious with pain.*)

Oh
Oh no
Oh no I'm so sorry
Please stop

FRANNY: Ppppllllleeeaaasssseee Piiiilllllllllll // pplllllllease

CHERYL: They won't give us more pills
You know that don't you
I would do anything
But I –

> *(CHERYL tries to resume her knitting. She knits she knits she knits to control her rage. FRANNY moans with more quiet agony.)*

Oh Mom
Oh Mom please
No shhhh No No

> *(She holds FRANNY like a baby.)*

No no
Shhhhhhhhh
Shhhhhhhhh
It's going to be just fine
I'm so sorry
So so sorry
I'm
I'm
Ta ta
I can't stop hearing her voice
In my head
Ta ta
*Ta t*a
Over and over
I hear her say it
(CHERYL is crying silently with rage.)
Ta ta
She said
Ta ta
Change your life
Change your life
Ta ta
Why do you get to change your life?

> *(CHERYL grips her knitting needle with intensity before a quick light shift.)*

SCENE FOUR:
VIOLET

Behind VIOLET, we see the vestiges of the old, electronic billboard towering in the background like the skeletal remains of a past species. It is difficult to make out what it once advertised, or even the purpose it once served. There is a piece of flapping plastic or shellacked microfiche that hangs off of it like sagging flesh.

VIOLET: *(She holds a gold-embossed, print published book in her hands.)*
None of the adults ever talked about it
I don't know that they ever even thought to explain
But when I was around eleven or twelve
I suddenly needed to know

Why are we called Tradepacks?

I asked my caretaker
And she picked me up and she said:
We are people who get sick
Maybe not today
Maybe not tomorrow
But eventually
All Tradepacks get sick

And it's true
Because when I started high school
I would wake up in the morning and see it:
My caretaker would stop
Breathless
On her way up the stairs
My caretaker would sit and rest on the couch
In the middle of the day
She would sleep for twelve hours
Fourteen hours
Bruises on her back
Dark circles round her eyes
My caretaker wouldn't get out of bed

When I sat with her
In the evenings
When I knew that she was getting near the end
I told her I thought it was unfair.
I knew that some people got doctors
I knew that some people got pills
Why not us?

She told me to read the good book
(*She motions to the gold-embossed book in her hands.*)
She told me to follow the serials
We are Tradepacks
She said
And we are proud
Our bodies carry disease away from this world
So that others might live
Longer
Happier
Healthier
Lives

Not everyone has a purpose, Violet
She told me
Not everyone is so lucky
Some people search their whole lives
Without ever really knowing what they believe
Why they exist
Some people don't ever even know how they feel
You will meet them
She said
Flailing lost souls
Looking for the light
And you will feel sorry for them
Lost in a sea of choices
Not like us:
We have only one choice to make
When
When to depart this world for the next
And for that, we are special

It's all in the book
She said

She died that year
So did my closest friend
And some of my classmates
They started closing down the schools
When too many of the students stayed home sick

Me?
I kept waiting to get a cough
Or an ache
A fever
Or dark bruises

All Tradepacks get sick
Eventually

Don't they?

SCENE FIVE:
MACY & CLAIRE

A dramatic light shift to MACY and CLAIRE in CLAIRE's office: a leather sofa, an obelisk sculpture, not a book in sight. From the soaring views of the city, the Inspector Ovid billboard sits like a tiny flag on the horizon. CLAIRE has her back to us. When she turns around to face MACY, she is visibly pregnant.

CLAIRE:
Sit down
Sit down
Here or here
(Motioning to her leather sofa.)
That's a Rofra
Thanks to Inspector Ovid
And his talking dog
What I did with
Digi-Direct Downloads
Corporate gave me a Rofra

It feels like butter
Feel it
Just feel it
Butter right?
I know that's a cliché
But I felt it and I really thought
My god! This actually feels like butter!
Who said that
First?
That butter thing
Who made that up?

MACY: I don't know

CLAIRE: Well I know it's a cliché
But I really don't care
Things are cliché
Because they're true
They've been tested
Originality is overrated
Really
Don't you think?
No one understands it
It's too busy being original
To communicate anything
Me, I like communication
Butter right?

MACY: Hmmmmm
Wow!
Just for Inspector Ovid
And Digi-Direct?
Wow
Wow

CLAIRE: Inspector Ovid
And my Digi-Direct series of self-help
Seven secrets to something or other
A collection that aggregates celebrity DNA
And sells to women of like code
It allows Perseus Publishing to completely double dip

Fucking fantastic
Fucking fantastic
Right?
We get paid by the cosmetic industry as well as selling retail to the the the
Consumers
The Readers, I mean, sorry
The people who actually buy the crap
It's like paying to see an ad

>*(Pause.)*

MACY: So

CLAIRE: So

>*(MACY is waiting for CLAIRE to say something about her pregnancy but she hears nary a word.)*

MACY: Um
Congratulations

CLAIRE: Hmmmm
For what?
What are you talking about?

MACY: For
For
For Digi-Direct…?

CLAIRE: Oh!
Yes!
For Digi-Direct!
For that!
Well
You know how everyone is these days.
In my day –
When I first arrived –
Well the whole business
Had gone to crap.
No one was buying books:
Books were quaint little objects that sat on the desks
Of twee little people;
The kind of people I hated –

Then and now –
The kind of people who said phrases in French
Like "It's so lovely when we travel en famille!"
Twee people like trinkets lifted from some flea market in some
Godforsaken seaside town.
Covered with dust
All moaning and groaning:
"Oh! I just love books!"
"Oh I just want to live in a home surrounded by books!"
"Oh I don't trust people who don't have books!"
Books books books

MACY: Books books books…

CLAIRE: You know what I call it?
    A fetish:
    It's freakish, I think
    Fetishizing these outdated packs of information
    The majority of which people no longer even open
    Sitting on shelves gathering mites and mites and –
    What did you just say?

MACY: Nothing

CLAIRE: No really though
    You just said something

MACY: No
    No I didn't

CLAIRE: Let's just say you did
    Okay?
    Just for fun
    Let's just say you said a word
    What word did you say?

MACY: I
    I don't know

CLAIRE: The word you said was
    "Digitize"

MACY: Okay

CLAIRE: Say it
Say it Macy

MACY: Say it
Like
Now?

CLAIRE: Yes
Say it

MACY: Ah
Okay
Digitize

CLAIRE: Exactly!
That's exactly what I said
And that's where my Digi-Direct innovation comes in
They're text yes okay but they're
They're
Condensed
Digitally condensed
Digi-D is only the most essential
Digi-D is only the most necessary
Data
We've number crunched the themes
We've number crunched the characters
And you simply punch in what you want to know
From the algorithms
Narrative that is *data-driven:*
Do away with interpretation
To help offset the miscommunication
Remember me?
Remember how much I like communication!
Butter
I am not a fan of miscommunication
Are you?
Macy?

MACY: I'm
No.

CLAIRE: *(She breaks into a "pep talk".)*
　　My editors ANALyze
　　My editors THEORize
　　And then
　　When all the analog work is done
　　My editors DIGItize
　　In order to SYNTHEsize
　　That's my little pep talk
　　To them of course
　　To them not to you
　　Ha ha ha ha ha

MACY: Ha ha ha ha ha
　　(Fake laughter giving way to some concern.)
　　Who
　　Who
　　Who is editing my novel?

CLAIRE: I am
　　I am dear
　　Didn't Astrid tell you
　　I am of course
　　I'll have my line editor step in
　　Laura
　　You'll meet her later
　　She'll do some of the heavy lifting
　　But this project, this is all mine
　　I'd like to keep the big picture work between the two of us

MACY: Because
　　She said
　　Well I don't mean to sound presumptuous
　　But Astrid said you
　　Loved it

CLAIRE: Loved it?

MACY: So
　　I'm
　　I'm really just thrilled to be here
　　To be working on my book with someone who –

CLAIRE: She said I loved it?

MACY: She did
    Uh
    Is that wrong?
    You don't
    Love it?

CLAIRE: No no
    No no no no no
    That's not what I'm saying
    Terror's Peon is our last
    Print published novel ever
    Ever ever
    Ever in fiction
    Ever
    So
    So
    To *Terror's Peon!*
    Congratulations!

MACY: Thank you!
    Uh
    Congratulations to you too!
    That is
    I'm doing all this
    (Vague gesture.)
    Or I did all that
    Because I really just want people to read my book

CLAIRE: Oh course you do
    Why else would you have written it?

MACY: So I guess
    Well what I'm asking is
    What did you think of it?
    When you read it?

CLAIRE: I thought it was
    It was
    Well to begin with
    I should say

We're publishing it
We're moving forward
You got the contracts
You got the cover art
By now you must have received the whole
Kit and
Kit and
What's that other word
Kit and whatever
Thousands, millions
Of copies of you
You to the nth degree
So there
Okay?

MACY: No no
That's wonderful
But what did you think?

CLAIRE: I think
I thought
(She smiles at MACY.)
It's
Not really
It's not my thing
There
That's all
Oh one other quick thing
We might want to change the title
Don't you think?

MACY: You don't like the title *Terror's Peon?*

CLAIRE: Hmm:
We'll see
TBD
Yes
That's all really
Just a title change consideration
And maybe you know maybe working a bit with *(A vague gesture.)*
So that's it.

MACY: Working a bit with *(Trying to imitate the vague gesture.)*

CLAIRE: The the
(Doing the gesture.)
You know
That

MACY: How should I work on it?

CLAIRE: You know
The
The
(Vague gesture.)
Maybe you can just tweak that climax a bit
Where it all comes together
That's all
Oh and then change the title
But I mentioned that already

MACY: Do you mean when the…

CLAIRE: Yes?

MACY: When the
(Doing the gesture again.)
Happens
Tweak that?

CLAIRE: Uh
Well sure yes that
Maybe just look at that more closely
It feels like you could spend more time on it

MACY: Right *(…I am gonna be sick.)*

CLAIRE: Excuse me?

MACY: I think I'm gonna be sick
Right here on your Rofra

CLAIRE: Uh excuse me
Miss Blonsky
Are you all right?

(A little pause.)

MACY: You haven't read it have you?

CLAIRE: What?
    Of course I've *read* it

MACY: !I don't think you have!

CLAIRE: I'm not going to *argue* with you
    I've read it //
    So there

MACY: Ohmygod Ohmygod
    I don't think you've even read my book
    What is it about?

CLAIRE: You know as well as I do what it's about

MACY: What is it about?
    You haven't read it have you?

CLAIRE: It's a
    A
    A biting satire with dystopian leanings
    So

MACY: !So!
    !So you've read the *back flap copy*?!
    !SO?

                (CLAIRE stands up, further emphasizing the state of her very pregnant belly.)

CLAIRE: Miss Blonsky
    You are making it very difficult to have any kind of
    Logistical conversation
    Maybe you want to
    Take a breath
    Take a walk even
    Maybe you want to reconsider
    Your approach?

MACY: *(Recovers herself.)*
    Excuse me
    I
    I was just
    Excuse me

CLAIRE: I have read it Macy. *I have*

MACY: Yes

    Of course you have
    How could you be my editor if you had never read my book?
    How could you –
    (Her disbelief leads to a slightly panicked laugh.)
    How could that ha ha ha ha ha happen?
    Let's continue

CLAIRE: So

    You'll be receiving a full copy of your
    Book Tour schedule
    Sometime
    They'll arrange all that
    In publicity
    And you know it's our biggest
    Offering
    This season
    Our last offering
    In print
    I told you that
    Did I tell you that?
    So you'll do *The Talk of the Town*
    And then we'll get you on *Morning Muse*
    With Paulina Petrovsky
    She's very short
    Just FYI
    Don't be surprised because she is extremely short but they shoot her
    Standing on a box
    So there's that
    I always like to tell my authors that
    You know, it will be my biggest push this year so
    So all is well
    Isn't it?

MACY:

    All is //
    Well
    Thank you

CLAIRE: This is what you wanted
    Correct
    This is what you asked for correct?

MACY: Is that what Astrid told you?
    What did Astrid tell you?

CLAIRE: Astrid
    Sold us
    She sold us a deal
    We couldn't refuse
    That's all
    That's the way agents work though
    You know how they are
    They lie
    Everyone lies
    In some way or another
    Don't they Macy?

MACY: Do they?
    (A quick change of subject.)
    So
    Is there anything
    Else
    What else should I do?

CLAIRE: You just sit tight
    And Laura will get in touch with the line edits
    That's all
    That easy

MACY: Claire.

CLAIRE: Yes?

        *(There is a pause but MACY hesitates. CLAIRE is distracted by a message
        on an "electronic gizmo doo-dad" machine. She scrolls down and tsk tsks.)*

CLAIRE: Tsk Tsk
    RSS e-flash
    Hmmmm....
    Oh dear
    Seems some border clerk

Went home and killed her sick mother with a
(Facial expression of shock and disgust.)
Knitting needle
(She scrolls down further.)
A *knitting needle?*
It's just so
So depressing
(She snaps her machine shut and looks up again at MACY.)
Well you know these poor Tradepacks
What choice do they have
With The Transition?
(She stares at MACY. Is it some kind of challenge?.)
It calls for great compassion
What choice do they have Macy?

MACY: Are you really asking me?

CLAIRE: *(The moment ends and CLAIRE moves on.)*
But still a knitting needle?
Seems a bit much doesn't it
(She busies herself with something else. After a moment, she looks up, surprised that MACY is still in her office.)

CLAIRE: Something else?

MACY:
Yes I –

(MACY is speechless.)

CLAIRE: It's going to be a huge hit Macy
You'll see
Terror's (Vague flappy gesture.) will make you a star
This novel will change your life

MACY: *Change your life*
That's what I wanted

(MACY is about to leave the office when CLAIRE makes a gesture to the floor.)

CLAIRE: Uh
Macy
I think you dropped something
Down there

MACY: What?
> *(She looks at the floor and sees her scan card.)*
> Oh
> My scan card

CLAIRE: You dropped it
> Didn't you
> On your way in?

MACY: *(Looking at CLAIRE and picking it up.)*
> I
> Did
> I'll
> I'll
> See you soon

CLAIRE: I'm looking forward to the day it comes
> Out Macy

MACY: The novel you mean?

CLAIRE: Yes yes of course!
> The novel!

SCENE SIX:
BENITA & YARROW
CLAIRE
MACY

Somewhere, out of focus on stage but occurring simultaneously, MACY is visible for a moment. We might also see a shadow of CLAIRE working away at her desk.

In another part of the city, our main focus is on a luxurious skyscraper where we see BENITA & YARROW through a frame of windows. We are so high up and so close that the windows reveal just the pupil of INSPECTOR OVID's eye from the billboard. At this close range, his eyes pixellate a bit like the abstractions of a Chuck Close painting.

The flashing lights of the billboard dance across the fine bamboo floors of the penthouse.

BENITA is listening to "Inspector Ovid" on a speaker somewhere in the house. She chuckles in delight at the voices.

THE SNOUT: There were plenty of other owners before you and some of them were pretty smart fellows. The difference is that none of them *believed.* None of them *believed* that I could really talk.

INSPECTOR OVID: So you're saying I'm more gullible?

(YARROW enters and snaps the speakers off.)

YARROW: Please Benita
I can't concentrate

BENITA: I like this one

YARROW: Please
Not again //
!I can't listen to this one again!

(BENITA snaps it on quickly and we hear the voices again.)

THE SNOUT: I'm saying you have a better imagination Inspector Ovid. If you can't allow for it in your imagination then you'll never see it come true in rea –

(YARROW snaps it off.)

YARROW: NO!
No more

BENITA: But you know why they're playing this one
Don't you

YARROW: I don't care why they're playing this one
I'm gonna be up all night
I don't want to be thinking about *Inspector Ovid*
In the middle of my // brief

BENITA: But they always play the first Ovid
When they're about to display
The new downloads

YARROW: Why don't we talk about it //
Later

BENITA: Just come online
　　Just take a second
　　We should look at them now
　　Unless we want to wait until –

YARROW: Until when?

BENITA: Until
　　I don't know
　　Loooooooooong time
　　They say new downloads can take years

YARROW: They say?
　　Who is they?
　　Where did you hear that?

BENITA: I don't know
　　I've just heard that around
　　Forget it
　　We can do it another time

　　　　(Pause.)

YARROW: No no
　　Let's look
　　At the very least we can look

　　　　(Their faces are alight against the glow of an illuminated screen.)

BENITA: See I think they display our matches
　　Here
　　Or
　　Ohmigod!

YARROW: Wow
　　You didn't tell me they had pictures

BENITA: They're just approximations
　　But
　　Woah //
　　These are

YARROW: These are dangerous!
　　These pictures are are are
　　Oh!
　　Adorable!

BENITA: Maybe we shouldn't look at this
    If we look at this //
    You know we're gunna wanna download

YARROW: Click back
    Click back //
    I saw something

BENITA: Did you hear what I said?
    I said: if we look at these photos
    We're going to download //
    Looking at these photos is totally different than looking at the counts

YARROW: Just click back –
    I want to –
    Oh! //
    See! See!
    That's what I wanted to show you!
    Look at her!

BENITA: Wow!
    Oh!
    Wow! //
    She's perfect

YARROW: She even looks like us
    Is that my imagination?
    Look
    That's your nose

BENITA: That's your // nose

YARROW: Look at how perfect she is in the photo!
    Is she sleeping?
    Is that a simulation of her sleeping?
    Ohmygod!
    This button makes her move!

BENITA: Oh look
    They have more photos
    More simulat –

YARROW: She's perfect
    And her code couldn't be better for us

BENITA: Well sure but she's
  (Reading small print.)
  She's only available this season //
  That means we –

YARROW: !Just this season!
  !You mean we might not be able to get her next year?!
  That won't work
  That doesn't work for me
  (Deep breath.)
  Maybe we *should* download now.

BENITA: Are you sure you want to –

YARROW: Look at her
  Have you ever seen anything so perfect?

BENITA: No no
  But remember it's just a –
  (Reading more small print.)
  "This is a simulation of what your baby download will look like.
  Be prepared for subtle discrepancies:
  Babies in photograph may appear larger than
  Babies at various stages of birth development..."
  Blah blah blah
  RSS really should get a better copywriter on these sites //
  Don't you think?

YARROW: She's the one
  She's perfect

BENITA: Yarrow
  I know that look
  I know that obsessive look //
  Are you okay?

YARROW: I want her
  She's ours
  She looks like she was made for us //
  Don't you think?

BENITA: Well you know me
  You don't have to twist my arm

I mean
I love all of them
And her
She's
What is her sequencing code again?
Ru13772656378
It has a great reputation
That code
It's a perfect match for our counts
(Really looking at the photo.)
I mean sure
Absolutely
But I thought you weren't ready

YARROW: So did I
But then
Look
Look at those eyes
That nose!

BENITA: *(Reading carefully to begin the dowload.)*
It's just a simulation remember
"Subtle…" whatevers may apply
(Looking up at YARROW.)
Okay
Okay then
You're sure?

YARROW: Yeah
This is it
She is definitely it

BENITA: Okay

> *(BENITA takes out her own scan card – similar in size and shape to MACY's card – and places it on some designated spot to begin her "download".)*

Here we go
I'm clicking
I'm clicking
I'm doing it

It's
It's //
It's
Yes and now
Okay
I clicked
It will arrive
And

YARROW: *(Jumping with excitement.)*
Oh god
Please
Here we go!
Here we go!
Here we go!

BENITA: Okay it will
It says it will
Arrive in a week
So
Ohmigod next week
Next
Week
September //
I love September

YARROW: September?!
Here we go!
Holy shit!

BENITA & YARROW:
(Not in unison.)
Oh
My
God

(A moment of tension breaks once the "download" is complete.)

YARROW: We did it
We did our download

BENITA: *(Reading the screen for even "smaller print".)*
I just need to ingest it

Within 48 hours of delivery
And take some iron pills
Before seeing Dr. Franklin
And now
Oh there's
One more message
Maybe for the routing number?
No no
It's one more //
Message

YARROW: I'll get the routing number

BENITA: No no
    It's not that
    Oh
    Oh no
    It says there is some bug in the computer system
    They told us they got rid of all the computer // bugs

YARROW: What was that whole tax increase about then?
    They *promised us* no more bugs
    So what does it mean?
    Did our download go through?

BENITA: I don't know
    I don't –
    Wait the script is forming
    Oh okay here comes the
    Code
    Okay //
    Okay

YARROW: Phewwwwwwwww
    Breathe Breathe

BENITA: It looks like it went through
    Now it's
    It's
    It's //
    It's

YARROW: What?
    What?

(Pause.)

BENITA: It says:
> "Due to a current bug in the computer sequencing system
> You will be receiving an 'Error'.
> We apologize for any inconvenience this may cause you."

YARROW: Well that's ridiculous
We only get one download
They can't expect us to settle for
(Vague gesture for an "error".)
I'm sure we're protected legally
I'll go down to the office and see if –

BENITA: What does that mean?
Error
Does Error mean
Tradepack

YARROW: No Error does not mean Tradepack
Error means
Error means
Nothing
We are not even engaging in the possibility of
Error
We are going to cancel the shipping order
And we are going to pursue our legal
Rights
The system is on our side
I heard about a case like this
And the woman filed a complaint
And went to court
And she won
She got a brand new download
She has a perfectly healthy little girl
I mean look: It happened to *us*
If it happened to *us*, it could happen to *anyone*
So we are going to download
Again
That simple
We will

We will have a beautiful Keeper and –
It is absolutely within our legal rights to –
Oh no
Don't cry

BENITA: *You will be receiving an 'Error'*
What is it?
What are they sending us?

YARROW: Oh no
Don't cry
Please I can't
I can't stand it when you
Cry

(BENITA exits. YARROW watches her leave and then she does something violent to the computer. From the distance of another room, BENITA blasts "Inspector Ovid" on the speakers.)

INSPECTOR OVID: If we only just believe, we can make anything come true. Do you believe Snout?

THE SNOUT: I believe Inspector Ovid! I believe!

INSPECTOR OVID: Close your eyes and tell me you believe!

THE SNOUT: *(A cartoon whisper.)* I believe Inspector Ovid. I really be –

SCENE SEVEN:
MACY & LAURA
CHERYL

Somewhere on stage, a hand leads CHERYL to her "holding cell" in prison. We see her knitting, knitting obsessively throughout the following scene. She does not attract attention but her presence is palpable.

Our main focus is directed towards LAURA, MACY's line editor, speaking to MACY in some "public space" at Perseus Publishing. It is clear that there are other ears and eyes around them. The Ovid billboard is, again, a small white flag in the distance.

LAURA: !So you spoke with Claire!

MACY: I did

LAURA: Wonderful
Wonderful
Perseus Publishing is so happy to have you on board

MACY: Thank you
Ah
Claire is going to be my editor
I guess?
Along with you?

LAURA: I will be doing the nitty gritty yes but Claire will handle big picture
Yes
Claire Monsoon has over twenty years in the publishing business
She's the reason our entire library is digitized today
She's an incredibly efficient manager of information and data
She can get anything
Any piece of data into the system
And coded with copyrights
And you know
For licensing
She's brought in billions with our Digi-D selections alone
She's really a genius when it comes to –

> (LAURA speaks enthusiastically while shutting a door to her office. Once inside, shelves and shelves of leather bound books are revealed. When they are both safely inside the door, LAURA's manner changes drastically.)

LAURA: Phew
We managed to make it down the hall
Without any interruptions
And we're safe here in my office
Anytime I'm caught walking around out there
I might be pulled back in to one of Claire's insipid stomach stapling digital projects
Here
At least in here
I'm safe
(She breathes for a moment and then, suddenly, really looks at MACY for the first time.)

So
So
So Macy O. Blonsky!
At last!
I get a chance to speak with Macy O. Blonsky!

MACY: Books
You have
Books
You actually like books

LAURA: Of course I do silly
I'm in publishing
I love books
I'm a fool for books
Oh!
Did I even mention?
I love *your* book

MACY: You
You read it?

LAURA: Yes I read it
I read it nine times
I'm your line editor *remember?*
You're so silly
Now the artist character
I adore her
Let me guess:
Thinly veiled autobiography?
I love her –"M"
"M" is delightful
So lovely
But
"M" is *Familiar*
I've seen her before
Your real artistic breakthrough?
It's your Tradepack character
Oh Macy
She broke my heart
She felt like a *real* person

And the ending
I cried for days
I put down the last page and I started crying
I'll cry right now
Just thinking about her

MACY: (You read it
You actually read it.)

LAURA: Of course I *read* it
I love it

MACY: You read it
You love it
And
You read it
Wow
I'm just
That's such a relief

LAURA: Oh dear
What happened to you in your other meetings?
You're totally traumatized

MACY: No no nothing

LAURA: Really?

MACY: Nothing at all

LAURA: Look
Think of me as your friend
As your ally
Here in the trenches
I know these people
I know how they can be
If you are having any problems
You can talk to me
Do you need to talk to me?
Are you having any problems?

(Pause.)

MACY: *(Smiles brightly.)*
If you've actually read my book

LAURA:
> I love your book

MACY: If you've read it
> And you love it
> Then I don't have any problems

> *(LAURA begins to make tea for the two of them.)*

LAURA: Good
> So
> So
> What do you think about all of this?

MACY: Well
> All this
> You mean Perseus or?

LAURA: I mean all this
> This whole thing

MACY: The publishing culture?

LAURA: No silly
> I've been dying to talk with you ever since I read your book
> What do you think of all this?
> I mean
> *The Transition*
> It's really terrifying isn't it?
> *(She lowers her voice despite the fact that they are in her office.)*
> I just feel like our whole civilization is going to hell in a hand basket
> I wake up with nightmares
> Don't you?
> I mean
> Don't you?

MACY: *(Clearly uncomfortable with this level of intimacy.)*
> Well I think it's
> You know, RSS is moving forward –
> I'm perfectly healthy –
> We all are –
> And my book is coming out
> *Morning Muse*

Panet
The whole *(Vague gesture for "deal".)*
So I'd rather just let my book speak for itself
It should all be there in the writing
That's what real literature does right?
I suppose that's optimistic
But I feel like an optimist right now so –

LAURA: An optimist?
The writer behind *Terror's Peon* feels like an *optimist?*
(An odd intensity.)
Don't be an optimist.
Whatever you do, don't be an optimist.
Be a fascist, be an extremist, be an idealist –
By all means, yes, we should all be idealists –
But don't be an optimist.
The way RSS is handling this?
This is not for the best.

MACY: *(Taking a breath to choose her words carefully.)*
I
I
Sure
If you say so

LAURA: *If you say so*

MACY: I
I wrote a novel
Imaginative fiction
I'm asking questions
I'm not trying to answer them
That is
I don't engage in
I'm neutral
Politically
So

> *(Pause.)*

LAURA: Well then
Okay

Welcome to Perseus Macy
Consider me your friend, ally and
Above all else
Consider me the greatest advocate for your brilliant book.
Now
I rarely say this
I would only say this to dead writers
If I could talk to dead writers
But
You
You're here and alive
And your novel *changed my life*.

MACY: Thank you
I'm
God
Thank you

LAURA: More than anything, I think it changed Claire's life
You've done something
Something
Ineffable
To her taste
Powerful stuff

MACY: Powerful yes

(*Pause*.)

MACY: Actually: I don't think Claire read it

LAURA: What?

MACY: She had no idea what it was about
In our meeting

LAURA: All I know is that she sold it like the second coming at the
marketing meetings

MACY: She seems particularly good at that
Marketing

LAURA: (*A pause to assess MACY*.)
I don't know if you are aware of this but

You probably intimidate Claire
You and your refined reserve

MACY: Hmmmmmm
Maybe

> *(Pause. MACY goes to pull down some of the well-worn books from a shelf or a table.)*

MACY: These are beautiful
(MACY's finger follows all the offerings.)
Dante
Shakespeare
Locke
Swift
Goethe
Melville
Kafka
On and on and on

LAURA: They're all incredibly rare
Some of those don't even exist in print anymore
I have the only paper copy of a few of them
Originals in every way

MACY: Beautiful
Really
If I had more money
I would spend it all on books
Do you ever read them?

LAURA: They're quite fragile
Sometimes I'll pull them out and look
Just to have the old joy of print on paper

MACY: Can I touch?

LAURA: I think they might fall apart to be honest
They're really just
Gorgeous museum pieces

MACY: But you can still read them

LAURA: You can, yes
   You can

MACY: You don't sound very enthusiastic

LAURA: I love them
   Just like you
   But now I have a responsibility to think more
   Strategically
   What is the most strategic technology for the exchange of ideas?
   Truth is Macy
   I don't believe it's books anymore

MACY: Oh no
   Is this just another plug for Digi-Directs?

LAURA: No
   Macy
   Look at me
   No
   No no no
   Digi-Directs:
   Tacky, tasteless, commercial *(Vague gesture for something repulsive.)*
   Digi-Ds are flattening out all the nuance and rigor behind original thinking
   We –
   Macy: you and me –
   We still believe in ideas
   Independent thought
   Don't we?

MACY: I just want the story to be told

LAURA: We both do
   But we don't want *Terror's Peon* to sit on some shelf
   We want something more expedient for *Terror's Peon*

MACY: What is more expedient than a book?

LAURA: An experience

MACY: An experience…

LAURA: Imagine your Tradepack character
   What if people could spend time with her?

See her
Touch her
Feel her feelings
What kind of neurological change –
Oh but I forgot:
You're an *optimist*
You don't want to use your writing to change a thing
You're just happy to be here…
(MACY doesn't respond.)
Where did you say you went to school by the way?
Drink your tea dear
It will get cold

MACY: Oh thank you

LAURA: So where did you say?

MACY: Oh
   I didn't
   Why?

LAURA: Just curious

MACY: Um
   Prost
   And then Renwick

LAURA: Ohhhh
   Well
   Prost and Renwick
   Prost and Renwick
   Well that makes sense
   You're very Renwick
   Very very Prost
   So many of my good friends went to Prost
   And I almost went to Renwick
   My mother went there
   And my grandmother
   (She sings a corny little song.)
   Friend to all…
   Did you have to do that at the Arts Club initiation?

MACY: Oh I forgot about that
   That song

LAURA: *Friend to all*

MACY: *Friend to all*
   That's right
   (A bit more personality comes through.)
   !Those creepy, corny rituals and that –
   (She reins it in.)
   Sorry
   Yes
   I did have to do that
   And I did love my Arts Club

LAURA: I loved my Arts Club too
   And the rituals *were* creepy
   Creepy, corny, total elitist crap
   Right?
   But the values were
   Timeless:
   Love of learning
   Rigorous discourse
   Responsible Leadership
   What happened to those values?
   I just feel totally at sea with people in power today

MACY: (Me too....)

LAURA: Right?
   People in positions of power who can't even speak a coherent sentence
   People who put more faith in algorithms than they do in Aristotle –
   Claire –
   For example
   I mean
   Do you think Claire has ever even heard of –
   Nabokov
   de Tocqueville
   She probably thinks Locke n' Hobbes is a breakfast sandwich

MACY: *(Perhaps a fake laugh.)*
Claire and I –
We have other things in common

LAURA: *(LAURA does a "spot on" impersonation of CLAIRE's "pep talk".)*
We ANALyze
We THEORize
And then when all the analog work is done
We DIGItize
In order to SYNTHEsize

> *(MACY bursts out laughing despite her better judgment.)*

MACY: That's just
That's exactly what she said

LAURA: Are you kidding?
She gives us that pep talk every day...
Did she tell you about her Rofra?

MACY: Yes
She did

LAURA: *(Another "spot on" impersonation.)*
"Butter..."
"Who said that...Butter? Who said that first?"

MACY: *(Laughing.)*
Ohmygod
Ohmygod
How did
How did you know?

LAURA: Please!
I've had to listen to Claire Monsoon crank out
Corporate bullshit
For over ten years now
She's a hack
She's a hack who happens to hold court over the whole industry

MACY: !She is...!
!Claire Monsoon *is* a total hack!

LAURA: Aha!
> I knew I would find a personality in there somewhere
> (Or at least a hint of one.)
> Were I not such an astute judge of character –
> And I am –
> You don't spend more than a decade decoding
> Digital downloads of Dostoyevsky without understanding
> A little something about human nature –
> But were I not –
> I might look at you and feel a bit disappointed –
> You can trust me
> I am on *your* side...

> *(A small pause.)*

MACY: *Butter*

LAURA: *Who said that?*
> *Who said that "Butter thing"*
> *Who made that up?*

MACY: She started giving me notes
> On my novel
> A novel she's never even read

LAURA: She gave you notes?
> She never gives notes
> What did she say?

MACY: Nothing
> She said absolutely nothing
> She made a little doo-dad loop-de-loo
> Motion
> And said: Fix that
> And I said: Fix what?
> And she said: You know, *that //*
> And that was the only thing she could say

LAURA: Terrifying
> Totally terrifying

MACY: *(The full head of steam finally releases.)*
> !Because she has never even read the book!

LAURA: Will you please behave this way in your next meeting?
I would pay money to see how Claire responds to
The real Macy O. Blonsky

MACY: (The real Macy O. Blonsky) //
Right

LAURA: *"Things are cliché // because they're true"*

MACY: Um
Laura

LAURA: What's wrong?

MACY: *(A deep breath.)*
There is something

LAURA: What?

MACY: I –
Never mind

LAURA: Macy
I already know

MACY: You know
You know
About
You know about my book?

LAURA: It's *me*, Macy
Don't play that weirdo well-mannered schoolgirl with me
Just tell me the truth

(Pause.)

MACY: I
I
Didn't mean to get involved in something like this
But –

LAURA: But you couldn't resist
I understand
You had to act

MACY: I did have to act
　　I did
　　Because I just wanted people to read it
　　That's all

LAURA: But that's more than enough

MACY: So you understand?

LAURA: Of course I do
　　I would have done the same // thing
　　Right
　　Because

LAURA: Because we both believe // in –

MACY: Yes
　　Exactly
　　The // book

LAURA: The // book

MACY: Phhhhew
　　God //
　　I feel like I can breathe again

LAURA: And what it can do for
　　The Tradepack Resistance

　　　　(Pause.)

MACY: Excuse me
　　The Tradepack Resistance
　　Did you just say
　　The Tradepack Resistance?

LAURA: *(She goes to check her door: is anyone listening?)*
　　It's okay Macy
　　I know
　　I already know
　　I've been doing my research
　　I've been digging deeper into the RSS eflashes
　　And I *know* that there is Resistance written all over your book
　　Your political activism
　　The secret codes you are communicating to the underground Tradepack cause

So
So
That's what I've been trying to tell you this whole time
We're on the same side

   (*Pause.*)

MACY: Wow
   I'm

LAURA: You don't have to say anything

MACY: Okay
   But –

LAURA: Not another word
   You are safe here
   Okay?

MACY: Okay

LAURA: I believe in what you're doing
   I'm working from *inside* to help

MACY: I'm not involved
   Laura
   Really

LAURA: I also understand that this is what you have to say

MACY: I'm really not involved
   I could
   You know
   I could have you arrested for this, Laura
   For this kind of conversation

LAURA: You could
   Yes
   You could
   But you won't
   Something tells me that you won't
   Friend to all
   As corny as the song is
   We both believe in our responsibility
   So you needn't bother denying anything

Just consider my office a safety zone
And our work on *Terror's Peon* –

MACY: What does *Terror's Peon* have to do with this?

LAURA: *Terror's Peon* has everything to –
Well
We'll talk about that later
For now
For now
Let's just dig into these line edits

MACY: Laura
I
I
I have nothing to offer you

LAURA: You're too modest Macy
You are the author behind *Terror's Peon*
You have everything
Everything in the world to offer
So let's begin then
Shall we?
(She begins reading from a galley proof of "Terror's Peon".)
Chapter One

SCENE EIGHT:
CHERYL & JOAN

Further down, in the dark heart of the city, CHERYL sits in the bowels of a holding cell. Only the spindly legs of the billboard are visible through the bars of the windows. She knits. She knits. She knits. Someone yells in to her.

VOICE OF JOAN:
Hey lady!
They're gunna let you go!

(CHERYL knits and knits.)

Did you hear me?
They're coming down here to let you go!
"An act of mercy", that's what they called it.

> *(Knitting and knitting.)*

You killed your Mama?
Is that right?

> *(Knitting and knitting.)*

What'd she have?
She have The Cancer or somethin' else?

> *(Knitting knitting.)*

My sister had The Cancer and they wouldn't give us any drugs.
Not even a pill for the pain.
Not even a single pill for the –
(The anger overcomes JOAN. She contains it and moves on.)

You got nothing to be ashamed of around here honey.
There are no judgments under my watch.

> *(JOAN enters and takes in the sight of CHERYL knitting. She tries to pull away the knitting needles from her hands but CHERYL grips them instinctively.)*

Your hands are gunna cramp honey.
You better let those go.

> *(When she finally pulls away the knitting, CHERYL continues to make the knitting motions with nothing in her hands. JOAN holds up her shawl to see what she's making but it no longer has any shape or pattern to it: just a huge pile of knotted wool.)*

Was it a sweater?
Or a blanket?
You can talk to me.
Just tell me what it was.

CHERYL: *(In a trance.)*
    I lost the
    Pattern

(JOAN wraps her arms around CHERYL in an unexpected gesture of comfort and CHERYL collapses into her and shakes. JOAN holds her for a moment and then she stands up to go back to her desk.)

JOAN: I'm supposed to take away these needles you know

    Seeing as you used 'em as weapons

    Okay?

    Okay?

    (JOAN pauses to consider the safety of what she is about to offer before leaning in.)

    You helped us.

    Do you know that?

    Your desperation: your anger.

    Your story's giving us the courage to get organized:

    The Resistance is finally getting organized

    We're not gonna take this.

    We do not have to take this.

    (She slides her a little card cautiously.)

    I'm getting together all of the groups.

    We're all underground.

    We're all hush hush.

    But soon

    Very soon:

    There are gonna be marches

    There are gonna be protests

    We're protesting because of you:

    You: your Mama

    Your story

    You have no idea how much strength your story has given us.

    (She looks at CHERYL, trying to assess if she can hear the following.)

    You can't just act once

    And shut your eyes

    And go to sleep.

    You gotta act

    Every day

    Every day honey

    Every day

    (Another gesture of comfort.)

    When you're ready

    You dial this number and ask for Joan

(JOAN disappears around the corner and CHERYL is left alone. The bulbous knitting ball is now lying on the ground and CHERYL knits with imaginary needles in her hands. She counts under her breath in some semblance of a pattern.)

CHERYL: *(Looking off in the direction of the JOAN.)*
    Ta
    Ta

END OF ACT ONE

ACT TWO

SCENE NINE:
VIOLET

She delivers the following lines in "performance mode".

Every one of you has a purpose.
But you don't believe that.
I know how you feel.
You don't think anyone is watching.
I know how you feel:
You feel angry.
You feel upset.
You feel...

    (She makes a vague motion for "and so on..." The performance breaks. She speaks as herself.)

That was my "TLT":
My tough love talk.
I delivered that one to the Tradepacks with bad attitudes
Former Resistance members
Old underground protestors
Not that there were ever that many of those.
They were pretty much defeated by the time I came around.

Like old beat up alley dogs
Those ladies

They would scowl and they would snarl
But by the time I was giving speeches,
Their will had been broken.

They knew their will had been broken.

By the time I was giving speeches –
Going on tours for the RSS,
Delivering the word,
Staying "on message" –
By that time, most of the Tradepacks were already gone

And the ones left standing
The ones who could even make it to the events
By that time
They were eager to hear about departing early
They wanted to move on from this world
Move on to paradise
Painless with purpose
It felt like fate
Inevitable:
What we were doing here
Where we were going
Why

Why

Of course, *I* was always a bit of a mystery.
And maybe that was a part of my special draw.
I was the Tradepack –I am the Tradepack– who never got sick
Not just the Tradepack with a more mild disease
Or the Tradepack with a bit less weakness
But the Tradepack who was perfect
Perfectly healthy
Perfectly immune

That's why the RSS asked me to be their ambassador
Come one! Come all!
Come and meet "the miracle."
Experience the prophet sent from a paradise beyond.

I almost believed it myself.
Or I wanted to.

How could I be a Tradepack
Spending countless hours in the company of
The infected, the wounded, the cancerous, *the dregs* –
How could I be a Tradepack while my body resisted all disease?
How could that be?

Experience the prophet sent from a paradise beyond…
It makes for such a good story but –

One day I snuck into an RSS bureau
Stole a password to the system
And tried to find out for myself

My name appeared
Violet:
Sequencing code: 470982809

And then there it was
Mystery revealed
Right before my very eyes
It didn't say "Special Ambassador"
It didn't say "Prophetess"

Systems don't produce miracles, you see
Systems don't have faith
Or fall to the will of angels
We believe that they do but…

My name is Violet
I wasn't born from the clouds or beamed in on a ray of light
The story of my life is much simpler than that
Simpler than anything I could have ever imagined

SCENE TEN:
BENITA & YARROW
MACY & LAURA

Somewhere in the spacious penthouse, YARROW is arriving home from work. She enters in and out, putting things away. Her eye catches sight of a small cardboard box, prominently placed and decorated with large cartoon storks. She stops dead still and stares at it while Inspector Ovid's billboard eye peers through her window.

Over in LAURA's office, we see MACY and LAURA beginning the process of a major editing effort.

YARROW: Why didn't you cancel the shipping order?

BENITA: …

> *(BENITA walks over to turn on the unseen speaker or sound system. We hear Inspector Ovid and The Snout for just a moment.)*

INSPECTOR OVID: So you're saying I'm more gullible?

THE SNOUT: I'm saying you have a better imagination Inspector Ovid –

YARROW: Turn that crap off!
> *(BENITA turns off the sound.)*
I asked you to cancel the shipping order

BENITA: Well I didn't

YARROW: Yes
> I can see that
> And now we're stuck with with
> The Error

BENITA: Don't call it that
> I don't want you to call it that
> Call it
> A name // at least

YARROW: A name!
> Call it a name!
> I don't want to call it anything
> I don't want to think about it
> I assumed that I wouldn't have to think about it

Because I assumed that you would have canceled
The shipping order
I asked you –

BENITA: I didn't

YARROW: I asked you to do one thing

BENITA: And I didn't
I didn't
I didn't do it

YARROW: What do you do here
All day long?
I ask you to do one thing
And –
So what *do* you do?
If you don't do the one thing I ask you to do? //
Just out of curiosity

BENITA: Don't be mean
You're being mean

YARROW: I'm not being mean
I'm being reasonable
I reasonably asked you to do something
And now I am reasonably asking you why –
Forget it
I'll send it back

(Pause.)

BENITA: It's our only chance

YARROW: That is not true
I filed the complaint
And now we'll just see
And if it doesn't go through
I'll file another one //
I'll keep filing until –

BENITA: What if
What if
This really is our only chance

YARROW: Well now you're just being
     This is totally typical
     You're being totally
     Unreasonable
     We have every chance of success
     If we just work within –

BENITA: Work within what?
     Work within *the system*?

YARROW: Yes
     Work within the system

BENITA: *(More to herself?)*
     I am
     I am being totally unreasonable

YARROW: What?

BENITA: I am feeling something
     Without reason //
     I want
     Let's open the box
     Let's do it

YARROW: What?
     No: we are not going to open the box
     Just stop
     Stop thinking this way

BENITA: I
     I
     I can't

YARROW: Well I won't tell you how to think
     But if you think this way
     You shouldn't all right
     Don't think this way
     It's
     Dangerous
     It's misguided
     We're in an *ideal* situation so why would we
     Open
     This

This
Pandora's Box
It's *an Error*
We have no idea what that means
Why would we
When we don't –
Desperate people make these kinds of decisions
We are not desperate
We have choices //
That's all

BENITA: Maybe we don't
Maybe we think we do but an Error
Is some amazing lesson
Some amazing possibility
For something
Unforeseen
Something
Beautifully //
I don't know

YARROW: No
No I refuse to let you
Get romantic and Airy
Fairy
I will make you
See the real
The real
Situation as it stands
And that means –
What if
What if
It's a Tradepack
This Error
We don't know
Error could mean
Tradepack
And if it's a *Tradepack*
What
What then?

What will you do if it gets sick?
You take care of her
Day and night
And what do you get in return?
All day all night
You don't get shit
You might not get smiles
You might not get fingers //
You might not get
Who knows?
You have NO IDEA

BENITA: That's a lie!
That's a lie!
Who told you that?
Who told you that Tradepacks don't have fingers?

YARROW: I don't know
Someone
I heard it at work
Not the older ones but these last few
This last generation
That's what everybody // says

BENITA: Everybody who?
Everybody lies
I don't believe everybody
I believe myself

YARROW: Well what if it's not just fingers
What if it's feelings
You might not get Love maybe
Maybe you don't even get Love
From it
And you say that's
Beautiful
But I say that's cruel
I say that's not even
Half a life
I say that is no //
Life

BENITA: No life
    No life!
    Who are you
    To say No Life
    Who are you
    To know what a half life
    Even is
    What a no life
    Even is
    Who are you to know
    What a real
    Feeling is
    A real feeling
    Have you ever even felt a
    Real feeling
    FUCK YOU!
    FUCK YOU! //
    HALF LIFE
    YOU'RE A HALF LIFE
    YOU LIVE A HALF LIFE

YARROW: OH NOW WE'RE AT IT
    NOW WE'RE ON IT
    THIS IS WHAT IT'S BEEN
    THIS WHOLE TIME
    MAYBE SO HALF LIFE
    BUT I CAN MAKE IT TO THE END OF MY LIFE
    AND TAKE CARE OF MYSELF
    AND TAKE CARE OF OTHERS //
    WITHOUT TAXING
    TAXING
    THE SYSTEM

BENITA: YOU HAVE NEVER
    YOU HAVE NEVER
    Taken care of me
    Ever
    In a real way
    Apart from a roof

And some silk shirts
On my birthday

> *(Long Pause.)*

YARROW: Well then

> *(BENITA looks down at the box. She opens it and furiously shovels out an absurd amount of packing peanuts. At the very core, in a protected gauze shell, is a little white pill. She looks directly at YARROW and pops it in her mouth. And swallows. In the window, the eye of INSPECTOR OVID blinks. There is a pause.)*

BENITA: Not over this
I can't be reasonable over this
Yarrow

> *(Pause.)*

YARROW: Okay

SCENE ELEVEN:
MACY & LAURA
CHERYL

> *MACY and LAURA are working on TERROR'S PEON in LAURA's office. They have stacks and stacks of paper all around them. They are clearly in the midst of an all-night editing reconstruction. The white flag of the Ovid billboard is lit up and glowing in the far, far distance of the night.*

LAURA: Okay
So in this moment –

MACY: What time is *Morning Muse?*

LAURA: We have to be on the set at eight

MACY: Urgh
Eight
That's in
That's in

LAURA: Don't think about it
Focus

So in this moment
Near the end
When you have this –
Well it's almost stream of consciousness

MACY: The end of Chapter Nine
Or the Start of Chapter Eleven

LAURA: The beginning of the end
You know: In Chapter Nine
And your Tradepack is talking about her life
And about what she remembers

MACY: Right
What about it?

LAURA: It's nice
I mean: I appreciate the literary flourish
But –

MACY: But what?

LAURA: I don't buy that those are her memories
They feel too –
Look: her life
Her memories
It's all just a waiting game
Until she gets sick
She knows that she's going to get sick
She knows that she's going to die
She's a Tradepack

MACY: She's a Tradepack sure
But that's just a given circumstance of her situation
That's not her whole life

LAURA: But her given circumstances *are* her life
What else is her life *besides* her given circumstances

MACY: Well sure no
Of course
I'm just saying that
First off I'm saying that she doesn't remember certain things
BECAUSE she's a Tradepack

She remembers certain things
BECAUSE she's a character
She has those memories because they –
They mean something to her –
They're the details that make up her life –
And the fact that she's a Tradepack
Well
I don't even know what to say to that
Not all Tradepacks would be thinking about sickness and death
Because
Because
Not all Tradepacks are the same

    (Pause.)

LAURA: Is that what your own Tradepacks tell you?

MACY: My what?

LAURA: You know: your own Tradepacks
    Your secret sources

MACY: No
    I
    This is just how I feel
    As a person

LAURA: As a *person*
    How quaint
    So who did you base this Tradepack character on?

MACY: No one

LAURA: Do you actually know any?
    Tradepacks?

MACY: Of course I do
    You do too

LAURA: No I don't

MACY: They make up
    I don't know
    Thirty –
    Or twenty percent of the population now

LAURA: By the time we graduated
    They had been slotted into different school tracks

MACY: Well
    At work
    Or
    You'd be surprised

LAURA: I mean
    Sure
    People I run into on the streets
    Sure
    But –

MACY: What does it matter?
    My novel is not about Tradepacks
    My novel is about a woman
    Who *happens to be* a Tradepack

LAURA: Do you though?
    Do you know any *real* Tradepacks?

MACY: Yes

LAURA: Well enough to really know what goes on in their minds?

MACY: Yes

LAURA: Who?

MACY: I'm not saying

LAURA: Who?
    Who do you know?

MACY: It doesn't matter

LAURA: I am trying to help you Macy
    But you refuse to give me what I need

MACY: Who I *know* is not the point
    It's what I can *imagine*
    My imagination is the point

LAURA: But do you actually know one?

MACY: Yes I know *one*

LAURA: Who?

MACY: Someone

LAURA: Who?

MACY: Someone
Someone you know too
I can't tell you who
But if you knew, you would completely change your –

LAURA: Whhhhhhhhhhhhooo?
You're bluffing
Now you have to tell //
Who?

MACY: No one
Forget I said anything

LAURA: Who
I don't believe you
Who who who

(Perhaps the tiniest intake of air.)

MACY: Claire Monsoon
Claire Monsoon is a Tradepack
So there

*(MACY is terrified at her revelation. LAURA looks at MACY in shock
and then she bursts out laughing.)*

LAURA: *Claire Monsoon*

MACY: Claire Monsoon
Ha ha ha

LAURA: Claire Monsoon
Ha ha ha
Can you imagine

MACY: Claire Monsoon
Ha ha ha
I can't imagine

LAURA: Claire Monsoon
(*Perhaps taking a moment to consider it.*)
Can you imagine
(*A quick shift from that thought.*)
The truth about *Tradepacks* Macy
Is that we'll never really understand them
Because they need too much
They're in too much pain
They're just
They're too sick
To have any kind of real life

MACY: *Real life*
What does that mean?

LAURA: You know what I mean
A life that is not
Totally dominated by desperation
They're not like us
Their desperation makes them
Different

MACY: I've always thought
Tradepacks were like us
They're they're just like us
They are us

LAURA: But then
They're different
You know they're different
C'mon

MACY: I thought you were involved in The Resistance
Friend to All

LAURA: I am
Or I was
I studied them at university
I even did one of my thesis papers on them
An eighty-page in-depth study
Highest Honors with Distinction
But if you're working with them –
And I still think that you are –

Then you already know how disorganized they are
This last year or so
I've grown totally disenchanted with their whole movement
Their goals are completely muddled
Muddled and
Misguided, quite frankly
They have no idea how to shape a message
It's not their fault really
They just haven't been properly educated
They're not fit for leadership Macy
I think
I think
We have a responsibility to help

MACY: To help how?

LAURA: To help –
Women like that border clerk

> (*Somewhere, in another part of the city, we see CHERYL arrive back home in her garret apartment. It looks oddly empty and haunted without FRANNY. CHERYL appears in shadows and silhouettes as she walks through the space where she killed her mother. She begins taking off her coat or sweater, emptying her pockets. She sits and makes the knitting motion with her hands.*)

LAURA: You know:
The one who killed her own mother with the knitting needle.
We need to help *her*
And the hundreds of thousands of women
Just like her.
Women who want to end the pain.

MACY: But the only way for anyone to end the pain is to
Fight back
Resist The Transition
What else is there?

LAURA: Surrender
There is no shame in surrender
Let's surrender and help The Transition go *faster* –

MACY: *Help The Transition go faster*
  No
  What?
  The point is
  The point is
  To
  To slow down
  To stop –

LAURA: That is what you –
  A member of the privileged elite – say
  What are the actual Tradepacks saying?
  Think of that border clerk and her knitting needles:
  Is she out there asking for a revolution?
  No:
  She is mercifully trying to release her loved ones from pain.
  We have to encourage her
  Encourage more of this kind of mercy killing
  Help these Tradepacks to leave this world of suffering
  Give them a new story
  A new mythology: something better to believe in:
  Tradepacks are departing this world with Purpose
  Painless: with purpose
  We work in publishing for God's sakes
  We're in a perfect position to use *Terror's Peon* to convey these ideas

MACY: Aren't we just doing line edits

LAURA: But this is our one chance to fix your Tradepack at the end

MACY: I thought
  I thought you loved this book

LAURA: I do
  I love its potential

MACY: … Potential

LAURA: What is your message
  At the end?

MACY: I don't –
  The

The
Details
The details of what she sees when she walks home
And we know she's going to die
And she knows she's going to die
But she's feeling things
All sorts of things that –

(Pause.)

Potential?
Why did you tell me you loved it?
You lied
Why does everyone lie?

LAURA: All right
You know what
I'm terrible at offering generous feedback
There is some really worthwhile writing in here
But the ending is not communicating anything
The last few chapters feel like
Well
How shall I put this?
Sort of like
Mmmmmmmmm
A black hole

(MACY grows more and more upset.)

MACY: !A black hole?!

LAURA: Just the last few chapters
So I'm not saying it's a big black hole
Think small:
A small three-chaptered black hole

MACY: (A small three-chaptered black hole…)
So even if people actually go to the trouble
To pick up my book
Browse through it
Buy it
And then start reading it
Maybe even enjoying it

By the time they make it to the final three chapters
They won't understand a word of it?

LAURA: *(She considers briefly.)*
Yes
I think that's probably right
But this is just my opinion
It's *your* book
What do *you* want to do?

MACY: I don't want to end with a "black hole"
That's my worst –
Like a horrible nightmare I used to have
Where I write all night
Night after night
Night after night
And then
Just at the moment I'm about to turn in the pages
I look down and see that it's all
Everything I've written
It's only zeros and ones
Zeros and ones
Page after page
Nonsense
Nonsense
Page after page of meaningless code
Not a single pattern in any of it
(Some kind of panic sets in.)
Ohmigod

LAURA: Are you okay?

MACY: *(Perhaps reaching for a stiff drink or a whole bottle in desperation.)*
Let's fix it
Let's fix it right now
What would that mean?

LAURA: Well it would mean
We just reshape this chapter here
And then you would need to rewrite all of nine
Nine, ten, and eleven

MACY: Why?
> Why exactly?

LAURA: Why?
> Well
> Okay
> Because we need to give your Tradepack a
> Purpose
> She's not dying
> She is *departing*
> In a
> A
> *Painless* manner
> Are you with me Macy?
> I'm seeing something
> Majestic
> Happening in the imagery here at the end
> The reader takes the story in with a larger scope
> Because maybe she
> Maybe she is part of a movement
> A movement helping all the Tradepacks
> To *depart early*
> A movement
> A movement
> To lead them onto paradise

MACY: I just
> I really can't hear any of that in my head
> Those words

LAURA: Okay
> Well let me
> Do you mind
> Let me just write it out a bit
> And then you can finesse

> *(LAURA sits down and begins to write something.)*

LAURA: Come sit by me
> I'll show you what I'm doing

MACY: Only add a little

LAURA: I'll work for a bit
    And then you work for a bit
    Tag team
    Right Macy?

MACY: Remember
    Only add a little
    Only enough to address
    That
    That
    "Black hole aspect"

LAURA: I'm just working on this section here
    The shape of the end

MACY: You're writing so fast!
    How can you write so fast?

LAURA: I've been thinking about this ending
    For a long, long time
    We'll wrap up "M" so we can end with The Tradepack
    Following her final days
    Throughout The Transition
    And then the narrative will break open
    To reveal something
    Shimmering
    Imagine experiencing that word
    Shimmering
    Shimmering possibilities for our society
    What do think of that?
    Macy?

MACY: I don't even know what that means

LAURA: It will make sense in context
    I'll work for a bit
    And then you can see it

MACY: Of course I can see it
    Laura
    It's mine

LAURA: You're completely fried
　　Look at your eyes
　　Just put your head down for a minute and relax
　　I'll be done before you know it

MACY: Okay but
　　I can't fall asleep
　　I can't fall asleep until I see
　　The context

　　　　　(*MACY puts her head down.*)

LAURA: Of course you can't fall asleep
　　Macy O. Blonsky
　　You're the writer

SCENE TWELVE:
CHERYL

We see CHERYL sitting in her home –her hands still making knitting motions– at a loss for what to do. She turns on an unseen speaker somewhere and listens for a moment.

INSPECTOR OVID: If we only just believe, we can make anything come true. Do you believe Snout?

THE SNOUT: I believe Inspector Ovid! I believe!

INSPECTOR OVID: Close your eyes and tell me you believe!

THE SNOUT: *(A cartoon whisper.)* I believe Inspector Ovid. I really believe.

INSPECTOR OVID: If we all believe in The Transition, we can change the world!

(Suddenly CHERYL turns the speaker off with a violent anger. After a moment, she takes out Joan's little white card and she considers it. She dials the number on her cell phone device. It rings and she hangs up.)

SCENE THIRTEEN:
MACY

In LAURA's office, we see MACY sit up suddenly, shocked out of a nightmare. She looks around the office with groggy recognition but it is empty.

MACY: !Morning Muse!

MACY furiously searches the office for her manuscript but there is no sign of it. She grabs her bag and runs out the door.

SCENE FOURTEEN:
MACY, LAURA, ASTRID & CLAIRE

The "digital programming" set for MORNING MUSE. ASTRID stands alone reading the final pages of the manuscript – perhaps on some kind of digital device? LAURA enters.

VOICEOVER: *(Perhaps we hear this voiceover just to indicate location.)*
Soundcheck '*Morning Muse*'
Soundcheck '*Morning Muse*'

(A violently chipper theme song plays for just a moment and then ends: this is the Morning Muse theme song that will continue to play in brief bursts throughout the scene.)

ASTRID: Laura!
We have to talk about this new draft!

LAURA: *(Turning around and approaching Astrid.)*
Excellent!
So you read the changes

ASTRID: My god the changes
You didn't tell me about all the changes
Where is Macy?
I'm starting to get nervous

LAURA: We had some new ideas
Some new directions
So I helped to tease them out

ASTRID: Well it's
It's beautiful –
Brilliant even –
It is –
But if I didn't know Macy better –
It reads like a religious handbook for The Transition //
Laura

LAURA: It's not a handbook for anything
It's just the shape
Of the story
Claire liked it
Loved it //
Claire loved it in fact

ASTRID: Really?
Claire loved it

LAURA: *Loved it*
The politics –
You're out of touch Astrid –
People my age love the politics –
They can't get enough

ASTRID: We used to say that literature was the highest calling
Higher than politics
Higher than god
Good writing was above good peopl –
(She catches herself.)
!Oh listen to me!
!Send me to the taxidermist!
!I'm already dead and stuffed!
If Claire loved it, then I love it

(LAURA exits towards the edge of the set.)

Where is Macy?
Did you try all her numbers?

(MACY comes running in, breathless, confused.)

ASTRID: There you are!
  I love it
  All right
  Do you love it?
  Just tell me that?
  Do you love it?

MACY: Wait: What?

ASTRID: Do you love it?

MACY: I love it

ASTRID: Then *I* love it

MACY: *(She starts laughing and suddenly, she can't stop.)*
  I love it
  I love it Astrid
  I
  I
  I
  Haven't even read it //
  I don't even know how it ends
  But I love it

ASTRID: What is she saying?
  I can't understand a word she's saying
  (To MACY.)
  Remember
  No one on *Morning Muse* is interested in *(Vague gesture.)*
  Are you all right Macy?
  For god's sake drink some water!
  You're positively slap happy
  (Eyeing the action on the set.)
  Oh look is that Paulina Petrovksy over there?
  She's so short
  Did you know she was so short?
  Shocking!
  Do they put her on a box or something?
  I'll be right back
  (ASTRID wanders offstage in pursuit of PAULINA PETROVSKY.)
  Yo hoo

Paulina!
Paulina Petrovksy!
I am Astrid Duncan
Of Astrid Duncan Literary Associates
You might have seen me at Panet?

(LAURA enters again. MACY sees her.)

MACY: You
You let me fall asleep
You promised to wake me up
To show me
To show me
Our book
My book
(MORNING MUSE music plays another test run.)
Ohmigod
(Beginning to crack.)
I can't go on there
I haven't even read the ending
It's my book and I don't even know how it ends

LAURA: Do you want me to go over it with you?

MACY: No
No
I have to read the ending
Tell them we have to reschedule
I'll go on in a few days
After I've read it

LAURA: I'm sorry I'm sorry
Did you say *reschedule?*
Paulina Petrovsky does not do reschedules

MACY: Then I don't think I should be alone with her

PAULINA: *(Offstage.)*
Where is my box?
I CAN'T GO ON WITHOUT MY BOX!

MACY: She really is short. Have you seen how short she is?

LAURA: Maybe I should go on for you at the beginning
    And you can join me later
    After you've read it
    Or at least looked at the ending
    You don't want to make a fool of yourself in front of the whole nation
    Do you?
    Maybe you do

MACY: No
    NO
    I don't

LAURA: Let me go ask about stepping in for you

MACY: Okay

        (LAURA rushes off to check. MACY watches from the side of the stage.)

    Wait!
    Laura!
    You need to leave me my novel so I can find out how it ends.

        (Suddenly, CLAIRE enters. She is no longer pregnant.)

CLAIRE: Oh good!
    I caught you
    You're about to go on then
    Good!
    I wouldn't have missed this for the world

MACY: Claire!
    You're here!

CLAIRE: Here?
    Of course I'm here
    Where else would I be?

        (MACY looks at CLAIRE.)

MACY: Wait
    Where
    Where
    Where is the baby?

CLAIRE: *(Bristling.)*
> What baby?
> I have no idea what you're talking about
> Miss Blonsky
> You really should get more rest
> You don't seem fully *(Vague gesture for "with it".)*
> Pats of cucumber and lemon zest on the eyes
> Have you ever tried it?
> It does wonders for the body and soul

> > *(CLAIRE leaves to go in and speak to the others on the set. MACY is left alone. ASTRID rushes back.)*

ASTRID: You're on in a minute
> Vite vite vite!
> *(She sees CLAIRE in the distance.)*
> So Claire did come
> What a steel turkey of a woman
> That Claire Monsoon

MACY: Did she lose the baby Astrid?
> What is going on?

ASTRID: Oh you didn't hear?

MACY: No
> No
> I didn't hear

ASTRID: Where have you been pet?
> It was all the talk at Panet

MACY: I was writing my book
> Laura's book
> Laura's brilliant political polemic

ASTRID: Shhhh
> Claire loves it

MACY: Nobody loves it
> Nobody has read it
> All I want to know is what happened to the baby?

ASTRID: Quiet please!
> *(Lowering her voice.)*

Rumors are running rampant
But I got the full scoop from her last night
Claire went into labor early
And she gave birth to a beautiful Keeper
Perfect
Perfectly healthy baby
Everything according to her plan
You know Claire: "ducks in a row"
So she was all set to take her home
When the RSS came calling
Seems someone leaked her Tradepack status –

MACY: !What?!

ASTRID: Someone leaked her Tradepack status
She doesn't know who
You don't have any idea
Do you?

MACY: No

ASTRID: You didn't tell anyone did you?

MACY: No!
Of course not!

ASTRID: I didn't think you would –

MACY: Only –
No
No
I didn't say a word to anyone

ASTRID: Well who knows
It could have been anyone
But the RSS found out and they came in and took her baby away
Like that *(A vague gesture for "poof".)*
If she tries to go and get her
The baby
They told her she could be incarcerated
Or worse

MACY: !Oh no!

ASTRID: I don't think any of it will actually happen
   Just so long as she doesn't make a fuss

MACY: So

ASTRID: So?
   What do you mean *so?*

MACY: So
   What is she going to do?

ASTRID: Macy
   She is not *going to do* anything
   There is nothing to do

MACY: She could
   She could
   Make a fuss

ASTRID: This is *Claire Monsoon*
   Why would she make a fuss?
   So she could moon her life away
   In some North Country prison
   Raising a baby on fresh goat milk
   And making hand woven pashminas in Prison Craft Class
   Claire Monsoon runs a media empire
   She does not don a baggy puce jumpsuit and wear a GPS lovelocket
   round her wrist

MACY: But –

ASTRID: And what if she does do something
   And they put her up for trial
   On ne sait pas
   She might even be executed
   With the goats
   The weird little goats in those weird little mountain towns
   You remember the goats

MACY: But –

ASTRID: All we want to do is publicize the last print published book
   Ever
   Leave politics to those pizza-faced ladies up North

MACY: No
I know
I know
(Perhaps even speaking to herself.)
But I just feel
(She is surprised and overwhelmed by feelings.)
I feel…

(The MORNING MUSE music again but this time, the show is actually beginning.)

PAULINA: *(Offstage/Voiceover.)*
We're here with Laura Miles of Perseus Publishing
And we'll be joined later by Macy O. Blonsky //
Authors of the last print published book
Ever
Terror's Goddess

ASTRID: Oh Macy!
You're on!
Go go go go go!

MACY: Did she just say *Terror's Goddess?*
Did someone change the title?

ASTRID: Macy!
Vite!

PAULINA: We'll chat more with Laura Miles and Macy O. Blonsky
Just as soon as we come back

(A break accompanied by more alarmingly upbeat theme music.)

ASTRID: !They're waiting for you !
Go go go

MACY: No

ASTRID: What?

MACY: No
I will not go on

ASTRID: !WHAT!?
YOU WILL GO ON

AND YOU WILL SMILE WHILE DOING IT
WHAT ARE YOU TALKING ABOUT?
LAURA is doing your interview
What are you –
GET ON THAT SET!

MACY: I
 I
 I don't think I can

ASTRID: *You don't think you can!?*
 STAY HERE
 I will go and get the PA to fetch you
 A pill of some sort
 And a stiff drink
 A whole bottle even
 She doesn't think she can
 Unbelievable

MACY: Wait Astrid!
 The draft Laura gave you this morning
 I didn't even write it
 Laura wrote it
 I haven't read a word of it
 I don't even know how it ends

ASTRID: But Claire
 Claire *loves it*
 Doesn't she?

MACY: No one loves it
 Not Claire
 Not me
 Not you
 No one
 And now it's going down in history
 As the last print published book
 Ever

  (CLAIRE enters.)

CLAIRE: !Oh god!
 !There you are!

!What are you doing!
They're looking for you everywhere

ASTRID: *(Starring at MACY and CLAIRE in disbelief.)*
I give up
I give up on all of it
!Farewell to Fiction Indeed!
Just let me retire with this one, Claire
Just give me a juicy cut of the residuals
Prop me up with a cocktail
And let me read my classics in peace
Honestly
In my day
In my day
Publishing was a two-martini lunch
Witty alcoholic writers
Books that actually created conversations
And a damn good time.
Do I look like I am having a damn good time
Macy
Claire
Ladies:
If either of you need to reach me
You will find me at
!Panet!

CLAIRE: Well don't just stand there
I'll deal with Astrid
You go and get that interview
!Up and At 'Em!
!Laura is stealing all your thunder!

MACY: I know Claire

CLAIRE: What

MACY: I know what happened
To your baby
How the RSS –

CLAIRE: *(Suddenly whispering.)*
>   What???
>   You've gone insane

MACY: We should
>   We should do something

CLAIRE: We should not *do something*
>   You should go on *Morning Muse* and you should chat about your book

MACY: But we have to do something
>   I'll help you

CLAIRE: And why would you do that?

MACY: Because
>   I'm responsible

CLAIRE: *(More whispering.)*
>   Oh please
>   Do you actually think this is your responsibility?
>   You've got quite some ego then
>   Macy O. Blonsky
>   Because there are millions of things in the world that have nothing
>   Nothing to do with you
>   They are the way they are
>   And they don't give a damn about your
>   Misguided idealism
>   Or
>   Even worse
>   Your *good intentions*

MACY: It
>   It
>   It's not intentions or ideals
>   It's

>   *(MACY offers up some gesture of comfort to CLAIRE. CLAIRE thaws in some subtle but profound way, if only for a moment.)*

MACY: This world
>   No one should be alone in this world Claire

CLAIRE: Oh
    I didn't know you felt –
    I didn't think it –

MACY: It does

        (CLAIRE reciprocates the gesture.)

CLAIRE: All right
    Well
    Yes
    And I'm
    I will admit
    I am
    I am
    Disappointed
    Very disappointed
    (A slight pause.)
    But life is full of surprising
    Disappointments
    Isn't it Macy?

        (Pause: Or perhaps a sound cue.)

MACY: We could
    We could
    We could try telling people

CLAIRE: Telling people what?

MACY: We could try telling people
    About you
    About the baby

CLAIRE: But I have my life Macy
    How would that work with my life?

MACY: Well we could both create
    Different lives
    We could be different people
    We could go out into the world
    And we could say
    Claire Monsoon is a Tradepack

And if Claire Monsoon is a Tradepack
Then anyone can be a Tradepack

CLAIRE: And then

MACY: And then

CLAIRE: And then what

MACY: And then we
I don't know
And then we
We go and claim your baby
And then we
Wait and see

CLAIRE: *Wait and see?*
We would be put in prison
At best
So what
What would we be?
Some pair of loony tune truth tellers trapped behind bars
No power
No access to-
To-
No
I can't
I can't Macy
Maybe you can imagine a life like that
The way you imagined a life for your Tradepack character
I can't
I honestly can't

MACY: You
You actually read my book?

CLAIRE: Of course I read it
Macy
Of course I did

> (*The two women sit in silence while we hear the interview between*
> *LAURA and PAULINA on the "set." CLAIRE and MACY slowly descend*
> *into their own forms of grief: perhaps just slumped and deflated posture.*
> *It is a moment of unified privacy. They are alone together.*)

PAULINA: *(Offstage.)*
Our regularly scheduled guest
Macy O. Blonsky
Will be joining us later
But for the moment
We are in the charismatic thralls of
Laura Miles
Laura essentially wrote *Terror's Goddess* with Macy
These are the authors behind the
The last print published book
Ever
Quite a lofty claim
Now Laura –
We all want to know:
Is this novel funny ha ha
Or is this novel very, very sad

LAURA: Paulina
This novel will change the nation

PAULINA: !Wooooow!
!Change the nation!
!Woooooow!
Serious stuff
Give us a sneak peek:
What will *Terror's Goddess* do for us?

LAURA: I'm glad you asked
We already have *Terror's Goddess* in print
But I'd like the story to take the form of
An entire system of experiences
Practices, say, and beliefs
Terror's Goddess will guide us through the upcoming changes in our Society
Series One to Who Knows How Many

PAULINA: FANtastic!
FANtastic!

LAURA: No market tests
No Digi-Ds

CLAIRE: *(Speaking over LAURA's interview.)*
    Would you listen to that?
    I think
    I think
    Laura is jockeying for my job
    Right there
    Live on the air with Paulina Petrovsky

LAURA: No, this will be beautifully done
    Beautifully subtle and beautifully
    Visionary
    We can shape this into something
    Seamless!
    Seamless experiential downloads
    Straight into the thoughts of the readers
    Let's do away with all the cognitive spaghetti of "reading"
    And bring *Terror's Goddess* directly into the hearts and minds of the
    people

PAULINA: Oh Ms. Miles!
    I love anything with a heart and a mind
    We're speaking with Laura Miles
    And we will finally be joined by
    Macy O. Blonsky
    Just as soon as we come back
    (The show cuts out again.)

CLAIRE: So now
    Hup hup
    Up and at 'em
    Are you going to go on or not?

MACY: I don't know
    What is our story?

CLAIRE: *(Looking at MACY with genuine regret.)*
    Our story
    I know it sounds absurd
    Don't think I don't know
    But I've already told the world my story:
    I am Claire Monsoon

Who are you?
(CLAIRE leaves quickly to avoid a display of emotion.)

PAULINA: Yooo hoo?
Macy O. Blonsky?
(The show begins again and Paulina speaks on the air.)
Welcome back to *Morning Muse*
I am beginning to think that our nation's most celebrated author
Is just a figment of our imaginations
Laura…
Did you just choose "Macy" as a nom de plume?

LAURA: *(Laughter.)*
That would be something wouldn't it?

PAULINA: Macy O. Blonsky
This is your last chance
Come and speak to your readers
Everyone is so eager to hear from you

> *(MACY chooses to join PAULINA and LAURA. She exits and appears offstage on the TV show. We hear the voices offstage or as voiceovers.)*

PAULINA: There you are!
FINALLY!
We have the second author behind *Terror's Goddess* here in the studio with us

How did you come up with a title like *Terror's Goddess?*

MACY: Well
I
I
I didn't
It just *appeared*

PAULINA: *(To the audience.)*
Creative inspiration is such a mystery!
(The interview fades into a blackout.)
Now Macy
They say this is the novel that will change the nation

MACY: Yes yes
That's what they say

(A transition occurs on stage. The Morning Muse set is dismantled and there is a feeling of change that occurs over the whole of the stage and, by extension, the whole of the city.)

SCENE FIFTEEN:
BENITA & YARROW

BENITA and YARROW are speaking with a BORDER GUARD. BENITA carries their baby in some kind of sling or stroller.

YARROW: You don't understand
  We're Keepers
  We don't
  Do this
  We walk through
  Because we live here
  On this street

BORDER GUARD: Not anymore
  Miss
  I'm sorry but
  Not until I read you

BENITA: Just give her your scan card Yarrow
  Who cares
  It will only take a minute

BORDER GUARD: We don't read scan cards anymore
  I'm going to need to read you
  The both of you

> *(The BORDER GUARD "reads" YARROW by taking a needle prick in the back of her neck. The conversation happens while they wait for the reading results.)*

YARROW: We never
  We don't usually do this
  Keepers don't –

BORDER GUARD: We're shifting into a new phase of The Transition

YARROW: A new phase?

BORDER GUARD: "More expedient"
    They say
    (She turns to BENITA.)
    Now you
    (She does the same reading and then checks the machine.)
    Fine
    You can go

YARROW: That's all?

BORDER GUARD: Yes yes
    That's all

        (BENITA and YARROW begin to walk away.)

BORDER GUARD: Oh
    The baby
    I have to read the baby too

BENITA: She's sleeping

BORDER GUARD: I have to

BENITA: It took us all day to get her back to sleep

YARROW: Look at her sleeping
    You can't ask us to…

        (Slight pause.)

BORDER GUARD: Oh fine
    Go
    Just go

BENITA: Thank you so much M'am
    Have a good day.

        (BENITA exits quickly with the baby.)

BORDER GUARD: *(Speaking to YARROW as she begins to follow BENITA.)*
    But I have to read her next time

        (YARROW stops still when she hears these words.)

YARROW: Next time?

BORDER GUARD: I'm stationed out here permanently now

YARROW: …Oh
…Why?

BORDER GUARD: All part of the new *(Vague gesture for "phase".)*
Changes
You know
They keep talking about the changes

YARROW: So you'll be reading us
Every day

BORDER GUARD: Every day ma'am
Every day

(YARROW stands motionless, silent.)

BORDER GUARD: Something else?

YARROW: No no
That's all

BORDER GUARD: So I'll just get your daughter tomorrow then?

YARROW: Yes
Yes
You'll get her…
Tomorrow

SCENE SIXTEEN:
CHERYL & MACY

The INSPECTOR OVID billboard that sits behind her in full view has been changed. It now reads: "TERROR'S GODDESS: Shimmering Possibilities For Our Society." There is an airbrushed photograph of MACY on it (Rendered à la Chuck Close.). The bottom copy reads: "This novel will change your life!"

We see CHERYL arriving for work at her post on the bridge. She stares at the billboard for a moment.

CHERYL: !Next!

(MACY emerges. This time, her outfit is more stylish and she wears big, dark sunglasses. This moment should read as a kind of circular repetition of their opening scene at the top of the play.)

MACY: Excuse me
　　I'm just
　　I'm just
　　(She makes a motion for "moving along".)
　　I'm meeting a friend for dinner
　　Across the bridge
　　And I don't want to hold you up
　　Or your line
　　So if you could read me
　　I'll just
　　(Same motion for "moving along".)

CHERYL: Wait
　　Hold up

MACY: I don't want to be late
　　And I know I should just take cabs
　　But

CHERYL: Take off your sunglasses

　　　　(MACY takes them off and looks at CHERYL.)

CHERYL: I know you

MACY: *(The moment of recognition.)*
　　I
　　I'm sure I've never seen your face
　　So

CHERYL: I know you
　　I know you
　　How do I know you?
　　You're the one who

MACY: You might have seen me
　　(She gestures vaguely towards the billboard behind them.)
　　On *Morning Muse*
　　With Paulina Petrovsky

CHERYL: *(Stops and then reconsiders.)*
    Oh
    Oh that makes sense
    I thought you were someone else
    Go ahead

MACY: Do you need to read me?

CHERYL: Oh
    Seems sort of stupid
    Considering the fact that *(Vague gesture for "it's all right in front of me".)*
    But we're shifting into a new phase of the Transition
    So I'll need to read your
    (She makes a gesture to move MACY's hair away. She "reads" her neck using
    a small little machine with a needle.)

CHERYL: Okay
    You can go

MACY: Well thank you
    Then
    I'm meeting a good friend
    At Panet
    And
    And
    Ah
    Thank you
    I'll be off now
    Ta ta!

CHERYL: Ta ta?
    (A bad feeling surfaces from somewhere in the reaches of her mind but she
    can't place it.
    Ta ta
    (She looks back at the billboard.)
    Ta ta
    Ta ta
    You said
    Ta ta
    You
    You

You got to change your life
(She is suddenly overcome. She walks away from her work area and stands, staring up at the billboard. She takes out the small card from Joan and dials the number on her cell phone device.)
Hello
Hello
This is
My name is
Please
Hello
Don't hang up
Please
Don't hang up
I am calling
I am calling
(An important decision is made.)
Hello
I am a Tradepack
And
I am asking for
Joan

SCENE SEVENTEEN: VIOLET

Name: Violet
Sequencing code: 470982809
But underneath my vitals
All it said was "UK"

UK
Unclaimed Keeper

All this time
I wasn't a Tradepack at all
All this time

The system thought I was a Keeper.
It must have been my own mother who disagreed.

Newborn Baby: 470982809
Taken custody by the RSS at birth
Mother requested to remain anonymous
Status: UK (Unclaimed Keeper.)

Unclaimed Keeper

I've tried to imagine it
I have
All the details inside her decision:

There was some download somewhere
A fancy woman
Or a couple, maybe
Mother requested to remain anonymous
Maybe she wanted to go back to the hospital
Maybe she wanted to go back and claim me
But she couldn't
They couldn't
Because
Because

I'm sure they've got some story in their mind for what they did
It might even be a good one.
A brilliant one: stranger than fiction
It could be
I'd like to believe that it is
I'd like to believe so many things

Me?
I've got my own stories now
I have my own reasons for being alive
My work
My speeches
Reaching out to the Tradepacks who need me

I'm really just a product of The Transition
And my mother? The mother who actually claimed me as her own?
Well that would have to be the system itself

So when I speak to these last groups of Tradepacks
When I get them ready to depart for the next world
When I talk to them about paradise

I always read to them from the good book.

(She reads from the same gold-embossed book. This time, we can see the cover clearly: Terror's Goddess.)

And I always choose the passage about possibilities.
Shimmering possibilities.

(Reading.)

Terror's Goddess: Chapter Nine
You aren't dying.
You are departing.
You are departing with purpose.
Painless: with purpose.
And what do you leave in your stead?
Not sorrow.
Not anger.

Certainly not sickness.

You leave possibilities.
Shimmering possibilities for our society.

(She stops reading.)

Shimmering possibilities

It's just a story
I know that
They do too
On some level

But if we didn't have stories
Where would we be?

If we didn't have stories
All we would have left is
…The truth…

(The lights go out. In the darkness, we hear the frequency of the Inspector Ovid serial playing.)

INSPECTOR OVID: If we all believe in The Transition, we can change the world!

THE SNOUT: That's right Inspector Ovid
So let's introduce some new friends
From the RSS serial *Terror's Goddess*
Stay tuned as all sorts of fascinating new characters
Are downloaded directly into your lives
Through this entirely new kind of imaginative storytelling.

Welcome to this next and final chapter of
The Transition

> *(The frequency fades out somewhat or cuts out entirely. The lights come back up quickly. VIOLET is gone. The only thing that remains is the worn copy of "Terror's Goddess" and the shreds of the old billboard flapping in the wind. And then, even those details disappear before our eyes until there is nothing but darkness.)*

THE END

THE COWARD

Nick Jones

Nick Jones is a performer and writer for theater, television and film. His new play *Vérité* received its world premiere at Lincoln Centre Theater's LCT3, directed by Moritz von Stuelpnagel. His play *Trevor* played a wildly sold-out run at Theater for the New City in the spring of 2013, and his play *The Coward* also received its world premiere at LCT3 in winter 2010, under the direction of Sam Gold. Nick's critically acclaimed madcap rock puppet musical *Jollyship The Whiz-Bang* played to sold-out runs at Ars Nova in 2008 and The Public Theater's Under the Radar Festival in 2010. Nick currently works as Writer and Producer on the Netflix original series *Orange Is The New Black*. Nick's play *The Coward* was nominated for four Lortel Awards (winning two) and is now being made into a motion picture with Big Beach/American Work.

Other plays include: *Salomé Of The Moon* (Waterwell/PPAS); *The Wundelsteipen* (the Flea); *Little Building* (Galapagos); *Straight Up Vampire: The History Of Vampires In Colonial Pennsylvania As Performed To The Music Of Paula Abdul* (Philly Fringe Festival, Joe's Pub); *Canada's Mid-Riff* (chashama); *Rockberry: The Last One Man Show* (The Brick); *The Nosemaker's Apprentice* (The Brick, with Rachel Shukert); *The Sporting Life* (Studio 42 at the Vineyard Theater, also with Shukert); and *The Colonists*, a puppet work for children (The Brick; "Best Puppet Show," L Magazine, 2009).

Nick was born and raised in Anchorage, Alaska. He earned his Literature/Creative Writing BA from Bard College and a Lila Acheson Wallace Playwriting degree from Juilliard, where he was a two time winner of the Lecomte du Nouy Prize. He has received theater commissions from Lincoln Center, Ars Nova, The Old Globe, Manhattan Theater Club, The Huntington, Center Theater Group and South Coast Rep.

More at nickjonesland.com.

Introduction

I first met Nick Jones through this very play, *The Coward*, which he submitted to Juilliard along with his application for admission. Christopher Durang and I took him in by the end of the first page.
So we can take no credit for his great wit and wondrous theatricality. Usually the Juilliard experience helps writers gain confidence and a sense of their "stuff." But Nick already had his voice and his agenda. He later told us that *The Coward* was the first play he had written for human actors, and that he only wrote it because he wanted to get into Juilliard. But it was fully formed, hilarious, completely eccentric and a great joy.

It is the story of a young man who wants to please his father. But his father will only be pleased if his son participates in duels, the precise activity that has killed his other two sons. Our hero, the coward of the title, decides to find and pay a surrogate to conduct duels in his place. And the plan works well until the surrogate decides he likes being the heroic son of the famous father, and uses his dueling prowess to even some scores of his own. When the "coward" intervenes to stop the surrogate's appropriation of his position, he proves heroic in his own unique way, and wins any last bits love we didn't already feel for him.

Nick is a serious writer, pushing the limits of playwriting in every venture. The worlds he creates are odd, the premises often fantastical, but he commits to them fully, and is absolutely prepared for the audience to turn away, though they never really do. A later play dealing with a medieval gang of no-good alchemists trying to create babies without women is pretty disturbing, but is finally so comically demented that you can't resist it.

The great humor of *The Coward*, however, comes from its inescapable humanity. People are afraid, ashamed, embarrassed, greedy, vain and stupid, but they are still capable of love and acts of great bravery. They select friends and stick with them. They confess to being weak, and yet they can be strong if they have to be. They hate their parents, but rarely kill them, preferring to hope they will change. Nick Jones knows we are all fallible, and that is his great subject in this and other plays. We are both less and more than we know. But it takes a great writer to convey that, and at the same time, make us laugh and carry us effortlessly through his tale.

Nick is an entertainer with serious questions to ask. His plays explore issues of gender identity, human callousness, and our place in the natural world. He is fascinated with history, and drawn to adventures. He would have been happy on the deck of a sailing ship bound for parts unknown, his scarf flapping in the sea breeze, his quill and paper waiting in his cabin below. But I am glad he is living in this time writing for the American theater.

I love this play, and I am so pleased to introduce you to it. Enjoy!

Marsha Norman

Production history

World Premiere at Lincoln Center Theater/LCT3 on November 22, 2010 under the direction of Sam Gold

Scenic Designer: David Zinn
Costume Designer: Gabriel Berry
Lighting Designer: Ben Stanton
Sound Designer: Jane Shaw
Fight Director: J. David Brimmer
Special Effects: Waldo Warshaw

Presented by Lincoln Center Theater
Artistic Director, André Bishop; Executive Director Bernard Gersten;
LCT3 Artistic Director, Paige Evans

Cast

ROBERT BLITHE:	Steven Boyer
OLD MAN/EGBERT/FRIEDMONT/	
SIR DEREK LANLEY:	Jarlath Conroy
FINN/EARL OF DORCHESTER/	
KING'S MESSENER:	John Patrick Doherty
GAVIN KLAFF:	Stephen Ellis
NATHANIEL CULLING:	Richard Poe
ISABELLA DUPREEE:	Kristen Schaal
LUCIDUS CULLING:	Jeremy Strong
HENRY BLAINE:	Christopher Evan Welch

Characters (7 men, 1 woman)

LUCIDUS CULLING	a rather delicate young noblemen of 20.
FATHER/NATHANIEL CULLING	40s.
HENRY BLAINE	Rake, scamp, duelist. 30s.
GAVIN KLAFF	a friend of Lucidus, 20s.
ROBERT BLITHE	a friend of Lucidus, 20s.
FINN	a friend of Henry Blaine's, 30s – 40s
ISABELLE DUPREE	a fine girl of 18, from royal stock.
THE EARL OF DORCHESTER 40s.	
SIR DEREK LANLEY	the Earl's friend and second.
OLD MAN	the father of the Earl. 50s –70s.
FRIEDMONT	the Butler.
EGBERT	the Bartender.
KING'S MESSENGER	

Old Man, Friedmont the Butler, Egbert the Bartender, and Derek Lanley may be played by one actor.

The Earl of Dorchester, Finn and The King's Messenger may be played by one actor.

THE SETTING
England, 1790. Sort of.

'/' indicates an interruption.

SCENE 1.

FATHER pours a glass of wine. His son, LUCIDUS, looks on.

FATHER: We are a family of gentlemen. As such, we are expected to act in accordance with our class. We are expected to behave nobly, and courageously, as befitting men with the right to bear arms. Lucidus, you are twenty years old. A man. By this time I should delight in hearing tales of your courage. At your age your brothers had already fought many duels. But you...you have fought nothing...

LUCIDUS: Father...

FATHER: I am not finished. The Baron approached me yesterday and told me that a man had been speaking slander against our family. He said this man said that you were a coward. That he saw someone call your horse fat and that you sought no satisfaction from him.

LUCIDUS: That is not true! I would never stand for that.

FATHER: Well, a man said this, so...I was then forced to seek out this man. To engage in a duel. At my age! Is it too much to expect that my son should protect the family honor? Or am I no more than a rock behind which you may be sheltered from all of life's tempests?

LUCIDUS: No! I would never let anyone talk like that. Tell me the name of the man, and I will settle the matter.

FATHER: It is settled. As it turned out, he was not a gentlemen, so was beneath my call to a challenge. I simply beat him with my riding stick and that was that. But I cannot stop all men from talking. And men *will* keep talking, unless you do something to bolster your reputation.

LUCIDUS: Father, I would never let anyone call my horse fat. You should know that.

FATHER: I do not know that. It is up to you to prove that to me.

SCENE 2.

In the park. LUCIDUS and his friends ROBERT and GAVIN are splayed upon a blanket, eating treats. An OLD MAN sits on a bench some distance away, enjoying the feel of sunshine on his face. His face is contorted strangely, as by a stroke.

GAVIN: Mm, I like the gooseberry. Of course I always like the gooseberry.

ROBERT: Oh but Gavin, the peach, the peach is colossal. I mean, the gooseberry is good, but it's *always good*. Peach, it takes some luck, to get a really good one.

GAVIN: What do you think Lucidus? Which cobbler do you think is best?

LUCIDUS: Oh, I can't say. I like them both fine.

GAVIN: Like them both not at all, you mean. Look, he's hardly touched his.

ROBERT: I say, Lucidus, are you feeling alright? *(LUCIDUS is not looking.)* Lucidus?

LUCIDUS: *(Surprised.)* What?

ROBERT: You look a bit wan.

LUCIDUS: What? Why do you say that? *(Getting to his feet.)* What do you mean by that?

ROBERT: Nothing. I just thought, if you're weren't feeling well, we could summon your coachman.

GAVIN: Lucidus, what's the matter?

LUCIDUS: *(Relenting.)* Nothing. I'm sorry.

ROBERT: What are you up in arms about? You're with your friends, and it's a beautiful day in the park.

LUCIDUS: I know. I'm sorry, my friends. *(Sitting back down.)* I was so looking forward to our weekend pie tasting. I suppose I'm feeling a bit out of sorts.

ROBERT: What is it? Is it Isabelle? Did she not return your handkerchief?

LUCIDUS: No, she didn't. But it's not about that. *(Noticing the OLD MAN looking in their direction.)* It's hard to talk about.

ROBERT: Well, it's a good thing she has that handkerchief, it means she hasn't made up her mind about you yet.

GAVIN: But she has not responded to his invitations.

(LUCIDUS becomes increasingly fixated on the OLD MAN.)

ROBERT: Well of course, because he's not known or respected yet. But his father is. That's probably why Isabelle hasn't rejected you outright. But I'll tell you this Lucidus: if Isabelle keeps turning down your invitations, but then keeps your handkerchief, that's not right. Then you need to demand she give it back!

LUCIDUS: Tell me friends, do you know that man over there?

GAVIN: *(Looking yonder.)* Who's that? Duke Pendleton?

LUCIDUS: No, that man there, on the bench.

ROBERT: Oh, you mean, the old man?

LUCIDUS: Yes.

ROBERT: No. What about him?

LUCIDUS: Does it seem to you that he's a making at face at me?

GAVIN: What sort of face?

LUCIDUS: A horrible face. A mocking face. He's not doing it now. But he was.

GAVIN: A mocking face, eh? Was it a face like this? *(Makes a silly face.)*

LUCIDUS: Quit that! I am serious! You mock my being mocked!

GAVIN: No!

ROBERT: Lucidus, calm down!

(LUCIDUS settles back down.)

ROBERT: God lord. Who put the bee in your bonnet?

GAVIN: Oh! Speaking of bonnets, we'd better go soon. Alexandra's party's going to start and we need time to change.

ROBERT: What? You want to leave already? We have a whole basket of pies we haven't even tasted.

GAVIN: But what if we're late?

ROBERT: We're not going to be late. Stop worrying about your clothes.

GAVIN: But I told Alexandra I'd wear my green waistcoat.

ROBERT: Well then why didn't you wear it to begin with?

GAVIN: I didn't want to risk getting it stained.

ROBERT: Oh Gavin…

GAVIN: What? As if you don't change your clothes between meals.

LUCIDUS: That's it.

>   (*LUCIDUS stands.*)

GAVIN: Lucidus what are you doing?

LUCIDUS: That man is definitely making a face at me.

ROBERT: What? No he's not. Lucidus, he's just an old man. Maybe he had a stroke. His face might just look that way.

LUCIDUS: *(So anyone nearby can hear.)* Well then, he shouldn't look in my direction. I am a gentlemen, and I won't stand for it!

>   (*He walks over to the OLD MAN, with purpose.*)

GAVIN: Lucidus? What is he doing?

LUCIDUS: *(To OLD MAN.)* You sir. You make faces at me?

OLD MAN: What? Who is it?

LUCIDUS: My name is Lucidus Culling. And I have just seen you making a horrible face at me. I demand an explanation.

OLD MAN: A horrible face? What are you talking about? Are you insulting me?

LUCIDUS: No sir. I believe it is *you* who is insulting *me*.

OLD MAN: What? If I wished to insult you I would do so plainly sir, not make faces like a child.

LUCIDUS: Oh a child am I?

OLD MAN: No, I didn't say that. Look boy, I do not wish to quarrel…

LUCIDUS: Well you should not have insulted me then. I challenge you sir.

OLD MAN: What?

LUCIDUS: I said I challenge you.

ROBERT: Lucidus, what are you doing?

OLD MAN: Leave me be. I did not make faces at you, I cannot even see you. I am blind!

LUCIDUS: You're what?

OLD MAN: I said I'm blind.

> *(Beat.).*

LUCIDUS: Well then, if you do not wish to fight, you should not go around insulting gentlemen sir.

OLD MAN: *(Getting up, trying to leave.)* Oh leave me be.

LUCIDUS: Not so fast – I demand your name, sir. So I may issue you an official challenge.

OLD MAN: Go away!

> *(LUCIDUS tries to stop him.)*

LUCIDUS: Not so fast.

> *(In trying to stop the OLD MAN, who resists, he gets tripped up and falls on him. ROBERT and GAVIN rush over.)*

OLD MAN: OOOW, my leg! Get off of me!

GAVIN: Lucidus, what are you doing?

ROBERT: Have you lost your senses?

OLD MAN: *(Continuing lamentation and pain.)*

LUCIDUS: Y-you have hurt yourself, sir..?

> *(ROBERT and GAVIN attempt to help the OLD MAN, while ushering LUCIDUS to leave.)*

ROBERT: Lucidus, what have you done?

LUCIDUS: *(In loud voice, for all to hear.)* Done? Nothing. It seems the gentlemen has broken his leg, accidentally.

ROBERT: Go, now – to the carriages.

LUCIDUS: In view of your accidental injury, I will consider my honor satisfied…accidentally.

OLD MAN: *(Furious.)* Honor? Honor?! You have no honor!

LUCIDUS: *(Again bristling.)* What's that, sir?

GAVIN AND ROBERT: Lucidus!

GAVIN: Leave!

SCENE 3.

LUCIDUS stands before his FATHER.

FATHER: You have been challenged by the Earl of Dorchester.

LUCIDUS: Who is that?

FATHER: The son of the old man whose leg you broke. Why did you break an old man's leg?

LUCIDUS: It was an accident. He had insulted me, and I was confronting him.

FATHER: Well, now you're to duel his son.

LUCIDUS: But I don't want to fight his son. The business is between his father and I only.

FATHER: His father is an invalid, and a hero, from the Seven Years' War. He does not need to fight you.

LUCIDUS: Then he is a coward!

FATHER: You will fight the Earl.

LUCIDUS: Very well. I will fight whoever is presented me. Who is this Earl?

FATHER: The Earl was a professional soldier, like his father. In the Army he was renowned for his skill with the sword. But they say that is nothing beside his skill with the pistol…

LUCIDUS: Oh?

FATHER: That's the word around Parliament. Fortunately, as the challenged, you will choose the weapon. There is luck involved in pistols. Despite his superior skill, a misfire is possible. So, you could get lucky.

LUCIDUS: Oh? Could I?

FATHER: Yes, it is possible. Don't tell me you're frightened…

LUCIDUS: Nay. Not I, father.

FATHER: You are frightened.

LUCIDUS: I am not frightened. *(FATHER waits.)* I am a little frightened.

FATHER: That is all well and good. Be frightened. There is no shame in fear. There is only shame in cowardice. To fight the Earl will take courage. If you live, you will be respected.

LUCIDUS: And if I die, father?

FATHER: You will be even more respected.

SCENE 4.

LUCIDUS is with his friends ROBERT and GAVIN. He is hysterical.

LUCIDUS: I don't want to! I don't want to die!

ROBERT: Lucidus, it's going to be alright! You may not die. Right Gavin?

GAVIN: Right. He might even…not be wounded.

LUCIDUS: Yes, yes but –

ROBERT: And they'll write of it in the paper for sure.

LUCIDUS: But –

ROBERT: Look my friend, It's a nasty responsibility, but one we must all face eventually.

LUCIDUS: But –

ROBERT: Your brothers all had to duel, didn't they?

LUCIDUS: My brothers are all dead!

ROBERT: Yes, well, learn from their mistakes. What did they do wrong?

LUCIDUS: Duel!

ROBERT: Not practice their marksmanship.

GAVIN: There you go.

ROBERT: Get a little practice in. How about that? Not so much as to seem unsporting of course.

GAVIN: Right. Just some familiarity with the weapon; so you can learn how to…you know…make it shoot.

LUCIDUS: I'm going to die.

GAVIN AND ROBERT: *(Not perfectly in unison.)* Nooooo…

LUCIDUS: I'm going to die.

> *(Beat. GAVIN and ROBERT look at each other.)*

ROBERT: Well…damn it Lucidus, if you're that scared of death than why'd you go around challenging people?

LUCIDUS: I didn't want people to think I was a coward.

GAVIN: But you are a coward.

LUCIDUS: I know! *Now!*

GAVIN: Well, then, maybe you shouldn't go through with it.

LUCIDUS: I have to.

GAVIN: Why?

LUCIDUS: Because! I'm a Culling!

GAVIN: So?

LUCIDUS: So you're not going to understand because you're not a real noblemen, but the Cullings have a reputation, as warriors. That's what got my father elected to Parliament.

GAVIN: Wait, what do you mean I'm not a real noblemen?

LUCIDUS: Well you know, you're just the youngest son of a royal lord. My father's the eldest son of a Baronet…

GAVIN: So?

LUCIDUS: So it's no big deal, but we're different quality people.

GAVIN: Oh.

LUCIDUS: Well…

GAVIN: Yes, I can see that.

LUCIDUS: Look, don't go and make this about you. I'm the one in trouble in here!

ROBERT: Wait, Lucidus, wait. I have an idea. Why not just hire someone to fight for you?

LUCIDUS: What do you mean?

ROBERT: The Earl is fighting for his father. So why shouldn't you find someone?

LUCIDUS: But can you do that?

ROBERT: Knights fought for kings.

GAVIN: *(Sulky.)* He's not a king. He's only the eldest grandson of a Baronet...

LUCIDUS: You're right, it's fair! I just need a champion! But who?

ROBERT: We could go to the pubs in town. We could interview commoners for the job. Who ever seems the strongest candidate, we'll hire.

LUCIDUS: What do I care? As long as they're strong enough to hold a pistol...

ROBERT: I'll bet most commoners will jump at the chance to duel for you. I mean, it isn't everyday you get a chance to fight for honor. Not when you don't have any in your blood to begin with!

(ROBERT looks askance at GAVIN, who is pondering his own situation now. GAVIN catches ROBERT looking at him. ROBERT quickly looks away.)

LUCIDUS: Yes! Excellent, excellent! Come! There's no time to waste. *(They start away. GAVIN does not follow.)* Gavin? Come, let's away!

GAVIN: Oh, why don't you just go on without me. I just went into town yesterday. I don't want to be seen there again so soon.

LUCIDUS: Gavin...

ROBERT: Oh don't worry about him.

SCENE 5.

ROBERT and LUCIDUS enter a pub. A BARTENDER leans against a bar, and two men, FINN and HENRY, play cards at a table some distance away.

LUCIDUS: Oh Robert this is wonderful. Just look at this. This is like, Ruffian City.

ROBERT: I know. Lord Quimby showed me this place. We come here for prostitutes. But there's all kinds of riff raff: stevedores, jugglers, pirates. It's like a riff raff rainbow. Now look, I think the best way to deal with these people is just lay down the facts. Don't embellish anything. Let your money talk.

BARTENDER: May I help you gentlemen?

LUCIDUS: Yes, sir, thank you. I am looking to enlist a mercenary.

BARTENDER: A mercenary? You mean, King's business? Most men round here aren't too happy with the King right now. Not after that hat tax bullshit. These men used to like to wear hats. Now they can't afford it.

LUCIDUS: This is not for the King. It is a personal matter. A duel.

BARTENDER: Oh, a duel, why didn't you say so! Wonderful! You'll find plenty people who will fight you, dressed like that.

LUCIDUS: No, it isn't an adversary I seek, it's a man to fight in my place. To fight a duel for me, in proxy.

BARTENDER: To fight a duel *for you?*

LUCIDUS: Yes. I will pay the man. Handsomely.

BARTENDER: But dear god, I've never heard of such a thing.

LUCIDUS: Nevermind! Have you a man for me?

BARTENDER: Aye. *(He points.)* There's your man. Henry Blaine. Rake. Scamp. And a fighter, if ever one was born.

ROBERT: Has he skill with arms?

BARTENDER: Yes, sir. He was an enlisted man. He fought them rebel Yanks in the colonies.

ROBERT: A lot of good that did.

LUCIDUS: Seriously.

BARTENDER: What makes a man is not what side he fights for, or what side wins. What makes a man is whether he fights.

(LUCIDUS and ROBERT approach HENRY and FINN's table.)

LUCIDUS: Excuse me, sir. Are you the man Henry Blaine?

HENRY: I am. Who are you?

LUCIDUS: My name is not important, for the time being. I come to you with a business proposal. If there is some quiet place we might adjourn?

(A pause, as HENRY appraises the two men.)

HENRY: Two pounds. Three if he's around to watch. I don't do double stuff.

LUCIDUS: No sir, you misunderstand. I am told you are gifted warrior. And I need a warrior. To fight on my behalf, in a duel.

HENRY: A duel? Over what?

LUCIDUS: It is a matter of honor.

HENRY: Well obviously it's a matter of honor, but what specifically?

FINN: Did he wear the same red boots as you? In the Snickerdoodle Parade?

(FINN laughs.)

LUCIDUS: What's the Snickerdoodle /Parade

(They laugh over him.)

No. He…The man, the man coveted my wife, sir.

HENRY: Hm. Well that is a taint on the old name. And what does your wife have to say, sir?

LUCIDUS: She…killed herself.

HENRY: At least she did the right thing.

LUCIDUS: Thank you.

HENRY: My condolences.

LUCIDUS: Thank you.

HENRY: But tell me sir, should you not seek redress, for this most terrible of injuries, by your own hand?

LUCIDUS: I would. I would, certainly. Were this not such a busy week. I have some business. Out of town.

HENRY: *(Smelling the lie.)* Ah yes. I'm sure you're a busy man. I can only imagine the sort of *busy life* you must lead. But tell me, my fair cuckold, what is the name of the man who did you this wrong?

LUCIDUS: His name is The Earl of Dorchester.

HENRY: The Earl of Dorchester you say?

LUCIDUS: Yes.

HENRY: But that can't be right sir…

LUCIDUS: Why not?

HENRY: Because the Earl of Dorchester is sitting RIGHT HERE!

FINN: *(Standing.)* I'm the Earl of Dorcester! And your wife sir, is a slut!

  (The two men laugh. The laughter will continue with each subsequent dig.)

A dead slut!

HENRY: *(Toasting.)* To your dead slut whore wife.

LUCIDUS: You …mock me?!

FINN: Yes.

ROBERT: *(Whispering.)* Lucidus, let's go…

LUCIDUS: You speak ill of my wife?!

FINN: Yes.

ROBERT: *(Whispering.)* Lucidus, you don't have a wife, what are you doing?

FINN: What are you going to do?! *Challenge me to a duel?*

BARTENDER: Pay me! I'll fight him for you.

LUCIDUS: You men are all rascals! Rascals I say!

FINN: Go on, throw a crumpet at me!

ROBERT: *(Pulling him away.)* Lucidus…

(LUCIDUS and ROBERT head for the door.)

HENRY: Lucidus. That's an unusual name. Memorable. I look forward to reading of your duel with the Earl, Lucidus.

BARTENDER: Yeah, in the obituaries, where you belong!

FINN: Bye-bye, Loo-cidus.

SCENE 6.

LUCIDUS is at home. From out of his desk, he removes a thin wooden case. He lays the box on the desk and opens it. Within is a brace of pistols, as well as accessories for loading and cleaning. He takes out a pistol and regards it gravely. He examines the accessories – a bottle of gunpowder, a ramrod – and tries to imagine how they work together to load the gun. He begins filling the pistol's powder pan with gunpowder, trying to teach himself as best he can. There is a knock at the door, which startles him, causing him to jump, and thus knock or blow the gunpowder out of the pan.

LUCIDUS: Yes? Come in.

(FRIEDMONT the Butler enters.)

FRIEDMONT: Your tea, Mr Culling.

LUCIDUS: Yes, thank you.

(FRIEDMONT comes and lays a tray of tea on the desk and begins to pour it.)

FRIEDMONT: Ah. Another letter has been returned to you, by Isabelle Dupree.

(He takes it from his inside pocket and hands it over.)

LUCIDUS: What? But I didn't send any new letter.

FRIEDMONT: I believe your father may have written this one sir. On your behalf.

LUCIDUS: I wish he wouldn't do that. I can do my own wooing.

FRIEDMONT: Of course you can sir. Perhaps he just thought his handwriting would more appeal to the lady…

LUCIDUS: Yes, well, obviously it did not. Thank you.

(FRIEDMONT *lingers, eyeing the pistols. LUCIDUS looks up.*)

FRIEDMONT: I see you have your brother's old dueling set.

LUCIDUS: Yes?

FRIEDMONT: Going out for some target shooting then, sir?

LUCIDUS: Yes. Just some target shooting. Nothing in excess. And it's been such a long time, I can't seem to remember how to load the damn thing.

FRIEDMONT: Will you allow me, sir?

LUCIDUS: You know of such matters?

FRIEDMONT: Of course, sir. May I?

(*LUCIDUS hands him a pistol.*)

Wogdon 22 Caliber. A fine piece of workmanship. Your brother quite knew his weaponry.

LUCIDUS: Yes, well we all have different interests. I had more the scientific mind.

FRIEDMONT: Yes sir. Technically, your bug collecting falls under the realm of science. Let me show you how to do that. (*He begins loading the weapon.*) You see, you simply place the main charge here with the ball, and load in the second charge here...

LUCIDUS: Ah yes, the second charge, now I remember.

(*Reaching to take the gun from him.*)

FRIEDMONT: It's easy to forget. Just let me do it for you, sir.

(*Turning away, denying him this.*)

LUCIDUS: That's all right. I will do it.

FRIEDMONT: No need...

LUCIDUS: (*Trying to take it from him.*) No, Friedmont, Just give it to me.

FRIEDMONT: No need...

LUCIDUS: Give it to me. Really. JUST LET ME HAVE THE BLASTED GUN!

(LUCIDUS puts his hand in FRIEDMONT's face, just as the doorbell rings.)

I'm sorry for touching your face.

FRIEDMONT: It's nothing at all sir. Excuse me…

(He goes to answer the door in the next room.)

(LUCIDUS struggles to load the gun. His hands shake. He can't do it. He is close to tears. In a short time, FRIEDMONT reappears.)

FRIEDMONT: Mr Culling, sir? You have a visitor.

LUCIDUS: Who is it?

FRIEDMONT: A Mr Blaine sir.

LUCIDUS: *(Not recognizing the name.)* Send him in.

(HENRY enters.)

HENRY: Good day, sir. You look well this morning.

LUCIDUS: What are you doing here? How did you know where I live?

HENRY: It's not difficult to find a gentlemen's house. You're a dying breed, after all.

LUCIDUS: So you've come to my house to mock me?!

HENRY: No sir. I was only joking. I've come to tell you I've reconsidered your proposal. Or rather, I was always inclined to say yes, but couldn't in front of my fellows. There's a different sort of code down in the pubs, you understand?

LUCIDUS: Oh yes, you just had to see to it that I was publically humiliated first…

HENRY: Yes, exactly, I had to, sir. Since you're a coward. I actually have nothing against cowards myself. But with the lads, there's a bit of a bias – unfair bias I think, since there's been many great cowards throughout history. Like…well the names escape me, but I'm sure they're there.

LUCIDUS: Yes, that's enough! I'll have you know I am not a coward.

HENRY: Oh, is that so, sir?

LUCIDUS: No. Yes. It's so! I will be fighting the duel myself. So I will not be needing your services; nor those of any man.

HENRY: *(Wryly.)* Oh. Well, I guess that business out of town has been postponed then?

LUCIDUS: I will now ask you to take your leave, sir.

HENRY: Okay, now just a minute…

LUCIDUS: I do not have another minute for you sir!

HENRY: Now look, I didn't mean to cause you offense. And I didn't come all this way to mock you. I only want to fight. I know you'll pay a fair price, and frankly, I need the money.

LUCIDUS: That is not my concern.

HENRY: But sir, you are not a fighter. And all I ask is twenty /pounds.

LUCIDUS: Did you not hear me! I asked you to leave!

> *(There is a beat. LUCIDUS takes the pistol, cocks it and points. But just as he has the gun out, HENRY has his own pistol out and pointed at LUCIDUS.)*

HENRY: Careful… Let's not do /anything

LUCIDUS: What do you want?

HENRY: I told you, I just want to fight for you.

LUCIDUS: And?

HENRY: And I like to duel. A lot. I'm quite good, you see. But people are usually good at things they enjoy; and no one I've yet met seems to take as much pleasure as I. And how do you like it, sir? How do you enjoy looking down the barrel of a gun? Being a twitch away from having your skull bashed open by a lead ball, or rending open your stomach? You can see it now, can't you? Your intestines in your hands? You'll fumble with them, try to shove them back in, but they'll never fit back quite right. And then you'll die, quickly sometimes, but usually slowly, bleeding to death, or of infection over several days; days you'll spend howling in agony; agony no opium could soothe; a pain like a thousand banshees. It isn't pretty, sir. Not the sport for everyone. Certainly not the sport for you.

LUCIDUS: I...asked you to leave...

HENRY: Let's put down our pistols sir. Let's talk it over. I can help you. Alright? Alright, I am putting my pistol away...

(As he lays his pistol down, LUCIDUS suddenly fires his own. HENRY flinches, realizes he is unstruck and then glares sharply at LUCIDUS who puts down his pistol, and backs away.)

LUCIDUS: Don't hurt me.

HENRY: That was very unsportsmanlike.

(Moving toward him.)

LUCIDUS: Oh please. Please don't hurt me. I'm sorry. Don't kill me.

(HENRY takes him by the shoulders.)

HENRY: I'm not trying to kill you! I'm trying to save your life, don't you understand, you damn fool!

(FRIEDMONT enters.)

FRIEDMONT: Sir? Is everything alright?

HENRY: Yes, everything is fine. Isn't it, Lucidus?

(LUCIDUS nods.)

FRIEDMONT: I heard a shot...

HENRY: It was nothing. It was just an accident – right Lucidus?

FRIEDMONT: Are you quite alright sir?

HENRY: Yes, he's fine! Aren't you fine!? Tell him you're fine!

LUCIDUS: Yes, Friedmont, I'm fine. Thank you...

(FRIEDMONT hesitates to leave.)

Thank you!

(FRIEDMONT leaves.)

HENRY: You see? I'm not as base as you think.

LUCIDUS: Very well. If it means so much to you, you may fight as my champion.

HENRY: Excellent sir. You will not regret it. I have fought many duels and won them all. Just tell me when and where.

LUCIDUS: My father is making the arrangements. The duel will take place sometime this week.

HENRY: Your father?

LUCIDUS: Yes. He will be acting as your second. It's alright, he knows all about these things. Oh you didn't think I was asking you to pretend that you were actually – that you would assume my name?

HENRY: I did.

LUCIDUS: No, you will *represent me*, as my *champion*. It is legitimate. The Earl is fighting for his father…

HENRY: I see. And was it the Earl's father who slept with your wife?

LUCIDUS: No, I don't have a wife. I may have misled you…

HENRY: I know. I'm just fucking with you, sir. Now listen here a moment. I don't know your father, but don't you think it would make him happier to imagine you settling your own affairs? I often wish I could turn back the hands of time, to prove to my father I'm a worthy man. And here you have this perfect opportunity, *to lie*…

LUCIDUS: You mean you would just…but how could anyone believe you are me? You are coarse and uneducated.

HENRY: Don't think we'll be speaking much Latin, sir.

LUCIDUS: Well probably not. You never know. *Auribus tenere lunum*. I mean, *lupum*. Wait…

HENRY: Trust me sir. All I need are some new clothes. And twenty pounds.

SCENE 7.

At FATHER's Manor. FATHER is in a good mood. LUCIDUS enters.

FATHER: Ah Lucidus, come in! Come in, my Lucey. Oh so happy to see you.

LUCIDUS: And I you, father.

FATHER: I was just about to go meet the Earl's man. We've been corresponding a bit by post but it's time to meet face to face, to muddle through the final details.

LUCIDUS: Yes father, actually I –

FATHER: But first, I have a present for you.

LUCIDUS: A present?

FATHER: Yes, one moment.

> (He goes and fetches a package which he hands to LUCIDUS. He opens it. It is a silk shirt.)

LUCIDUS: A new shirt…

FATHER: It's the finest silk. The absolute finest. It's important you wear good silk when you meet your man. Quite often when you are struck, the ball takes some of your clothing with it into the wound. Silk is the best and purest fabric and least likely to cause infection. Dying of an infected wound is the last way you want to go. Better right there on the battle field, if at all.

LUCIDUS: I will die as God sees fit.

FATHER: That's the spirit! Now put that back in the box. I just wanted you to see it.

LUCIDUS: Thank you father. It's very considerate.

FATHER: A trifle. I'm just so excited. My little boy's big day! I remember your eldest brother's first duel, and his last. What a day!

LUCIDUS: Father, about the preparations…

FATHER: Yes?

LUCIDUS: I have someone else I would like to act as my second.

FATHER: *(Taken aback.)* You don't want me to be your second?

LUCIDUS: Obviously, I would be happy to have you, but my friend… It has been his dream to second me. Since we were boys playing fighting games…

FATHER: But you never played such games. You played with ants…

LUCIDUS: I also played fighting games! Magnificent violent fighting games.

FATHER: But who is it? Gavin? That fop from the bullshit family?

LUCIDUS: No, it's someone else. A friend you don't know…his name is… Hanaroy Trudging.

FATHER: Trudging?

LUCIDUS: It's not an important family.

FATHER: Well, Lucidus, this comes as a bit of shock. I mean, obviously it's your decision, but it's a shock, and especially since I've already done most of the work…

LUCIDUS: I know, father. I'm sorry I didn't tell you earlier…

FATHER: I was looking forward to meeting the Earl's second. Derek. He seems very nice. Excellent handwriting. Well I guess I'll get to meet him tomorrow. I was going to bring a few colleagues from work, if that's alright…

LUCIDUS: Actually, father, I'd rather it be a private affair.

FATHER: Very well, quite right, I'll come alone then.

LUCIDUS: Actually, I'd rather you weren't there, either.

FATHER: What?!

LUCIDUS: If something should happen to me, a parent should not have to witness that.

FATHER: Well I am not like other parents! I want to be there!

LUCIDUS: Father, it's my affair.

FATHER: It's our family's honor at stake.

LUCIDUS: I need for you to trust that I can uphold that honor on my own. Isn't that what you wanted?

FATHER: Well, yes, but…

LUCIDUS: So I need you to trust me.

(FATHER *looks over his son.*)

FATHER: I do trust you, Lucidus. I didn't before. But I see now that you are very brave.

LUCIDUS: Father, I only want to make you proud.

FATHER: *(Overcome with emotion.)* Oh, Lucey, what a man you've become.

(They shake hands.)

SCENE 8.

LUCIDUS meets DEREK LANLEY, THE EARL's second. They will sit to discuss the details.

LUCIDUS: Are you Derek?

LANLEY: Yes. You are the boy's father?

LUCIDUS: Ah, no. My name is Hanaroy Trudging. I will be acting as Lucidus's second.

LANLEY: Oh? But I had thought that /Mr Culling...

LUCIDUS: Mr Culling has been dispatched to attend to other duties. Regrettably.

LANLEY: I see. No matter then. It's Trudging, you say?

LUCIDUS: Yes.

LANLEY: Where is that /from?

LUCIDUS: Don't bother trying to think of my family. They're nothing. I'm sure you've never heard of them.

LANLEY: No no, but I'm sure I have met a Trudging before. Sausages? You make sausages?

LUCIDUS: No. Once, maybe.

LANLEY: Oh well, no matter. Please have a seat, sir.

LUCIDUS: Thank you.

(LUCIDUS sits at the nearest chair, which is not at the table.)

LANLEY: No, bring it over.

LUCIDUS: Ah.

(LUCIDUS brings the chair over, sits.)

LUCIDUS: My understanding is that we have only to choose a spot...it's pistols, yes?

LANLEY: Yes, so we had agreed, but before we get into that...

LUCIDUS: Yes?

LANLEY: The Earl would like to express his sincere regrets about the whole affair. He has great respect for the boy's father.

LUCIDUS: Oh, well you may thank him for that.

LANLEY: It has also not escaped our notice that the Cullings have lost two sons to dueling already. And that there are no more male heirs left.

LUCIDUS: Yes?

LANLEY: It is my hope, on behalf of the Earl, to resolve this matter without bloodshed.

LUCIDUS: Mm-hm. And what would satisfy the Earl?

LANLEY: A simple apology, to both he and his father. It was a misunderstanding, and can be shown publically as such.

LUCIDUS: Hmm...

LANLEY: Certainly we don't wish to destroy a noble family...

LUCIDUS: You may thank the Earl for his concern, but Lucidus Culling cannot accept a retraction at this point. A slander has been made and honor must be restored.

LANLEY: Yes, but this business of dueling, sir – it is barbaric. And had the Earl known of the boy's situation, he most certainly would not have challenged him...

LUCIDUS: You speak of Lucidus? What situation?

LANLEY: Only we have heard that Lucidus is rather inexperienced and perhaps...a bit slow, sir. In the head. Which is to say, in the brain. The Earl is an experienced fighter. It is perhaps beneath him to fight such an unfortunate soul.

LUCIDUS: This is further slander, sir!

LANLEY: But that is just what everyone thinks.

LUCIDUS: Then Lucidus Culling will demand satisfaction from *everyone!* Lucidus Culling is the bravest smartest man I ever did meet, and if the Earl will not fight him, his name will be posted as a coward!

(He stands up abruptly.)

LANLEY: Very well.

LUCIDUS: And that is that…

LANLEY: But –

LUCIDUS: Is that!

LANLEY: *(Firmly.)* We are not finished, please sit back down.

(LUCIDUS sits back down.)

Though I feel this decision extremely unwise, I have been given authority to proceed.

LUCIDUS: Excellent.

LANLEY: I'm sure we are all eager to put this all behind us…

LUCIDUS: Maybe you. Not Lucidus. He's relishing it all. Because he's that brave.

LANLEY: Be that as it may, we need to settle this swiftly. The Earl must be back in Oxford to inspect proofs for the Quarterly.

LUCIDUS: The Quarterly? The Oxford Quarterly? The science review?

LANLEY: Yes. He is the editor?

LUCIDUS: Whhhaaaaaat…

LANLEY: May I propose the principals meet tomorrow morning, behind Harper's Abbey.

LUCIDUS: …I love the Oxford Quarterly!

LANLEY: *(Brusquely.)* Behind Harper's Abbey, sir?

LUCIDUS: Uh, that will be fine.

LANLEY: Very good. Behind Harper's Abbey then. We will see you tomorrow at seven sharp.

LUCIDUS: Seven? In the morning?

LANLEY: Is that too early for you sir?

LUCIDUS: Certainly not. *(Stands.)* Getting up early is no problem for Lucidus Culling.

> *(He wants to leave, but hesitates, wonders if maybe he stood up too soon.)*

Are we done?

LANLEY: Yes.

LUCIDUS: Good!

> *(He turns on his heel and marches out.)*

SCENE 9.

> *The next morning. LUCIDUS and HENRY have shown up first to the spot. HENRY is loading the pistols, as LUCIDUS reads a letter. HENRY is collected but nervous. LUCIDUS has a little picnic banquet set up to the side.*

HENRY: Are you still reading that letter? You're a slow reader.

LUCIDUS: I'll have you know that I am *re*-reading this letter. And you would too, if you knew who it was from… *(Wait for him to ask; he doesn't.)* Isabelle Dupree. Heard of her?

HENRY: Can't say I have.

LUCIDUS: Well you wouldn't. Needless to say, she's from very good stock. She wrote to wish me luck. All of a sudden, not only does she know who I am, but she's wishing me luck. She says she's sorry not to have accepted my invitations in the past. She says she wanted to, but her father would not allow it…

HENRY: *(Uninterested.)* How interesting.

LUCIDUS: …she said her father said, that by the sound of my letters, I sounded inadequate for a lady of her station. But the thing is, I didn't even write half those letters – it was my father, and he's a *member of Parliament!*

> *(He is amused by this, alone.)*

HENRY: Oh.

LUCIDUS: …and my father thinks that Isabelle's father is the one writing her letters, and *he's a chamber minister.*

HENRY: I see. Funny.

LUCIDUS: Isn't it?

HENRY: So the letter isn't really from the girl, it's from her father?

LUCIDUS: Well…it's not clear. That's not really important.

HENRY: No. The important thing is that the old men hit it off, I suppose.

LUCIDUS: Well I didn't say that. But that is important.

HENRY: Well I think it's wonderful your father takes the time to control every aspect of your life. My father could've cared less whose knickers I took to ripping into.

LUCIDUS: Ew. Don't say knickers. It's gross.

> *(Beat.)*

What time is it? I told you we came too early.

HENRY: It's not too early. I needed time to prepare.

LUCIDUS: All these things take place too early. I don't see the reason in it.

HENRY: I like the morning. Before the woods start chattering, and the sun starts beating down. Everything all golden and still.

LUCIDUS: Well look at you. Who knew you were such a poet?

HENRY: *(Irritated, controlling himself.)* It is important that one has adequate time to survey the area and load one's pistols. Especially when one's second is incapable of doing it.

LUCIDUS: I'm not. I offered to do it. It's just…now my fingers are sticky.

HENRY: Nevermind. I don't want you near them. Things must be done right.

> *(LUCIDUS notices for the first time that HENRY is nervous and determined.)*

LUCIDUS: Henry. I hope you're not planning to actually kill the man?

> *(HENRY gives LUCIDUS a look.)*

LUCIDUS: No! Oh God no! We're just here to give the Earl *satisfaction.* Just let him shoot at you, that's all. I wish him no *harm…*

HENRY: I thought I was to battle the man.

LUCIDUS: It's hardly a *battle*, Henry. Maybe the sort of duels you've fought were different, but between gentlemen it's all pageantry. Almost a way to get to know each other. The Earl will very likely not shoot you. If he does, it won't be serious. And if it is serious, it will be an accident, probably.

HENRY: Well, I have already loaded the pistol...

LUCIDUS: That's fine. It is customary. And you should fire it, too. But fire it to the side. Yes. I think *that* should look rather gallant...

HENRY: To the side? And just let him shoot at me, undefended?

LUCIDUS: Yes! You see, I've found out a little more about this Earl. He is a scholar himself, and a poet; not like you, a real poet, with money. If we play this right, it could work out very nice. I think he could help me get my book published.

HENRY: Your book?

LUCIDUS: Yes. I haven't started it yet, but I'm writing a new rating system for insects. Butterflies specifically...

HENRY: Uggod...

LUCIDUS: ...one based not on physiology, but rather, on beauty. Did you know I was a naturalist?

HENRY: Sir, I thought this was a proper duel. I am not comfortable letting a man fire on me without an opportunity to defend myself.

LUCIDUS: But Henry, you will be undefended whether or not you return fire – you'll be firing at the same time. Oh look, I'm sure it's no worse than anything you faced in the army, walking in rows against those dastardly Americans.

HENRY: Against the Americans?

LUCIDUS: Yes. When you fought in the colonies.

HENRY: I fought for the Americans.

LUCIDUS: Good god. Have you no shame?

HENRY: Not lately, sir, no.

(THE EARL OF DORCHESTER arrives with LANLEY.)

LANLEY: Good morning gentlemen.

LUCIDUS: Ah, hello… Good morning. I am Mr Trudging, and you must be the Earl.

EARL: Good day sir.

LUCIDUS: I've brought some coffee and pastries if anyone would like…

EARL: No thank you. I will save eating till later, with luck.

LUCIDUS: Very good. We're almost ready. Mr Culling—him—was just inspecting the pistols which I loaded for us all by myself. Isn't that right, Lucidus?

HENRY: Yes, Hanaroy. And a right fine job you did.

EARL: You are Lucidus Culling? I thought you a man of twenty…

HENRY: I am twenty sir, and if you think me unhandsome we can settle that today with the other business.

EARL: That we will sir, though I doubt either of us will walk away looking more handsome.

LUCIDUS: Okay, ha ha, everybody calm down. No need to fight, verbally, on top of all else. Mr Lanley, would you like to inspect the pistols?

LANLEY: Actually, we will provide our own weapon – you may inspect it.

LUCIDUS: Oh. No need. I trust you. We are all gentlemen here. Let us just proceed. I have counted the marks at fifteen paces…

(He indicates some markings on the ground.)

EARL: *Those* are fifteen paces…?

LUCIDUS: On the short side perhaps. Typical Mr Culling…

(Moving the marks a little wider.)

EARL: Is Mr Culling typically suicidal?

LUCIDUS: No sir. Only immensely immensely brave. *(He laughs, alone.)*

EARL: It was my understanding Mr Culling, that you had never fought a duel before today.

HENRY: I've fought better men than you, sir.

EARL: Oh really? And what are their names?

LUCIDUS: It was no one important. You're certainly the finest man Mr Culling has had the pleasure to face. Isn't that right, Mr Culling?

HENRY: Oh yes, sir. In terms of status.

LUCIDUS: Which is all we care about. Mr Lanley, will you need time for loading your pistol?

LANLEY: No. We have already loaded our weapon. We are eager to be done with this.

LUCIDUS: Yes yes. The sooner we get this over with, the sooner we can have some pastries.

(LANLEY takes a coin from his pocket.)

What's that? Oh, you don't need to pay me for them – it's my treat.

LANLEY: No. We must flip a coin for places.

LUCIDUS: Places?

LANLEY: Which side. One is facing the sun.

HENRY: Oh come on. If you want even odds, you ought to have brought a slimmer man. The bloke's three times the target I am!

EARL: Pardon me?

HENRY: We'll fix that soon enough. Your guts'll be hanging over your dick, fat man!

LUCIDUS: Mr Culling!

LANLEY: Mr Culling I insist you conduct yourself like a gentleman!

LUCIDUS: I'm very sorry your Earlship, I think it's just nerves. Just his nerves…We…

(He walks over to speak to HENRY confidentially.)

What are you doing?

HENRY: What? I'm just having some fun with him. We're going to fight aren't we?

LUCIDUS: That is not how a gentlemen fights.

HENRY: No, you're right. I know. I've got a big mouth. In Boston they used to pillory me for my shit-talking. I can't help it sometimes. It's nerves; like you said.

LUCIDUS: Well try to control yourself, will you?

LANLEY: Mr Trudging! Is there a problem?

LUCIDUS: No, not at all, sir! Where were we?

LANLEY: We were choosing sides.

LUCIDUS: Oh yes. We will take the bad side. Mr Culling doesn't mind.

LANLEY: But that is not...

LUCIDUS: Please, I insist. He insists, *don't you?*

HENRY: ...sure, fine.

LANLEY: Very well. Let's get on with it. Gentlemen, take to your marks.

> (*They do.*)

Present yourselves.

> (*They turn so they are facing each other over their right shoulders, bodies turned to the side.*)

Cock your pistols.

> (*They do.*)

Raise your pistols.

> (*They do.*)

I will count to three. On the count of three you will fire your weapon. You may not fire before three. Your Earlship – are you ready?

EARL: Yes.

LANLEY: Mr Culling?

> (*Beat.*)

Mr Culling?

> (*Beat.*)

LUCIDUS: (*Whispers.*) *That's you.*

HENRY: Oh. Yes!

LANLEY: Very well gentlemen, Take aim...

(HENRY fires. He strikes LANLEY, who falls, dead. HENRY drops his weapon. THE EARL is shocked and horrified. He lowers his pistol.)

LUCIDUS: *(Uncomprehending, horrified.)* What?

EARL: You have shot my second sir, and before the count…

HENRY: Count?

LUCIDUS: You…

HENRY: *(To LUCIDUS.)* I was aiming wide.

LUCIDUS: You were supposed to wait for him to count!

EARL: *(Examining LANLEY.)* He's dead.

HENRY: *(To LUCIDUS.)* I was aiming wide, like you said.

EARL: He's dead… But I have not yet taken my shot.

> *(THE EARL raises his pistol. HENRY moves from side to side, preparing to duck or dive.)*

EARL: You will hold still while I take my shot sir…

HENRY: The hell to that…

LUCIDUS: Henry! What are you doing?

EARL: Henry?

LUCIDUS: *(Correcting himself.)* I mean Lucidus.

EARL: *(Comprehending.)* You are Lucidus Culling.

LUCIDUS: No, no…you don't understand. It was an accident…

EARL: *Accident?!*

HENRY: I was trying to shoot wide.

EARL: *(Turning to LUCIDUS.)* Assassins! If I had but two shots for the both of you! This is only half the justice you deserve…

> *(As he seems to be about to fire on LUCIDUS, HENRY takes another pistol from his back pocket and fires on him. As THE EARL is struck, a spasm shoots through his body, causing his pistol to fire in the air.)*

EARL: Urk!

(He falls, blood pumping from his gut. There is a long silence.)

(Softly.)

Wounded… Derek, I am wounded.

LUCIDUS: You have /shot the …

HENRY: Don't worry. There are other publishers.

(Pause.)

Good Christ, almost got the better of us didn't he? Fat bastard. Ha, look at me. Shaking. I had no idea this would be so intense.

LUCIDUS: What?

HENRY: This. Dueling. It's very intense.

LUCIDUS: I thought you had fought duels before!

HENRY: Well yes, but I've never done it this way, just standing and shooting at each other.

LUCIDUS: That is what a duel IS!

HENRY: Then maybe my duels were less duels than what you'd call… manslaughter.

EARL: Derek, I am wounded…

HENRY: I mean, very rarely did anything happen I couldn't blame on drink. That just happens sometimes. But this business of shooting at each other while sober, why it's just insanity. Absolute bleeding insanity…

LUCIDUS: Oh my god. I am ruined…

HENRY: No! No, don't you worry. This is all right honorable, my friend. On the face of it.

LUCIDUS: Honorable? You have blackened my name!

HENRY: No no, listen, We met with the seconds. Words were exchanged. The Earl was acting rather coarse. He was shit-talking, yeah? And what happened was, the seconds were drawn into the fighting. Both sides fired on the other. The side God favored least fell. Happens all the time.

EARL: Derek, fetch the doctor.

LUCIDUS: This is murder.

HENRY: No no no…

LUCIDUS: Cold blooded murder.

HENRY: Says who?

EARL: Derek, where is the doctor…?

HENRY: Derek is dead, remember?!

LUCIDUS: Oh god, what are we doing? We can still save him.

> (LUCIDUS starts toward THE EARL but HENRY grabs him and holds
> him back.)

HENRY: *(Firmly.)* No. We can't.

LUCIDUS: But…

HENRY: Shhhh. No.

> (He approaches THE EARL.)

LUCIDUS: Henry, what are you doing?

HENRY: Quiet. Pack up the pastries.

> (HENRY gets down on his knees to strangle the dying EARL.)

LUCIDUS: Henry, what are you doing?

HENRY: *(Strained from the effort of strangling.)* Pack up the pastries.

> (LUCIDUS takes the other loaded pistol from his set, still unused.
> He cocks it, and points it at HENRY.)

LUCIDUS: This one is loaded, Henry. You loaded it yourself.

HENRY: So I did. But what will you do if you fire it? What will you tell
your father? Put down the pistol, Lucidus. There's been enough violence
for one day.

> (LUCIDUS puts down the pistol and HENRY resumes strangling THE
> EARL. HENRY strangles THE EARL until he is dead.)

There we are. All done.

> *Intermission (if necessary.)*

SCENE 10.

FATHER is with LUCIDUS. He reads from the newspaper.

FATHER: "Lucidus Culling, a young fire eater previously unknown to polite society, made a fairly bloody impression on the Earl of Dorchester Tuesday, when he shot and killed him, in a duel behind Harper's Abbey. Lucidus is the son of Nathaniel Culling, recently appointed to Parliament, and himself a notoriously pugnacious figure, both politically and personally. Also killed in the duel was the Earl's second, Derek Lanley, a courteous man known for his generosity and intelligence. Both men leave behind large families left reeling from – dubba dubba dubba *(skipping ahead)* – it is in the opinion of this paper that if the reader should encounter a Culling on the street, do let them pass, for they are hot blooded and not to be trifled with…

(He has finished reading.)

Oooo, that's quite a notice… Pure political currency right there. I've been congratulated so many times this week I can't even remember.

LUCIDUS: Is no one upset?

FATHER: Many are upset about the Earl. He was a fine man, by all accounts. But they also sympathize with our family, for having been placed in a position where we *had to* kill him. And I think everyone takes comfort that it was done correctly, and honorably. And this business with the seconds?! Well, that's just wonderful! This friend of yours must be quite the gallant knight, fighting alongside you in your personal affair.

LUCIDUS: Yes, well, I wasn't expecting him to show such, um/…

FATHER: *Sangfroid?* I know! That's the sign of greatness. I must meet this Trudging. We must have him over for dinner!

LUCIDUS: Ah, I am not sure he will accept. I think, ultimately, he found the whole affair rather gruesome. And I share that opinion.

FATHER: Oh, well, that's true these things can be awful. But they are necessary. How else are we to know who the best men are, eh? That reminds me, there's been more letters from Isabelle. Very passionate woman. Or at least her father is. I've arranged for a meeting.

LUCIDUS: Father, I don't know if I'm up to that right now…

FATHER: Of course you are. You must strike while the iron is hot. A young gentleman cannot while away his whole life with prostitutes, bearing illegitimate children…

LUCIDUS: I've been having nightmares.

FATHER: …There comes a time when he must begin to think about bearing *legitimate* children too, children worthy of his name. Isabelle is quite beautiful. And her father is a chamber minister – an advisor to the king himself!

LUCIDUS: Yes father, I know.

FATHER: *(Not listening.)* Grandchildren. That's my priority now. To carry on the family legacy. It's important.

LUCIDUS: Yes father, I know. Of course it is.

SCENE 11.

LUCIDUS is at home. FRIEDMONT knocks.

LUCIDUS: Yes?

(He enters.)

FRIEDMONT: Mr Culling. Mr Klaff is here to see you.

LUCIDUS: Send him in.

(GAVIN enters, carrying a document.)

LUCIDUS: Gavin. So good to see you.

GAVIN: And you too, my friend.

(They embrace.)

So much has happened. Your name is everywhere. I had hoped to see you at Roger's party last night. I fairly well expected it.

LUCIDUS: I haven't felt like conversation.

GAVIN: Just when you're the toast of the town? Well if you can have it that easy, I suppose it's not worth bothering with, is that it? I would die to be in your shoes right now. Admired, respected…

LUCIDUS: It is just talk.

GAVIN: True. Real honor comes from within. In the blood I suppose.

(And then, his smile fades.)

LUCIDUS: Gavin, I'm sorry about what I said. About your family.

GAVIN: Oh, it was nothing. Look, I respect you Lucidus. And I know you will respect me, if presented with the right information...

(He lays out the document, a visual representation of lineage.)

Therefore, I have prepared a lesson to educate you on my ancestry, and clarify a few minor errors you may have made in your assessment of us.

LUCIDUS: Gavin, this is not necessary.

GAVIN: Please, Lucidus, indulge me. It will take but twenty minutes.

(FRIEDMONT knocks.)

LUCIDUS: Yes?

FRIEDMONT: You have another guest, sir. Mr Blithe.

GAVIN: Robert? Oh Lucidus, I didn't know Robert was coming over. Have I intruded?

LUCIDUS: No Gavin, of course not.

ROBERT: *(Entering.)* Lucidus! Gavin! What a surprise. I didn't know you were coming over.

GAVIN: Nor I you.

ROBERT: Just stopping by. Lucidus and I have been carousing all week, haven't we?

LUCIDUS: Well, you've come by a lot.

ROBERT: That I have. Because we're friends. Some might even say we're *best friends*. Together all the time.

GAVIN: Oh.

ROBERT: Lucidus, are you doing anything? Let's go riding. Where's that fat horse of yours? Oh, don't shoot me! No, no, I hope I'm not making a weird face. Hahaha, I'm just kidding, you're wonderful...

GAVIN: I didn't bring my horse. For riding.

ROBERT: Damn. Well, maybe next time for you then. Lucidus, riding?

LUCIDUS: Well, I'm not sure.

GAVIN: Oh you should go, Lucidus. I was just on my way out. I'll leave this here. It's a copy, you can keep.

LUCIDUS: Thank you, Gavin, I'll be sure to look it over.

GAVIN: Yes, excellent, thank you. And maybe sometime we can all go out and have a pie tasting, the three of us.

ROBERT: *(Noncommittal.)* Yes, perhaps. It is getting rather late in the season for pie…

GAVIN: Pie or some other activity. Good day to you, my friends.

LUCIDUS: Goodbye Gavin.

    (ROBERT nods. GAVIN leaves.)

LUCIDUS: Why did you do that?

ROBERT: What?

LUCIDUS: Act so coldly towards him.

ROBERT: Oh he's just become so dreadfully boring, that's all. He's such a little boy. Remember when we went to the brothel? How pathetic was he? Giggling every time some one so much as touched him…

LUCIDUS: I didn't like the brothel.

ROBERT: …I don't want to be around people like Gavin anymore, these fey fancy boys. We are men. We should only be around other men.

LUCIDUS: Gavin is our friend, Robert.

ROBERT: Oh it's fine when you're a child, to play with the servant brats, and people like Gavin. But when you get older you need to associate with a better class of person than the youngest son of a royal lord. You said it yourself, remember?

LUCIDUS: I spoke rashly.

ROBERT: You spoke only what we both were thinking. Let him go…you have new friends.

(Hands him an envelope.)

LUCIDUS: What's this?

ROBERT: I've spoken to my uncle, Lord Dukingham, on your behalf. He owns several literary journals. I told him about your book proposal. He loves the idea of a gentlemen bug collector. He said if you self-publish it he will give a good review in the Cambridge Quarterly. It's not as good as the Oxford Quarterly, but you probably don't want to send them anything for a while.

LUCIDUS: Then all I have to do is write it?

ROBERT: That's right. And I could probably get the King to read it, too. He was at my sister's wedding you know...

LUCIDUS: I know, you told me. This is wonderful news! Thank you, Robert!

ROBERT: I'm sure you would've done the same for me.

LUCIDUS: You see this, this is how a gentlemen proves himself. Not through strength of arms, or silly challenges, but by the strength of his intellect.

ROBERT: Write your book my friend. I already know it will be great. A treatise that shall live for a thousand years!

SCENE 12.

LUCIDUS is waiting in the park for Isabelle, wearing a hat. She enters.

ISABELLE: Are you Lucidus Culling?

LUCIDUS: Yes.

ISABELLE: Enchanted to meet you, sir.

LUCIDUS: We've met.

ISABELLE: Have we?

LUCIDUS: Yes. Many times. I lent you my handkerchief – It doesn't matter...

(He helps her take a seat on the bench. They sit in silence a moment.)

ISABELLE: So you're a Culling...   LUCIDUS: My father tells me...

(They stop, smile.)

ISABELLE: You have a lovely hat.   LUCIDUS: Have you seen my hat?

ISABELLE: It is a lovely hat.

LUCIDUS: Thank you.

ISABELLE: Oh Lucidus, I have so enjoyed your letters. I have boasted to all my friends about them.

LUCIDUS: You have?

ISABELLE: Oh yes. Lady Elizabeth is beside herself with envy. Everyone is clamoring to know who you are and what you look like. Like this, I suppose.

LUCIDUS: But I know Lady Elizabeth. She came to my house, for my birthday bash.

ISABELLE: Oh, well, it's hard to remember every man you meet. And Lucidus, you are not at all… like one might suspect.

LUCIDUS: What do you mean?

ISABELLE: Well, after reading your letters I expected a man who was a bit more…ferocious.

LUCIDUS: I can be ferocious.

ISABELLE: I am sure you can be. I believe a man can be anything he sets his mind to. The secret is to ignore the actual reality of the situation. Do you read Descartes?

LUCIDUS: No.

ISABELLE: Me neither. He's too French for me.

LUCIDUS: Isabelle, I hope you don't judge me by what I wrote in my letters.

ISABELLE: Oh don't worry Lucidus I don't judge anyone by their politics. I judge them mostly on their handwriting. And you have very nice handwriting.

LUCIDUS: Well thank you. I do like to write. In fact, I am writing a book.

(HENRY enters, dressed in finery, with a grand hat. LUCIDUS has his back to him.)

ISABELLE: A book? Do tell.

LUCIDUS: Yes, it's going to be a long one…

ISABELLE: *(Interested.)* Oh!

LUCIDUS: …on insects…

ISABELLE: *(Less so.)* Oh.

LUCIDUS: …Butterflies specifically. I am creating a rating system, based on the beauty I perceive in them. Sort of a study of zoology, but less rigorous.

ISABELLE: Fascinating. And you *touch* these insects?

LUCIDUS: Well, Friedmont kills them first – but yes, I touch them. It's no big deal.

ISABELLE: *(Notices Henry.)* Incredible. A revolution in France and you write about insects. Oh dear, Lucidus…

LUCIDUS: What?

ISABELLE: That man there, he is staring at me.

LUCIDUS: Who?

> *(LUCIDUS sees HENRY, starts.)*

He must have recognized me. Because I'm Isabelle Dupree.

LUCIDUS: Ah…Will you excuse me for a moment?

ISABELLE: Oh Lucidus, you don't need to hurt him for me. It's quite alright.

LUCIDUS: I'm not going to hurt him, I'm just going to have a word with the man.

ISABELLE: Although if you did kill him, I *would* find that awfully romantic.

LUCIDUS: I'll be right back.

> *(Goes to HENRY.)*

LUCIDUS: What are you doing here?

HENRY: That's a fine looking doxy you've got there, sir. Is that the girl you told me about?

LUCIDUS: What do you want?

HENRY: Sorry to bother you sir, but I have some bad news. Looks like we might have to fight again.

LUCIDUS: What?

HENRY: There's been loose talk, about how you might have taken shooting lessons before the duel with the Earl. Some gentleman by the name of William Bridgeworth was running his fucking mouth off.

LUCIDUS: You challenged a man?!

HENRY: Nay, I could not. It was you who challenged him. But I had no problem passing off as a gentlemen, with these new clothes. Even paid the hat tax, fair and square.

LUCIDUS: You must be joking! I will not fight this man! I have no wish to participate in anything so ghastly and pointless again.

HENRY: But sir, it's not pointless now. You've got to quell these rumors before they get out of control. Believe me this is not a man you should worry about. He's a pig. He deserves to die.

LUCIDUS: You know him?

HENRY: No. Well I know of him.

LUCIDUS: How?

HENRY: He's my landlord. But that's just a coincidence. He was talking about you, sir. It cannot go unavenged.

LUCIDUS: Oh yes it can! Call off the duel, Henry!

HENRY: But he questioned your honor sir...

LUCIDUS: As he might, with you posing as me. Why it's unimaginable. To think anyone would believe you were a gentlemen. In that ridiculous hat.

HENRY: Is this hat ridiculous, sir?

LUCIDUS: Yes. On you it is.

(Beat. They are wearing comparable hats.)

ISABELLE: (Calling from afar.) Mr Culling. I require entertainment.

LUCIDUS: (Firmly.) Call off the duel.

HENRY: Are you sure, sir? All you need to do is serve as second, as before. I'll take care of everything. As /before.

LUCIDUS: Call it off! And do not speak to me again. Our business together is through. You are dismissed.

(HENRY leaves, as LUCIDUS returns to Isabelle.)

ISABELLE: Who was it, Lucidus? Why was he staring at me so?

LUCIDUS: Oh it's alright Isabelle, it was a misunderstanding. He wasn't looking at you. He was looking at my hat. He wanted to know where I purchased it.

ISABELLE: Oh. Well, he probably was also staring at me, because I'm Isabelle Dupree.

LUCIDUS: Yes I suppose he might have been. I would have. If I was not so polite.

ISABELLE: You are very polite, Lucidus. Please. You were telling me about your book.

LUCIDUS: Well…

(They continue on, getting to know each other.)

SCENE 13.

LUCIDUS is at home, at his desk, quill in hand, trying to write. He is having difficulty. ROBERT bursts in, followed by FRIEDMONT.

ROBERT: Why didn't you tell me?

FRIEDMONT: Mr Blithe, sir…

LUCIDUS: Tell you what?

ROBERT: You know what…

(ROBERT presents a newspaper.)

That you had another duel. I can't believe you didn't ask me to second you? You and this mysterious Mr Trudging, you're thick as thieves aren't you…why haven't we met him?

LUCIDUS: What?

(He grabs the paper and reads.)

ROBERT: William Bridgeworth? It does not sound like the name of a worthy opponent for you. Still, it's a lovely notice.

LUCIDUS: Robert, I didn't duel this man! It's not true!

ROBERT: It's not? But why would they write such nice things about you then.

LUCIDUS: They aren't nice things, Robert. It's a horrible thing to kill a man!

ROBERT: Well perhaps you're right. In that case, it's libel. You should challenge the editor of the paper. And let me second you.

LUCIDUS: I have to go…

(He goes and puts on a coat.)

ROBERT: Where are you going?

LUCIDUS: I have to go. I have to fix this.

ROBERT: *(Blocking his path to the door.)* Are you going to challenge someone? Let me come with you.

LUCIDUS: No! Robert, you can't come.

ROBERT: You're going to go run to this Trudging again aren't you?

LUCIDUS: No…I'll explain later.

ROBERT: Don't forget your friends, Lucidus. I was there for you. I stood by your side, tried to comfort you, and help you, when you didn't have the courage to fight… And when you cried after your toy boat wrecked, and when you cried after your violin teacher said you had no ear, and when you cried after you were stung by a bee. And when you cried because there were no more tickets left to see the Magic Flute. I was there for you. And now that you've mustered courage in your life you're going to shut me out?! I need to make a reputation too, you know…

LUCIDUS: I have to go.

(He exits through a different door.)

SCENE 14.

LUCIDUS enters the tavern, and approaches the BARTENDER.

LUCIDUS: Where is he?

BARTENDER: Who?

LUCIDUS: Henry Blaine!

BARTENDER: Blaine, eh? I'm not sure I know any man by that name…

LUCIDUS: Do you not know me then, sir?!

BARTENDER: Should I?

LUCIDUS: You should! It is you who directed me to Henry Blaine, you rascal!

BARTENDER: Rascal?!

> *(He comes from behind the counter with a terrifying looking medieval spiked club, or 'Morning Star.' Just then, HENRY enters with FINN, well dressed, as before.)*

I will not be spoken to that way, sir.

LUCIDUS: Oh, no! Wait, I apologize, please I apologize!

HENRY: Egbert! Lower thy morning star. It is my friend, Mr Trudging.

BARTENDER: But he called me a rascal.

HENRY: I assure you Mr Trudging meant no harm. His tongue is too quick for his brain that is all. And besides…you *are* a rascal…

BARTENDER: *(A smile breaking.)* Well, that's true. Heh.

> *(Glaring again at LUCIDUS.)*

You're lucky I have dishes to do, knave, or I would not brook such infamy…

> *(Laughs again as he returns behind the bar.)*

HENRY: Mr Trudging. What brings you so far from Trudging Manor?

LUCIDUS: What brings me? You brings me, blast you! What is this?

> *(Throwing the newspaper before his face.)*

HENRY: Ah the post is out. Well come then, let's talk privately.

(Leading him away.)

LUCIDUS: I told you to call off the duel! Was I not clear?

HENRY: No sir you were clear enough. But matters are complicated.

LUCIDUS: What is complicated?

HENRY: My emotions are complicated sir. I have been enjoying the ways of a gentlemen. And the satisfaction I have received on your behalf.

LUCIDUS: I have received no satisfaction. Only anguish.

HENRY: Do not worry, sir. Entrust all to me. There are only a few more encounters to be had.

LUCIDUS: What do you mean, a few more?

HENRY: There are some more people I do not like. This evening I will duel Father McRoy by Edward's Oak in Victoria Park.

LUCIDUS: Father McRoy? A priest?!

HENRY: A rector. From my childhood. An overly stern and vicious man. He jostled me in the street the other day and made me drop my groceries. The fiend.

LUCIDUS: You think I will abide by this? That you can use my honor as a shelter for your petty crimes?

HENRY: Well the way I see it, your honor and I had more of a mutual exchange of services.

LUCIDUS: And I paid you, but now this must end!

HENRY: It will end when it ends.

LUCIDUS: *(Pleading.)* Henry, it is my name. It belongs to me!

HENRY: For the time being, we must share it.

LUCIDUS: But /why?

HENRY: I'll tell you. Back in Boston, when I started dueling – or what I would call dueling – the ground would be so frozen you couldn't bury the bodies; you'd have to chop them up and feed them to the pigs; or else row out and dump them in the harbor. It's a great big hassle. And why did I go to such trouble? Just because I was not born rich. Well I am forty-three years old now. I have served in the King's Army, and

General Washington's army, and General Arnold's army. I have proven myself a great fighter – if not in any of those armies, then on the streets, in the Army of Hard Knocks. So why should I not duel now? Because I am not a gentlemen? Well poor though I may be, I am still a man. I live, I breathe, I feel. And I have to kill to get ahead, just like any man.

LUCIDUS: Oh my god.

HENRY: Maybe I won't ever be a member of Parliament. Maybe I won't ever own my own land, or write a book. Maybe I won't ever have a father who loves me. But I have a right to kill, just like you.

LUCIDUS: Henry! You can't do this! You can't!

HENRY: Oh, but I can. And I must. I have ambitions to glory, Lucidus. And only as a Culling can my urges be seen as such. Now. Mr Finn. Will you please escort Mr Trudging to his coach?

FINN: It would be my pleasure.

SCENE 15.

LUCIDUS has just returned to his home, where FRIEDMONT is waiting to take his coat.

LUCIDUS: Friedmont!

FRIEDMONT: Yes sir?

LUCIDUS: I want you to contact the police. Tell them that a duel is taking place tonight by Edward's Oak, and they must stop it.

FRIEDMONT: Yes sir. And who shall I say will be fighting, sir?

LUCIDUS: It will be me. And a priest. Father McRoy.

FRIEDMONT: Yes, sir. Would you like me to try and stop you, sir?

LUCIDUS: No.

FRIEDMONT: I'm fairly certain I could.

LUCIDUS: No! Let me clarify: it will not be me, but a man who claims to be me…

FRIEDMONT: Why would anyone claim to be /you?

LUCIDUS: Will you just communicate the warning, please? And hurry! It could take place any moment. Perhaps I should just go myself. But that might implicate me…um…

FRIEDMONT: Yes, sir. While you are deciding, I should inform you that Miss Dupree has been waiting on you.

LUCIDUS: What?

> *(He turns to see ISABELLE as she enters from the other room. FRIEDMONT takes his leave.)*

ISABELLE: Mr Culling, you are fighting another duel?

LUCIDUS: No, no, I'm not.

ISABELLE: Was it the man who dared stare at me then dared not stare at me?

LUCIDUS: No, Isabelle, I'll be fighting no more. And you wouldn't be so eager to see me fight if you knew how awful these things truly are.

ISABELLE: *(With love in her eyes.)* No, I know.

LUCIDUS: Duels are horrible things!

ISABELLE: Yes, of course they are.

LUCIDUS: It proves not courage or valor. It proves nothing!

ISABELLE: Yes. I know. It's practically suicide.

LUCIDUS: You don't look particularly upset.

ISABELLE: I can't help it. You've inspired me Lucidus. You've inspired everyone. Lady Elizabeth is biting at the bit to meet you. And father went down to the gentlemen's club, hoping to see you at the lecture on table manners. But they told him you don't go to the club too often.

LUCIDUS: No, I don't like the tea there.

ISABELLE: Quite right, And a man like you doesn't need to be taught such things. He is born with innate moral knowledge.

LUCIDUS: Isabelle, I'm sorry but could we speak another time, I /was just –

ISABELLE: Oh Lucidus, I feel so lucky to have found you. I feel like I've known you forever.

LUCIDUS: You haven't.

ISABELLE: Oh no? Was that not you in my dreams last night?

LUCIDUS: I don't know.

ISABELLE: *(As she comes toward him.)* I think it was you. And that was you the night before. And the night before that. Every night, ever since I was little girl. Only you were taller, and you had a different face.

(She kisses him, then runs away coquettishly.)

No Lucidus it's too soon!

LUCIDUS: Yes, you're right. Actually, Isabelle, this is not the best time. I /have to –

ISABELLE: But Lucidus I'm Isabelle Dupree. Don't you want me?

LUCIDUS: Yes, of course. You are Isabelle Dupree…

ISABELLE: I know!

LUCIDUS: I have fancied you for so long.

ISABELLE: As I have fancied you, Lucidus.

LUCIDUS: Ever since I first saw you.

ISABELLE: Ever since I first read about you in the paper.

LUCIDUS: But I don't know if I'm the man you fancy. I don't know if that man even exists – I'm sorry, can we meet and talk another time?

ISABELLE: Yes of course Lucidus; but not before I get what I came here for.

LUCIDUS: What's that?

ISABELLE: Why your solemn pledge, of course.

LUCIDUS: Pledge?

ISABELLE: You are a hero. And I am almost 18. So now the time has come for you to claim me.

LUCIDUS: You mean, married?

ISABELLE: Yes.

LUCIDUS: To you?

ISABELLE: Right.

LUCIDUS: But Isabelle, shouldn't we wait a little bit to see…what our chemistry's like.

ISABELLE: Who cares? So long as we're talked about. *We'll be a power couple.*

LUCIDUS: All the same, I would rather not rush into things. We should wait.

ISABELLE: Til what? Till I'm 19? When I'm old and dried up, and your father no longer wants to write to my father? What's the problem? I thought you fancied me!

LUCIDUS: I do. It's just I need some time. I need to…finish my book.

ISABELLE: Your book…

LUCIDUS: My book will be a great success, Isabelle, I'm sure of it. It will help me become respected.

ISABELLE: But you are already respected. I wouldn't be here if you weren't. I'm /Isabelle Dupree.

LUCIDUS: Isabelle Dupree, I know. But if you wait until I finish my book, I will be *even more respected.* And then we'll be an *even more powerful* power couple.

(Several beats as she thinks about it.)

ISABELLE: Very well. Finish your book. I will wait for you. For like a week, or maybe another week.

(She rings for Friedmont, who soon enters.)

LUCIDUS: Thank you for understanding, Isabelle.

ISABELLE: I understand nothing but duty. And duty understands you don't always need to understand anything.

LUCIDUS: Ooh. Epigrammatic wit. Isabelle, you should write that down.

ISABELLE: Why? To prove I'm clever. I'm Isabelle Dupree. Of course I'm clever – and rich and beautiful and everything else. I have nothing to prove. Why you should still feel the need to prove yourself is beyond me.

(She exits out the door, stopping one last time to say:)

One more week, or like, maybe one week after that.

LUCIDUS: Friedmont?

FRIEDMONT: Yes sir?

LUCIDUS: Did you tend to that business? Stopping the duel?

FRIEDMONT: Yes sir. I sent the chambermaid. The police will be informed.

LUCIDUS: Good. You're sure?

FRIEDMONT: I'm sure she left five minutes ago.

LUCIDUS: Good, good. Is she smart?

FRIEDMONT: Compared to what, sir?

LUCIDUS: Nevermind. I better go myself. Ready the carriage.

(FATHER enters.)

FATHER: The carriage? But Lucidus where are you going?

LUCIDUS: Father. I was just on my way out.

FATHER: So I see. Going to Edward's Oak perchance?

(Beat.)

To fight another duel?

LUCIDUS: How did you hear about that?

FATHER: The Baron told me. His family priest is involved. He came hoping I'd try to talk you out of it. Can you imagine? I told him that's out of the question. I'd never stand in the way of my son.

LUCIDUS: Well, yes, thank you. Actually, father, I should probably go. People get rather upset when you're late for these things. You understand.

FATHER: Oh yes, of course...

LUCIDUS: And I want to make a good impression, especially with a member of the clergy involved.

FATHER: Lucidus...

LUCIDUS: Let's have dinner later...

FATHER: The duel already happened.

(Beat.)

LUCIDUS: What?

FATHER: About half an hour ago…I went down there to see it myself. Bad enough I missed two of your duels already. I wasn't going to miss a third. So I went down there… Knowing you might object – I couldn't help myself. And that's where I met your friend.

(HENRY enters.)

HENRY: Good evening.

LUCIDUS: No. You shouldn't believe this man, father. He lies!

FATHER: Well I know. I figured that, when he introduced himself as you. But then he explained everything. How you were frightened. How you wanted to do right by the family name, but knew that deep down inside, you couldn't. That you would probably end up running away, or firing before your turn. And that is why you called upon Henry here.

LUCIDUS: Father, listen to me…

FATHER: Shhhh, it's alright. I understand. Deep down I always knew you didn't have it in you. But my foolish heart, wanted what it wanted; it made demands you could not meet. But I want you to know that I'm proud of you for putting family first, and for admitting to yourself that you are a coward. That took courage, sort of.

LUCIDUS: Thank you, father. That's so…

HENRY: It's alright, Lucidus. No one will ever know. And no one will ever bring shame to your name.

LUCIDUS: Wow, that's so –

FATHER: That's right, because from now on, Henry will bear your name.

LUCIDUS: What?!

FATHER: Henry fought bravely today in his duel with the slanderous rector. He proved to me that he could be the son I always wanted. A brave noble son.

LUCIDUS: Father, he is a murderer!

FATHER: As you are not! And you never will be! But there's no point getting upset about it. Not now.

FATHER: Stay in your manor. Collect your buggies, and eat your treats. Live by the expectations you set for yourself. Henry will live up to the expectations I set for Lucidus Culling.

LUCIDUS: But you can't – you can't just use my name! People know me! They won't believe you!

HENRY: Will they call your father a liar?! If they do, I will challenge them. And I will fight them every one. I will be as an impenetrable rampart to defend this family from slander and infamy.

LUCIDUS: Father!

FATHER: Son, you know there is nothing more important to me than family. That is why I must do this.

LUCIDUS: But I'm your only surviving heir! I am your flesh and blood!

FATHER: I'm not talking about children. I'm talking about *our family's name*! It's true, I do want grandchildren, but I'm sure New Lucidus can tend to that.

HENRY: Absolutely, dad.

LUCIDUS: What?! No!

FATHER: Goodbye son. Live well on next month's allowance. It will be your last.

(They turn and leave.)

LUCIDUS: Wait! Father!

(He tries to run after them but HENRY pulls a knife on him.)

HENRY: Stay away!

(HENRY backs out of the room. Shortly, FRIEDMONT re-enters.)

LUCIDUS: What will I do? Where will I go?

FRIEDMONT: I'm sorry, sir.

LUCIDUS: This can't be happening. It must be some grand practical joke.

FRIEDMONT: It would be hilarious, sir. Were that so.

LUCIDUS: Friedmont, they'll come to take me from the manor! They'll come and take away everything. They'll take away you! And without my allowance, I can never self-publish. What should I do?

FRIEDMONT: Is it is not obvious sir? You have a very nice set of Wogdons.

LUCIDUS: There is no other way, is there?

FRIEDMONT: So it seems, sir.

LUCIDUS: So be it.

FRIEDMONT: Shall I load a pistol for you?

LUCIDUS: What? I haven't challenged them yet.

FRIEDMONT: Oh, you're going to challenge them, sir?

LUCIDUS: What were you suggesting?

FRIEDMONT: Nothing sir. Your idea is better.

> *(Pause.)*

FRIEDMONT: Though I don't imagine they're much afraid of you. Or that they'd feel the need to accept your challenge, since now they're asserting you don't exist.

LUCIDUS: You're right… so what can I do? What was your first /idea?

FRIEDMONT: Never mind that sir. I'm sure you can call out Mr Blaine. And it does not matter how much stronger or skilled he is. Pistol duels have nothing to do with such things. When I was a young man, it was all about swordplay.

LUCIDUS: You used to fight with swords?

FRIEDMONT: No sir, I didn't have a sword. In Manchester we just had short knives, for stabbing.

LUCIDUS: Were you ever stabbed?

FRIEDMONT: Yes, but it was a long time ago, when I was a child.

LUCIDUS: That's awful.

FRIEDMONT: Well yes, but I don't blame mother for it. I was willful. Can't say I'm worse off for it now. In fact, if I hadn't been bleeding so profusely, I would never have attracted the notice of kindly old Miss Burbank, the schoolteacher who found me in the snow. She mended me up, adopted me; taught me to read, and eventually, speak properly, like someone not from Manchester. If not for her, I would never be where I am today. So, in a way, that stabbing was the single greatest thing that ever happened to me.

LUCIDUS: Friedmont, I'm not going to fight.

FRIEDMONT: What will you do then sir?

LUCIDUS: I have a plan. I'm /going to…

FRIEDMONT: No need to tell me sir. I'm sure it's excellent, as always.

SCENE 16.

LUCIDUS has assembled his friends, GAVIN and ROBERT.

ROBERT: I should have known, there was no way you could have done it!

GAVIN: But why did you lie to us, Lucidus? We're your friends.

LUCIDUS: I'm sorry my friends. You all just seemed so happy to believe it was true. I didn't want to disappoint you.

ROBERT: It's true. I had begun to see the world differently. I was looking at people on the street and wondering if they all contained hidden reservoirs of strength and virtue. Now I can just judge them at face value again.

GAVIN: I know. Lucidus, doing all those things; I kept thinking if Lucidus found courage, then what the hell have I been doing wrong?

LUCIDUS: You haven't been doing anything wrong, Gavin. Dueling is senseless, and it's only a matter of time before people realize that.

(He takes out a letter.)

GAVIN: What's that?

LUCIDUS: My account of the events which have transpired. In an essay against dueling.

(Hands it to ROBERT.)

ROBERT: You want to publish this?

LUCIDUS: Yes.

ROBERT: Are you sure my friend? It won't reflect well on you.

LUCIDUS: I don't care. The truth must be known. If people can't see the horror of dueling with their own eyes, let them be moved by the horror of my prose. I mean, the horror *depicted* in my prose. Take this to Lord Dukingham. Take it all the way to the King.

ROBERT: The King?

LUCIDUS: Yes. You know the king, right? He was at your sister's wedding right?

ROBERT: Well yes I think so, I mean I think that was him.

LUCIDUS: Set this before his eyes.

GAVIN: No, don't! Lucidus, you don't know what will happen if this news gets out. The public is fickle, and unforgiving. You could destroy your reputation forever. Not to mention ours, if we're involved.

ROBERT: Well no offense Gavin but you don't really have a reputation, so…

GAVIN: Shut up Robert, you don't even know what you're talking about!

LUCIDUS: Yes please, Robert…

GAVIN: I may not have a reputation, but that doesn't mean I don't have honor. And when the honor of one man is tarnished, so does it tarnish the honor of all.

LUCIDUS: Well yes that's cute, but what does that really mean?

GAVIN: There's only one way to prove yourself Lucidus. And you don't have to do it alone. I will challenge Henry for you.

LUCIDUS: No, Gavin, I don't want you to fight.

ROBERT: Yes and besides, they probably won't even accept a challenge from a Klaff.

LUCIDUS: Shut up Robert!/

ROBERT: I'm just stating a fact. I'll do it. I think I am probably more respected, anyway.

GAVIN: But I said it first. It's my /idea!

LUCIDUS: No. I don't want either of you to fight.

GAVIN: It wouldn't be just for you. Please, let me prove myself a friend. A true friend. A best friend.

SCENE 17.

The next morning, a public square, the appointed time. GAVIN and LUCIDUS wait anxiously.

GAVIN: Well where are they?

LUCIDUS: There's no hurry, Gavin. In fact, the longer it takes the better off we are. There will be more people around. That's why I arranged to meet in the public square.

GAVIN: It seems like it's rather dangerous to be firing pistols in a public square.

LUCIDUS: Yes well, at least this way there will be witnesses. In case Henry tries to do anything…horrible.

(FATHER and HENRY enter. They are not surprised.)

FATHER: Are you the men who dare accuse my son of lying?

LUCIDUS: Yes father.

FATHER: Father? Who is he speaking to? I have received your letter. We are here to meet your challenge. Fine place for a duel though I must say. If I didn't know better, I'd think you'd never done one of these things before.

LUCIDUS: Just wanted to make sure everything is done honorably.

FATHER: Of course. Well let's get on with it. You said you have some proof of nobility? Klaff, is it?

(LUCIDUS goes to take out the heraldry chart.)

GAVIN: Yes. Gavin Klaff. Of the clan Klaff. You took Lucidus and I apple picking when we were children.

FATHER: Mm, I don't seem to remember that.

HENRY: I don't remember either.

LUCIDUS: That's because you weren't there!

FATHER: Alright calm down. It doesn't matter.

(LUCIDUS presents the heraldry chart. FATHER looks it over.)

FATHER: Let's see. King Philip…a Baron… Two sons…alright we'll kill you.

(He walks back to where he has lain his box of pistols.)

I brought the pistols…

LUCIDUS: That won't be necessary, father. I have an excellent set of Wogdons right here.

(He presents the wooden box containing the Wogdons.)

FATHER: Your brother's set.

HENRY: *(Almost inaudibly.)* My brother's...

LUCIDUS: I inherited it.

FATHER: So you did. Do you know how your eldest brother died?

HENRY: My brother...

LUCIDUS: Screaming in pain, I believe, in bed, after 2 days of internal bleeding.

FATHER: Nobly. Nobly, screaming in pain, in bed, after 2 days of internal bleeding.

LUCIDUS: He got in an argument over whether snails could become ghosts.

FATHER: And he never backed down! You don't deserve to so much as *hold the box* for these pistols. Look at you; you've not even the stones to defend your own name. You have your little friend fight for you.

LUCIDUS: That's not true.

GAVIN: That's right. He's only here because you wouldn't accept his challenge otherwise. But Lucidus is here prepared to fight. We both are!

LUCIDUS: Well, that's not what we talked about...

HENRY: Yes. We are gentlemen. We can't just fight at the drop of a hat. Send a letter if you wish to fight me. And pick a different second. This one, I could barely read his handwriting.

GAVIN: Excuses are for the craven.

FATHER: What?

GAVIN: Why put off the inevitable!? There's a score to settle and one way to settle it. All four of us, to the death!

LUCIDUS: Gavin!

HENRY: Why you little knave.

GAVIN: Unless Mr Culling is somehow above fighting his own battles?

FATHER: You dare speak to me like that, in public?

LUCIDUS: Gavin, I appreciate your enthusiasm, but what the fuck are you doing?

GAVIN: Don't worry my friend. This is what we need, for our self esteem.

LUCIDUS: No, it isn't!

HENRY: Father, you need not fight that way. We are gentlemen.

FATHER: Gentlemen nothing. You think I can abide such talk? With all these people here? In an election year? No, I want to do it. *(To GAVIN.)* I accept your challenge.

LUCIDUS: But you would be shooting at me.

FATHER: So?

LUCIDUS: I am your son. The same blood courses through our veins.

FATHER: There is nothing in your veins! Your veins are full of little girl-baby urine.

LUCIDUS: What is the matter with you?

FATHER: Nothing is the matter with me. I am a man, and I accept my responsibilities. *(Quieter.)* Even if it means killing my own son.

HENRY: I'm your son.

FATHER: Even if it means killing some nobody. Let's get on with this.

GAVIN: Very good. We will do a four way then.

FATHER: A four way..? It's called a Chesterton.

(A KING's MESSENGER enters.)

MESSENGER: Wait stop!

HENRY: What?

MESSENGER: I bid you quit this deadly business, by order of the King.

GAVIN: The King? How did the King hear of this?

LUCIDUS: *(Unconvincingly.)* Oh no!

(GAVIN notices his insincerity.)

Oh Gavin, you didn't really think I'd let you come into harm's way? Or me?

GAVIN: What?

FATHER: Sir, this is a personal affair.

MESSENGER: Are you Nathaniel Culling, of Parliament?

FATHER: Yes.

MESSENGER: Then you are to cease immediately. His Majesty cannot spare more noblemen to the field of honor.

LUCIDUS: Oops.

MESSENGER: Now come at once, as gentlemen.

LUCIDUS: Very well. But first…

(Indicates his essay.)

MESSENGER: Sir, what are you doing?

LUCIDUS: I'm going to read my essay. That's the real reason I arranged to meet in the public square.

MESSENGER: Essay?

LUCIDUS: Against dueling. And why it is bad. The very same treatise Robert Blithe delivered to the King.

MESSENGER: No sir. Any statement you have you can make to the magistrate.

FATHER: The magistrate?! I am from a noble family!

MESSENGER: Yes. And if you are slighted, you must act through the courts.

(ISABELLE runs in. She is breathless.)

ISABELLE: No! You mustn't!

LUCIDUS: Isabelle…?

ISABELLE: If there is a gentlemen among you, you will not submit your honor to be decided by the courts. For satisfaction, blood must be shed.

MESSENGER: Isabelle? Miss Isabelle Dupree?

ISABELLE: Yes yes. Oh Lucidus, I know everything. Robert came to visit mother and I. He came, thinking we'd help him pass on word to the King. He was trying to keep you from dueling!

LUCIDUS: Ah, regrettably, I think he may have succeeded.

MESSENGER: I am a messenger from the King, Miss Dupree. His Majesty wishes no more noble blood spilt for petty grievances.

ISABELLE: Petty grievances? Do you not know, this man has been defamed and stripped of his name? He must be given an opportunity for satisfaction. And besides, there is a principle involved.

LUCIDUS: Well yes, there is a principle, / actually…

ISABELLE: *(Stepping in front of him.)* This is about your right, as nobles, to seek justice by your own hand. If you give up your right to fight, then what is to distinguish you from the common rabble? From the common stevedore, or juggler, or pirate.

FATHER: Yes. Exactly!

LUCIDUS: But Isabelle, there may be more to the picture than you can grasp…

ISABELLE: Oh, I see the picture. I see the picture quite clearly. We're going the way of France! First goes dueling, then goes table manners, and chivalry, and all that is good in this world.

LUCIDUS: Isabelle, can we talk about this later?

ISABELLE: When? After the last nobleman has fallen into moral turpitude? After the last noblewoman has been beheaded and defiled by gin-guzzling madmen? Look around you gentlemen. The public is watching now. *This* is our moment. *This* is our opportunity to prove we nobles are beyond reproach. That we are of a higher moral substance. That we are *half-divine super humans*, governed by higher principles than matters of the flesh.

MESSENGER: But Miss Dupree, the King…

ISABELLE: I know the King. I'm Isabelle Dupree. Don't you think I know what the King wants better than some *messenger*?

ALL: Yes!

MESSENGER: Well…I'm just doing my job.

LUCIDUS: Yes and His Majesty's orders…

ISABELLE: If our liege were here, I have no doubt he would fight.

MESSENGER: Perhaps.

LUCIDUS: What? No…

ISABELLE: Unless you say our King is not brave?

MESSENGER: Of course I would never.

ISABELLE: Public, the seed of justice is in you all! And the justice of a nation is a great lawn, constantly mown. Only through dueling, do we keep it neat and tidy. So says the family Dupree.

FATHER: So says the family Culling!

GAVIN: So says the family Klaff!

MESSENGER: Who?

HENRY: For the honor of England! We must be allowed to fight!

MESSENGER: Hear, hear!

LUCIDUS: What?

MESSENGER: I beg the pardon of the gentlemen assembled. This lady's words have moved me. I now see the goodness of your fight, and ask that you may allow me to serve it as well...

LUCIDUS: *What are you talking about?*

MESSENGER: Will you please provide me with a pistol and an opponent?

ISABELLE: I will fight you sir.

LUCIDUS: Isabelle, NO!

GAVIN: In light of new circumstances, I suggest we adjust our engagement for a simultaneous duel between six.

MESSENGER: A duel between six? You mean –

GAVIN: Yes, sir.

FATHER: A Windemere.

GAVIN: All in favor say aye.

LUCIDUS: Nay!   EVERYONE ELSE: Aye!

LUCIDUS: Nay.

FATHER: The majority has it. Will the lady require a pistol?

ISABELLE: Not at all, sir. I have my own.

(Producing a brace of pistols, and passing one to the MESSENGER.)

LUCIDUS: No Isabelle, you can't do this!

ISABELLE: And why not, because I'm a woman? I think a woman should have the right to die for her country just like any man.

LUCIDUS: For your country? Against who? We're all English!

ISABELLE: Shhhh, darling, don't think.

GAVIN: Who shall give the count now? No one remains outside ourselves.

FATHER: Then we should count together.

GAVIN: But when will we know when to begin counting?

FATHER: We'll count to three.

GAVIN: So we'll count to three and then begin counting to three.

FATHER: Yes.

GAVIN: Agreed.

MESSENGER: For the glory of England, I shall count my loudest.

FATHER: Are you ready son?

HENRY: Yes, father.

(The assembled take up their pistols. All save LUCIDUS.)

GAVIN: This is the best way to duel. With friends and family around to give support. This really couldn't be better.

(LUCIDUS begins stripping his clothes off.)

FATHER: What..?

ISABELLE: Lucidus? What are you doing?

LUCIDUS: I just remembered. Clothes can get in the wound. I don't want to get an infection.

FATHER: No no. None of that. Put your clothes on. Don't make this undignified.

GAVIN: You've got no claims to dignity sir. If he wants to fight you naked, he'll fight you naked.

HENRY: All the same to me.

FATHER: No. There's too many people here. It doesn't look right, firing on a man like that.

ISABELLE: Lucidus, come on now darling, let's try to be civilized.

LUCIDUS: I don't want to be civilized.

FATHER: Oh blast it.

> *(Comes over, then softly.)*

Son, put your pants on. Try to be brave.

LUCIDUS: I don't want to die.

FATHER: You might not die.

LUCIDUS: I don't want to.

FATHER: But the longer you put this off, the more people will be watching, and the more I'll feel the need to not miss.

LUCIDUS: Why don't you love me?

FATHER: *(Moved, but mastering himself.)* Love is a big word son. People show their love in many different ways. Now please, let's just get this over with.

> *(LUCIDUS takes the pistol, resigned at last.)*

LUCIDUS: Yes father.

FATHER: Do you need help cocking your pistol?

LUCIDUS: I can do it.

ISABELLE: I love you Lucidus.

GAVIN: Don't worry Lucidus, we're all here supporting you.

LUCIDUS: *(Without enthusiasm.)* Huzzah.

GAVIN: Ladies and gentlemen, on the count of three, we will count to three. Do not begin counting to three before the count of three. On the count of three the second time, you may fire. Do not fire before three, and don't fire the first time you hear 'three,' but when we're counting altogether, the second time. Is that clear?

ALL: *(Overlapping.)* Mm…yes…I guess…

GAVIN: On three then. Ready? One…two…three.

(Assembled on two sides, the slightly confused combatants turn to the side and raise their pistols. Before the second count of 2, HENRY will flee.)

HENRY: *(Fleeing.)* You know, actually…

ALL but HENRY: One…two…three…

(Everyone fires. The MESSENGER falls. ISABELLE falls. FATHER falls. GAVIN falls. LUCIDUS falls. A great moan of pain swells up from the fallen, as blood begins to pool under them. Except for LUCIDUS, who is huddled, moaning, but actually physically unhurt…ISABELLE begins to crawl her way to him. GAVIN, wounded slightly in his side, gets up and staggers away.)

GAVIN: Someone get a doctor! Someone run and find a doctor!

(HENRY returns on stage and kneels beside FATHER.)

HENRY: Father? Father are you struck?

(He discovers his head bleeding, and seemingly bashed in.)

Oh Father! Father!

(Bereaved, he empties FATHER's pockets, and staggers away. ISABELLE reaches LUCIDUS, and feels over his body.)

ISABELLE: Lucidus. My Lucey…where are you hurt?

LUCIDUS: My head. My head…

ISABELLE: Where? Let's have a look at you.

(Looks him over.)

You are unscathed.

LUCIDUS: But my ears…

ISABELLE: It was loud, darling.

(ISABELLE sits back and removes a handkerchief which she uses to dab her forehead gingerly. LUCIDUS sees, for the first time, the blood pouring out of her…)

But we came out alright.

LUCIDUS: Isabelle, you're bleeding.

ISABELLE: Oh am I? Oh no that's nothing, just a…it's just…

> (*She pulls up her dress and her intestines fall from her gut, grotesquely.*)

Oh dear.

LUCIDUS: Oh god. Oh god, Isabelle!

> (*ISABELLE tries to shove her intestines back, with difficulty.*)

ISABELLE: Ahhhhh…

LUCIDUS: Someone get a doctor! Isabelle, you're going to be fine, just hold on!

ISABELLE: Lucidus, sweetheart, it looks like I might have to die.

LUCIDUS: No, you'll be fine, just hold it, hold them in.

ISABELLE: But if I die, I die for something great. For honor, Lucidus. Your honor.

LUCIDUS: Yes yes…

ISABELLE: Isn't that beautiful?

LUCIDUS: Oh Isabelle, you don't even know me…

ISABELLE: I know the idea of you. It's the Age of Enlightenment. It's the ideas that are important.

> (*Dabbing her forehead.*)

Oh god, I'm sorry, this is it, isn't it? – your handkerchief.

> (*She hands him the bloodied handkerchief.*)

LUCIDUS: It's not important now.

ISABELLE: Quite right.

FATHER: Lucidus…

LUCIDUS: Father?

FATHER: Lucidus, come here…

LUCIDUS: I'm busy father. Just wait a moment.

FATHER: Who is that? Isabelle?

ISABELLE: Mr Culling, hello!

FATHER: Oh, you don't look very good.

ISABELLE: I know.

LUCIDUS: No Isabelle it's going to be fine. Modern medicine can do anything. They'll patch you up, and then we're going to get married.

ISABELLE: Oh good.

FATHER: But Lucidus, I need to speak to you, too. I'm dying too.

GAVIN: I'm dying too. Lucidus, give me /your hand...

FATHER: Lucidus /please, come here...

ISABELLE: Lucidus. /Lucidus

LUCIDUS: Okay, I can't understand when you all talk at the same time! Father?

FATHER: I don't want to be alone.

LUCIDUS: Well then you can come here then. I'm not coming to you.

GAVIN: Lucidus, give me your hand.

FATHER: But I feel so cold.

LUCIDUS: Or I can talk to you from here.

FATHER: I just want you to know I do love you. You'll always be my real son. And I'm proud of you.

> *(Beat. These words unleash a flood of emotion in LUCIDUS, despite himself.)*

LUCIDUS: Thank you.

FATHER: But I told Henry to burn down your house. To destroy any documentation you might have, proving your identity. I'm sorry. It seemed like a good idea at the time. But Henry isn't as strong as you, I see that now. He's all bluff and bluster. But you, you are a Culling!

GAVIN: *(Reaching for LUCIDUS.)* We're dying. We're all dying together. Best friends forever...

> *(LUCIDUS extricates himself from ISABELLE.)*

LUCIDUS: Will you excuse me a moment?

ISABELLE: Of course darling.

(LUCIDUS takes Isabelle's hand and gives it to Gavin to hold, then goes to FATHER. ISABELLE and GAVIN will both soon die.)

GAVIN: Best friends forever…

FATHER: She's a good woman, Isabelle. From a good family. You should marry her.

LUCIDUS: She's going to die.

FATHER: Then you should marry her quickly. That way you can still get some of her money.

LUCIDUS: Father, do you remember when I was little, and we spent the summers in Devon?

FATHER: Yes.

LUCIDUS: We'd go out hunting with the hounds remember? And Benedict and Kendrick would always come back with a hare, and I never did.

FATHER: Yes?

LUCIDUS: Well I did once. I shot a hare out in the glade. But I felt so bad about it, I cried. And while I was crying, just trying to pull myself together before I came back to show you, a fox came and took away my hare.

FATHER: Damn foxes. You should've told me.

LUCIDUS: I didn't want you to know. I was angry with you. I was angry with you for making me kill that poor rabbit.

FATHER: But rabbits are vermin. They pollute the landscape.

LUCIDUS: I like rabbits. I was afraid to tell you before, but now you should know. I love all living things. And if my horse is overweight, it's because I feed him so well.

FATHER: Why are you telling me this?

LUCIDUS: Because I want you to know who I am before you die.

FATHER: I might not die. I just wanted you to come over here.

LUCIDUS: I think you're going to die. And with you dies the last of the Cullings.

FATHER: What?

LUCIDUS: I don't want my name back. I don't want any part of your legacy.

FATHER: That legacy is all you have.

LUCIDUS: No it isn't. I have many interests.

FATHER: We are a family of warriors.

LUCIDUS: Well now we're going to be a family of naturalists, and pie makers...

FATHER: What?

LUCIDUS: Or maybe I could be a florist. Or a doily inspector.

FATHER: Stop! You're just saying all that to hurt me.

LUCIDUS: Well, maybe a little.

FATHER: *(Furious.)* You'll burn. Henry will burn you to the ground.

LUCIDUS: We'll see. God, I'm happy you're dying.

FATHER: *(Lunging forward.)* You've given me the strength to live. *(This is followed by a great pain, and he falls back.)*

LUCIDUS: I'll bury you with my brothers. But me, I want to be buried somewhere else.

FATHER: No one will bother to bury you. They'll throw your body to the dogs.

LUCIDUS: I like dogs. I told you, I like all living things!

FATHER: You don't know what it means to live, you coward. You worm.

LUCIDUS: Yes, I know you think little of me.

FATHER: Everyone thinks little of you. You little pussy shit! You little faggot pussy shit knave. You shit bag worm fuck! You little worthless fop –

> *(LUCIDUS stuffs the bloody handkerchief in his FATHER's mouth.)*

LUCIDUS: Your last words. I shall mark them well.

> *(ROBERT enters, out of breath.)*

ROBERT: Wait, stop!

> *(He takes in the massacre.)*

Oh, I'm too late.

LUCIDUS: It's all fine and well Robert. Everything's under control.

ROBERT: Oh my god. Is that Isabelle Dupree? And...Gavin?

LUCIDUS: Yes. But 'tis all well and good. They died a hero's death.

SCENE 18.

LUCIDUS returns home, his clothes still stained with blood. FRIEDMONT hears him enter and comes to greet him.

FRIEDMONT: Mr Culling?

LUCIDUS: Yes?

FRIEDMONT: You're alive…

LUCIDUS: So it seems.

FRIEDMONT: All is resolved between you and your father then, sir?

LUCIDUS: I should hope so. He's dead.

FRIEDMONT: Dead, sir?

LUCIDUS: Yes.

FRIEDMONT: And your estate?

LUCIDUS: It's still mine. Though Henry may come around and try to burn us down. I'm not sure.

FRIEDMONT: I'll keep a watch out sir.

LUCIDUS: Don't bother. It's insured.

FRIEDMONT: Still, I'd like not to burn to death. That would come as a blow.

LUCIDUS: Yes, of course. Maybe we should burn it ourselves then.

FRIEDMONT: And then what, sir?

LUCIDUS: Go away. Let's go away together. Live a simpler life. Just you and me. And the chambermaids, and the cook, and the stable hands.

FRIEDMONT: Go where, sir?

LUCIDUS: I don't know. Spain perhaps…

FRIEDMONT: Spain?

LUCIDUS: Yes. I've never been there. I hear there's beautiful women.

FRIEDMONT: I did not know you truly liked women, sir.

LUCIDUS: Of course I like women. Oh you're joking ha ha ha…
Ah, Friedmont, you've been such a friend to me.

FRIEDMONT: As you wish, sir.

LUCIDUS: Come there's not a moment to delay. Let's begin to pack.

FRIEDMONT: Yes, sir. But let me help you out of those bloody clothes first.

LUCIDUS: Ah yes, thank you.

(FRIEDMONT helps undress him.)

LUCIDUS: Friedmont, tell me, are there mountains in Spain?

FRIEDMONT: Yes, sir.

LUCIDUS: I'd like to climb one. Will you help me climb a mountain?

FRIEDMONT: If I must, sir.

LUCIDUS: That's a challenge worth taking, yes? That's a way to make a
name. Let every man know the name Hanaroy Trudging. The first to
climb a mountain.

FRIEDMONT: Trudging?

LUCIDUS: That's right. We're going to start fresh. The age of the Cullings is
over. Nathaniel is dead. Lucidus is dead.

FRIEDMONT: So who are you then, sir?

LUCIDUS: I am no man, and any man, not yet known.

FRIEDMONT: Very enigmatic sir.

LUCIDUS: Who am I? Ha. You tell me. Forget everything you know about
me, and look at me, but, and, forget how I look right now, but look at
me, and tell me, who am I? How do I seem to you?

FRIEDMONT: If I forget everything I know about you? And the way you look?

LUCIDUS: Yes.

FRIEDMONT: Well then I'd have to say, you look splendid, sir. Like a
perfect gentlemen.

(Fin.)

THE BOOK OF GRACE

Suzan-Lori Parks

Named one of *TIME* magazine's "100 Innovators for the Next New Wave," in 2002 Suzan-Lori Parks became the first African-American woman to receive the Pulitzer Prize in Drama for her Broadway hit *Topdog/Underdog*. A MacArthur "Genius" Fellowship recipient, she has also been awarded grants by the National Endowment for the Arts, the Rockefeller Foundation, the Ford Foundation, the New York State Council on the Arts and the New York Foundation for the Arts. She is the recipient of a Lila Wallace–Reader's Digest Award, a CalArts/Herb Alpert Award in the Arts (Theatre) for 1996, a Guggenheim Foundation Fellowship and the 2015 Dorothy & Lillian Gish Prize. She is an alumna of Mount Holyoke College and New Dramatists.

Her numerous plays include *Father Comes Home from the Wars (Parts 1, 2 & 3)* (2015 Pulitzer Prize finalist, 2015 Edward M. Kennedy Prize for Drama Inspired by American History, 2014 Horton Foote Prize), *The Book of Grace*, *Topdog/Underdog* (2002 Pulitzer Prize), *In the Blood* (2000 Pulitzer Prize finalist), *Venus* (1996 OBIE Award), *The Death of the Last Black Man in the Whole Entire World*, *Fucking A*, *Imperceptible Mutabilities in the Third Kingdom* (1990 OBIE Award for Best New American Play) and *The America Play*. Parks's work on *The Gershwins' Porgy and Bess* earned the production a Tony Award for Best Revival of a Musical in 2012. In 2007 her *365 Days/365 Plays* was produced in more than seven hundred theaters worldwide, creating one of the largest grassroots collaborations in theater history. Her work is the subject of the PBS film *The Topdog Diaries*.

Park's first novel, *Getting Mother's Body*, was published by Random House in 2003.

Her first short film, *Anemone Me*, was assistant-directed by Todd Haynes and produced by Christine Vachon. Her first feature-length screenplay, *Girl 6*, was written for Spike Lee. She has also written numerous screenplays, including the adaptation of Zora Neale Hurston's classic novel *Their Eyes Were Watching God*, which premiered on ABC's *Oprah Winfrey Presents*.

As a film actor, Parks has also appeared in the fictional-documentary *The Making of Plus One*, which premiered at the Cannes Film Festival in 2009.

In November 2008 Parks became the first recipient of the Master Writer Chair at The Public Theater. At The Public, and as she tours the country, she performs her innovative performance piece, *Watch Me Work*, a play with action and dialogue/a meta-theatrical writing class. She also serves as a visiting arts professor in dramatic writing at New York University's Tisch School of the Arts.

Holding honorary doctorates from Brown University, among others, Parks credits her writing teacher and mentor, James Baldwin, for starting her on the path of playwriting. One of the first to recognize Parks's writing skills, Mr. Baldwin declared Parks "an astonishing and beautiful creature who may become one of the most valuable artists of our time."

Introduction

Suzan-Lori Parks has always resisted categories. Her work is playful and deeply serious, formally inventive and profoundly moral, learned and casual, quirky and classical. The resistance to categories isn't just a formal description: it is at the center of her moral concerns. Freedom is her great subject, and the crossing of genres and mixing of tones, Parks' freedom of form, is a reflection of the great desire of her characters for their own liberation. Her most recent masterpiece, *Father Comes Home from the Wars, Parts One, Two* and *Three*, directly tackles the legacy of American slavery. Set in the American Civil War, Parks' characters dream of freedom, and understand that the absence of slavery is only the first step, vital though it is, in the achievement of freedom's promise.

When she first burst on the scene, 25 years ago, she remade our theatrical past: suddenly Adrienne Kennedy was part of a lineage, not an outlier. Suzan-Lori's astonishing linguistic pyrotechnics were fresh and powerful; they felt both completely new, and yet sprung from a classical tradition. In works like *Imperceptible Mutabilities In The Third Kingdom* and *The Death Of The Last Black Man In The Whole Entire World* she created powerful experimental plays that contained ravishing poetry and deep thought. Gradually her work began to take on more traditional narrative (without losing any of its theatrical and linguistic uniqueness), until in *Topdog/Underdog* she created an searing examination of race and family and history that is as deep a family play as the American theater has yet produced.

In *The Book of Grace* Suzan-Lori is struggling with the power of despair, and the immense difficulty of hope. Yet, the terrifying father/husband in *The Book of Grace*, is a border patrolman. The Border Fence he guards is a cage as well as a boundary, a repressive and powerful barrier that Suzan-Lori exploits for both its political and psychological resonance. The "Aliens" he guards against are both foreign nationals and members of his own family; once fences are built, everyone becomes the Other.

Grace invites her stepson Buddy back home in the hopes of brokering a reconciliation between father and son. Buddy, who changes his name to Snake, is being eaten alive by anger and shame. His Book, *The Book of Snake*, is a videotape, a video record of what becomes a suicidal mission of revenge against the father who abused him.

Against these angry, destructive men Grace has her Book, *The Book of Grace*. It is not taped, but written. It is her 'leaning towards the good', the manifestation of her belief that hope can be found in the darkest places. She is foolish and seemingly ineffective and often confused, but the strength of her hope is enough to bring her out of her grave and back to her kitchen, refusing to give up in the face of seemingly intractable hatred.

The Book of Grace is the rawest of Suzan-Lori's plays: reading it again, the desperation pours off the page. The language is still brilliant, the moral passion as fierce, but the hole in *The American Play*, which is 'an exact replica of the Great Hole of History', becomes in *The Book of Grace* a grave that Vet has dug in the backyard for his wife. This is a world stripped of poetry, where holes are not metaphors but places to bury people.

In *The Book of Grace*, Suzan-Lori Parks is fulfilling that ancient demand we make of our artists: to go to the darkest places, and bring back news. Fearlessly, she reports on a world where reconciliation feels impossible, forgiveness seems like weakness, and the only possibility of justice lies in bloody mutual destruction. This desert is a brutal and terrible place.

This world would be unendurable, except for Grace. Grace as the possibility of forgiveness; Grace as the collector of hope; Grace as the champion of narrative; Grace as a writer. In her struggle to find hope, she embodies a reason to hope.

Suzan-Lori Parks, now well into her third decade of writing for the American theater, loving mother to Durham and beloved member of the Public theater family, is our Grace, and our reason to hope. She has defied those who think that American lives don't have second acts.

The hope she offers is not reasonable, but it is not reason that makes us happy or unhappy. It is Grace.

Oskar Eustis

Production history

World Premiere at The Public Theater on March 17, 2010
under the direction of James Macdonald

Scenic Designer: Eugene Lee
Costume Designer: Susan Hilferty
Lighting Designer: Jean Kalman
Sound Designer: Dan Moses Schreier
Projection/Video Designer: Jeff Suff
Dramaturg: John Dias
Production Stage Manager: Amy McCraney

Presented by the Public Theater
Artistic Director, Oskar Eustis; Executive Director: Andrew D. Hamingson

Cast

VET:	John Doman
BUDDY:	Amari Cheatom
GRACE:	Elizabeth Marvel

Author's Note on the Productions

A Whole Can of Worms

In NYC, at The Public, we worked with a superb multiracial cast. In Austin, at ZACH, we worked with an equally superb cast, and chose to go ABC (All Black Casting). I feel that a monochromatic casting allows the production to embrace the more profound and thorny themes of the play. That said, I also understand that any casting choice will, especially with this play, open up its own can of worms.

Characters

VET
BUDDY
GRACE

SETTING
A house in a small town near the Border.

FROM THE AUTHOR'S ELEMENTS OF STYLE
I'm continuing the use of my slightly unconventional theatrical elements. Here's a road map.

• *(Rest.)*
Take a little time, a pause, a breather; make a transition.

• A Spell
An elongated and heightened *(Rest)*. Denoted by repetition of figures' names with no dialogue. Has sort of an architectural look:

BUDDY
VET
BUDDY
VET

This is a place where the figures experience their pure true simple state. While no action or stage business is necessary, directors should fill this moment as they best see fit.

• ((Parentheses around dialogue indicate softly spoken passages —asides; sotto voce.))

• [[Brackets indicate possible cuts for production.]]

For Buddy

and

For Stephanie Ellen

PROLOGUE

VET, standing outside near the Border Fence, wearing his uniform and, with his binoculars, scanning the horizon.

GRACE, in her kitchen, wearing her waitress uniform, and holding her red-marbled composition book, her Book of Grace.

BUDDY, outside, in a no-man's land, wearing t-shirt and jeans with a keychain on his belt. He's got his footlocker and a full-to-bursting plastic shopping bag.

VET
BUDDY
GRACE
     (Rest.)

GRACE: There's a lot of good in the world

VET: It's all about Us and Them

BUDDY: I can't forgive what he's done. What he's done to me. No way

GRACE: You just gotta look for it. The good. You just gotta look

VET: That's why Borders are good. They keep us contained

BUDDY: I can't forget it, but I could forgive it. Forgiving it will depend on him

GRACE: Sure there's bad. But there's good too. Like

VET: Borders keep Us on our side and Them on theirs. And that's a good

BUDDY: Forgiving it will depend on him not forgetting it. Funny how that works, huh?

GRACE: Like that baby hippo and that old turtle. They're friends. That's good

VET: And that's a good thing. Borders

BUDDY: I can't forget it

GRACE: Like the man who saved the lady when she fell into the river. He risked his own life to do it. That's good

VET: Borders and Fences, they say it all without saying a word: that is yours and this is mine

BUDDY: I can't forget it

GRACE: Why did he save her from drowning? 'Cause something in him was leaning toward the good

BUDDY: I can't forget it. OK?

VET: I see an Illegal trying to get in here and I say, "Stop in the name of the U.S. Border Patrol." That's my job

BUDDY: He's my "father." I use that term loosely. Let me be specific: he is my very own motherfucker

GRACE: There's so much evidence of good. So I write it down in my book.

BUDDY: I'm Buddy, Pop. Here I am. This is how I turned out

VET: I have contained myself. I've changed. I'm on the good foot now

BUDDY: Unspeakable. The things he did to me

VET: He'll try to make me admit to stuff

BUDDY: Unspeakable

GRACE: Looking on the bright side doesn't cost nothing

BUDDY: It can't be forgot but it can be forgiven

VET: I've contained myself

BUDDY: Three chances he'll get. Three strikes: 1-2-3

VET: I've contained myself

BUDDY: Hey, I am, after all, his son

GRACE: You just gotta look for it. The good. The good is all around

VET
BUDDY
GRACE
    (Rest.)

GRACE: *(Reading from her Book.) The Book of Grace. (Rest.)*

    A bell, thumb-cymbal sounding, rings.

    As the lights change, BUDDY hides his plastic bag. He hides it somewhere in the audience—silently asking folks to keep his secret.

CHAPTER 47

Early morning. A small one-bedroom house. Fairly well kept. Reading from her Book:

GRACE: *The Book of Grace*, Chapter 47: Aliens.

> *VET, working on his speech, recites while watching the TV and ironing his green uniform. He finishes one and begins ironing another.*

VET: "Aliens. That's what we're up against. Aliens. Not the ones from outer space although they might be. Although they could be. From another planet. From another land. Their land might as well be another planet. Because they're strange. They're not like us. That's why we've got to keep them out. And a Border alone won't do it. That's why the Fence, the Border Fence, that's why it's a miracle. The Border Fence is a modern miracle."

> *(Rest.)*

Yeah. That's it. Keep it simple. It's a speech. Talk about something they can all understand.

> *(Rest.)*

"This here. This is a crease. They see these creases and they know they're done for. We all wear the uniform. And we wear it proudly. Sometimes I even sleep in mine."

> *(Rest.)*

No, don't tell them that.

> *(Rest.)*

"This crease makes a Fence all its own."

> *(Rest.)*
>
> *(Rest.)*

"I caught those Illegals and their truckload of drugs and I did it single-handedly. So now I'm getting a medal for it. And I thank you."

> *(Rest.)*

"Aliens. Sometimes the Alien is right in your own home. Sometimes right in your own blood. And you've got to build a wall around it."

> *(Rest.)*

Maybe not that part but the first part. Yeah. OK. Lead with Aliens then keep it down to earth. All right.

> *He continues ironing.*

CHAPTER 48

Some time later. VET still ironing. TV still on. Reading from her Book:

GRACE: *The Book of Grace*, Chapter 48: My Version of Homeland Security.

> *BUDDY, standing in the doorway with his footlocker. He wears t-shirt and jeans.*

BUDDY: I've got I.D. Identification.

VET: That's good.

BUDDY: You need to see it?

VET: Are you really Buddy?

BUDDY: Sure, Pop.

VET: Just asking.

BUDDY: I've got I.D. Take a look.
> (*Rest.*)
I'll put it right here.

> *BUDDY sets his identification card down and glances at the TV. VET joins him.*

VET: The Border Fence. There it is.

BUDDY: That's where you work.

VET: That's right.

BUDDY: "Border Patrol Officer single-handedly catches 8 Illegal Immigrants and their truckload of drugs."

VET: You saw the news.

BUDDY: I knew it was you before they said your name.

VET: You recognized me. I've changed a lot.

BUDDY: Me too.

VET: For better or for worse?

BUDDY: That's a frame-of-reference question.

VET: How long you planning on staying?

BUDDY: Just for your Ceremony.

VET: That's tomorrow.

BUDDY: So I'll just stay the night.

VET: Grace says you might stay longer.

BUDDY: She home?

VET: She's at work.
>> (Rest.)
> I say we'll see.

BUDDY: About what?

VET: About you staying longer. We expected you yesterday.

BUDDY: I got held up.

VET: Grace baked you a cake. She wanted to have a party.

BUDDY: Yeah, she said.

VET: She said?

BUDDY: In her letter. I sent her a picture—

VET: —She showed me—

BUDDY: —So she'd know it was me. So you would too.

VET: It's been a while. 10 years.

BUDDY: 15 years.

VET: Point taken.

BUDDY: I got an honorable discharge. A few years ago.

VET: And you've just been doing what since then? Just kicking around?

BUDDY: Pretty much.
>> (Rest.)
> Can I get some water?

VET: Hold up.

> *VET approaches BUDDY. BUDDY raises his arms.*

VET: My version of Homeland Security. On the job and at home too.

> *BUDDY submits to VET's thorough pat-down. VET takes BUDDY's phone from his pocket. Looks it over.*

VET: You've got one of these, huh? A Smartphone.

BUDDY: It's a few years old.

> *VET hands the phone back.*

VET: You believe in the right to bear arms?

BUDDY: Sure. For self-protection. But I don't got a gun.

VET: Do you want one?

BUDDY: Not right now.

VET: You're not a liberal?

BUDDY: No, sir.

VET: Good. There's the sink. Help yourself.

> *VET goes back to his ironing and also watches as BUDDY goes to the sink, getting a few handfuls of water.*

VET: This heat makes me think of ice cream. Remember that time I took you for ice cream?

BUDDY: No.

VET: We had black walnut. My favorite.

BUDDY: OK.

VET: I got a single. You got a double-dip.

BUDDY: Triple-dip.

VET: So you remember. You got a favorite anything?

BUDDY: Nope.

VET: That ice cream was almost as big as you.

BUDDY: Almost.

VET: And your mother got vanilla.

BUDDY: Strawberry.

VET: Right.
>   (Rest.)
> Too bad she passed.

BUDDY: No one at her funeral but me. You could of come.

VET: What for?

BUDDY: Right. I got the condolence card Grace sent. I guess me visiting here was all her idea, right?

VET: The card was from both of us. And you visiting: we thought of it together.

BUDDY: Right.

GRACE: Footnote #1:

> *GRACE, waitressing at the diner, pauses from her work to speak to us.*

GRACE: So I said to him, "Vet, don't look at me like I'm crazy. You're getting a medal, he's got a medal already. You're doing pretty good, he's doing pretty good. It's the perfect time for you and Buddy to see each other again. You say you "can't see him." But you've got eyes, don't you? Of course you do. So you'll see him and you two will make amends. It'll be good for both of you. No brainer."

BUDDY: That Fence. It's something.

> *BUDDY watches the TV. VET watches BUDDY.*

VET: That's live-streaming video. But even live-streaming video doesn't do it justice.

BUDDY: Maybe you'll take me to see it.

VET: You'll see it tomorrow at the Ceremony with everybody else.
>   (Rest.)
> Grace says you're looking for work. She thinks you should work Patrol. With me.

BUDDY: There's a fast-track for military guys.

VET: But I'm guessing you've had a few blemishes on your record since you got out.

BUDDY: Nothing too serious.

VET: Still, you'll need my good word to smooth your path.

BUDDY: Yeah. I would.

BUDDY
VET
> (Rest.)

BUDDY: I got a favorite tree.

VET: OK.

BUDDY: The one we had in the yard on Myrtle Avenue was pretty good.

VET: Pine.

BUDDY: Elm.

VET: It was pine, I'm telling you.

BUDDY: When we lived on Elm Street we had a pine tree, but on Myrtle Ave we had the elm. But that was just me and Mom, when we lived on Myrtle.

VET: Right.

BUDDY: So you probably wouldn't remember it. The elm.

VET: That pine tree was something though, wasn't it? You practically lived up there. And then when that cone fell down and popped you on the head you took it personal. Stuck your firecrackers around the trunk and tried to blow it up.

BUDDY: I almost did too.

VET: Fire department had to come. Your mother blamed it on me.

BUDDY: Yeah.
> (Rest.)
>
> When's Grace coming home?

VET: In a couple of hours. She's at work, or at least that's where she says she is.
> (Rest.)
>
> You're grown and I'm old. Is that what you're thinking?

BUDDY: You're working that iron pretty good.

VET: 50 push-ups, 200 sit-ups every morning.

BUDDY: I do twice that.

VET: Want me to call Grace?

BUDDY: No need.

VET: You two talk on the phone a lot?

BUDDY: Nope.

VET: Just letters? Emails?

BUDDY: Just letters.
> (Rest.)
You wear Kevlar?

VET: Why you asking?

BUDDY: Just making conversation.

VET: A bullet-proof vest? We could, but the job doesn't go that way too often. Most Tonks don't hardly got shoes let alone a gun. Although I've got mine. Glock.

BUDDY: They make you keep it locked up at the station?

VET: They don't make me. That's my decision. Keeps things—contained.

BUDDY: You have changed.

VET: Yep.

BUDDY: You keep that Fence on all day?

VET: It feeds to the TV. From the "interwebs." So we can monitor the Border 24/7. Grace says I shouldn't bring my work home with me. The live-feed's mostly for volunteers, but I like it too.

BUDDY: It's interesting.

VET: You want a beer? I know it's early, but—

> VET takes two beers from the fridge, hands one to BUDDY who holds up his hand in refusal.

BUDDY: I'm all right.

VET: I could put an egg in it. Make it breakfast.

BUDDY: No thanks.

VET: Not your brand? It's American. The can's red-white-and-blue at least.

BUDDY: I don't drink.

VET: You drink water.

BUDDY: Not spirits.

VET: You a Muslim?

BUDDY: Nope.

VET: Next thing I know you'll drop down and be praying on the rug.
East is that way, if you're wondering.

BUDDY: I'm not.

VET: So you're a 12-Stepper?

BUDDY: Nope.

VET: Just a Teetotaler. OK. Your mother inhabited the opposing camp on
the subject of drinking if I remember correctly. I'm easy on the spirits.
So you're like me.

BUDDY: I guess.

VET: You're easy on the spirits, I'm easy on the spirits. We believe in the
same things. You got a footlocker. I got a footlocker.
I got private stuff in mine. What's in yours?

BUDDY: Private stuff.

VET: We're 2 peas in a pod. You turned out all right. Pretty much.

BUDDY: Thanks.

VET: Ceremony's going to be a social situation. Around here if you don't at
least hold a beer in your hand, people will think twice about you. Then
they'll think twice about me.

BUDDY picks up the unopened beer and holds it.

BUDDY: Should I open it?

VET: If we were in a social situation.

BUDDY: We're not in a social situation?

VET: No, Buddy, we're at home.

BUDDY: Your home, not mine.

VET: My home and we're glad you're here.

GRACE: Footnote #2:

Again, GRACE pauses from her work.

GRACE: And then I told him, "Vet, you'll know what to say. Say 'welcome home.' OK, so it's not his home. Say 'we're glad you're here.' Offer him a beer and a seat, Vet. It's not brain surgery. Or is it? OK, maybe it is brain surgery. Better get out your rubber gloves. No, don't get out your rubber gloves, Vet. Just offer him a beer and tell him to sit down. Forgive and forget. I mean, how bad can it be, right?"

VET: Grace wants you to stay. Longer than just the night. Christ, the things she's got going on in her head. She's thinking, together, the three of us can be some sort of family unit: me the Father, you the Son and her as the—Holy Ghost.

They enjoy that together.

VET: *(Rest.)* Stupid-dumb/   BUDDY: [[/Stupid-dumb.
                                            I remember that.]] You

and Grace?   Kids?

VET: Nope.

VET's finished ironing. He would go into the bedroom to change, but, to keep his eye on
BUDDY, he stays in the room, getting dressed.

VET: Look at that crease. Grace, she can't understand the importance of a good crease. It's just a boundary, just a line of demarcation. But that kind of understanding is beyond her. She came home one day. Reading one of those women's magazines and took one of the tests they've got in there, counted up her score and says the test says that she's got "boundary issues." Well, I could of told her that.

BUDDY is looking out the window.

BUDDY: It's nice here. Nice house. Nice yard.

VET: At night you can see the Fence from here. And when I'm over there I can see the house. From there, we're the closest lights in the distance. They wanted me to live on the base, with everybody else, but I don't like people in my business.

BUDDY: What's the hole in the backyard for?

VET
BUDDY
      (Rest.)

VET: How was the Service?

BUDDY: I qualified as "expert" on the M-16. I worked the M-79 for a while.

VET: Grenade launcher.

BUDDY: Yeah. I got out and I took some classes. A government class.
    "When in the course of human events it becomes necessary—"

VET: No need to school me.

BUDDY: I know the whole thing. The Constitution too.

VET: Grace said you were mostly a sort of army waterboy.

BUDDY: Water Transport Specialist.

VET: OK.

BUDDY: I got promoted. Got working as a Combat Engineer too.
    Building anti-tank ditches, laying landmines.

VET: Blowing up stuff. OK. You put your childhood inclination to good use.

BUDDY: I got the Bronze Star too.

VET: Tell the truth, now.

> *BUDDY takes off his boot.*
> *Empties out his medal.*
> *Shows it to VET.*

VET: Might as well take off the other one too.

> *BUDDY takes off his other boot. Shakes it out. Nothing in it.*

VET: Where's your name?

BUDDY: They don't put your name on it. It's like the Olympics. You get a
    medal in the Olympics they don't put your name on it.

VET: Grace would say we're finding our "Common Ground."
    (Rest.)
  I'm getting a medal too. The Governor's coming down. The whole town

will be there. The local news crew. The marching band. They're telling me I'll have to give a speech.

BUDDY: A speech?

VET: Yeah.

BUDDY: What's the hole in the backyard for?

VET: It's a deterrent.

BUDDY: You said you changed.

VET: Grace says I'm a work-in-progress.

BUDDY: What do you say?

VET: I say, are you in trouble?

BUDDY: In trouble? No, sir.

VET: Except for your stint in the Service you were always in trouble. Are you in trouble now?

BUDDY: I'm doing great.

VET: Mind if I take a look?

BUDDY: Yes.

VET: I've probably got a key that could fit it.

BUDDY
VET

> *BUDDY unlocks his footlocker, opening the lid. VET puts on some latex gloves before gently looking through the contents. Some bric-a-brac, old clothes, not much else.*

BUDDY: Just some old junk from Mom's house.

VET: Too bad you lost it.

BUDDY: They took it.

VET: Well if you don't pay the bill, they'll do that.

BUDDY: I could use a job.

VET: We'll see.

BUDDY: I need to get back on my feet. It's been hard.

VET: I said we'll see.

BUDDY: We'll see.
> (Rest.)
> Unspeakable. The things you did to me.

VET: I don't know what you're talking about.

BUDDY: Maybe we should just forget it.

VET: I don't know what you're talking about. What I do know is: I'm on the good foot now. Past behind me. Future in front. Like it should be, OK? OK. Hey, OK, maybe I'll have time later tonight. I could show you the Fence. See the Fence, meet the guys. Even a job—maybe.

BUDDY: "Maybe."

VET: You should get a haircut. So when you meet the guys you'll look correct. There's a barbershop—

BUDDY: You really don't have any recollection of it?

VET: It's past. I'm living today, OK?

BUDDY
VET
BUDDY

> *BUDDY holds up his thumb, like he's counting. It's Strike One.*

VET: What's that for?

BUDDY: I hitchhiked. From the bus stop.

> *BUDDY stands there with his thumb still extended.*
> *VET looks at the clock on the wall and then at his watch. He goes to the house phone, making a call.*

VET: Time at the tone is a real lifesaver.

> *He resets the clock, then his watch.*

VET: Past behind, future in front. All right?

BUDDY: We'll see.

> *He's still got his thumb out, but not brandishing it so obviously.*

VET: Well—"Welcome home, Buddy." I'll swing by the barbershop later. Pick you up if you're there. Then we could do the tour.

BUDDY: Sure.

> *VET goes.*
> *BUDDY stands there watching the Fence on TV.*
> *The sound of VET's truck fades into the distance.*
> *When the coast is clear, BUDDY goes outside and retrieves his plastic bag.*
> *Back in the house he opens his footlocker and transfers the bag's contents: several Army-issue hand grenades: very precious, very dangerous.*

BUDDY: Strike One.

CHAPTER 49

A few hours later.

GRACE just home from work. She wears her waitress uniform and carries old newspapers.

GRACE: *The Book Of Grace,* Chapter 49: Buddy. Grace. Right.

BUDDY sleeps on the couch. She stands there looking at him.

GRACE

BUDDY

GRACE

BUDDY

      (Rest.)
      She gets a closer look at his face. He doesn't wake.
      She sits on the edge of the couch, looking at him.
      BUDDY fidgets in his sleep. She keeps staring at him.

GRACE

GRACE

GRACE

GRACE

GRACE

GRACE

GRACE

GRACE

She scrounges around in her purse, pulling out a waitress notepad. Scrounges around for a pen.

Scribbles something on the pad. A fresh page, another glance at BUDDY, then more scribbling.

A glance at BUDDY's footlocker.

BUDDY gently wakes and watches her. She's absorbed and doesn't notice at first. When she does, she hops up, dropping her notepad, then toeing it under the couch.

GRACE: Buddy!

BUDDY: Grace.

GRACE: Right.

BUDDY: Well, hey.

GRACE: Hey.

BUDDY
GRACE
BUDDY
GRACE

> *They hug gently and then separate.*

GRACE: 15 years.

BUDDY: Yeah.

GRACE: You got here!

BUDDY: I did.

GRACE: Right on.

BUDDY: I guess.

GRACE: And you've come back to help celebrate your dad. Gold Star, Buddy.

BUDDY
GRACE

GRACE: What?

BUDDY: Nothing.

GRACE: Tell me.

BUDDY: No thanks.

BUDDY
GRACE
BUDDY
GRACE
BUDDY
GRACE

> *The distance between them feels like miles.*

CHAPTER 50

As BUDDY and GRACE are squaring off in the living room, VET, wearing his gun, is at work. He scans the horizon with his binoculars. He's still figuring out his speech.

GRACE: *The Book Of Grace*, Chapter 50: Marginalia: Sometimes I Don't See Anything.

VET: "Sometimes I don't see anything. Sometimes I can stand here for hours and look and look and—what am I looking at? The Fence. And nothing. The dirt. The rocks. The sand. The gophers. The lizards. The jackalopes. Just kidding. No such thing as a jackalope. No such thing as an honest Illegal. Honest Illegal is a whatchacallit. An oxymoron. Oxymoron. Funny word. If I didn't speak English I'd think that meant—'clean idiot.' Most of them don't speak English."
   (Rest.)
You're rambling. Your speech isn't a speech yet, it's a ramble. A babble. A wander. Give them something more substantial, Vet. Put the job in a nutshell.
   (Rest.)
¡SAL DEL COCHE! ¡SAL DEL COCHE! ¡VENGA! ¡VENGA! ¡YO SOY EL UNITED STATES BORDER PATROL! ¡SAL DEL COCHE! ¡SAL DEL COCHE CON LAS MANOS ENCIMA DE LA CABEZA! ¡AL SUELO! ¡AL SUELO! ¡VENGA! ¡CÁLLATE! Yeah. That's how we do it.
   (Rest.)
Nothing.
   (Rest.)
"Sometimes I turn a blind eye." No don't say that. But it's true. A misstep. An indiscretion. Ramirez taking an hour and 5 minutes for lunch. Flowers not filling out the paperwork like he should. Carter getting a little too friendly with some Tonk girl, and I know he's going to get intimate with her when he's pulling the night shift solo. "Hide it under the rug. Let the sleeping dog lie. Letting things slide sometimes is necessary for the greater good. Of course, strictly speaking, letting things slide is just the beginning of the slippery slope. But what can you do. We're like a family, us Patrol guys, out here." Yeah, say that. "Us against them. Gotta do what I can to maintain that. I set the example. I bend and flex up to a point. I make accommodations. I don't overdo it, but I do what I can. Because, hey, we are family, after all."

He continues scanning the horizon.

CHAPTER 51

BUDDY and GRACE still squaring off.

GRACE: *The Book Of Grace,* Chapter 51: The Luxury of Perspective.

GRACE's notepad is visible from where she dropped it earlier. She picks it up, tucking it in her pocket.

She turns on some music. Something upbeat. She dances around.

GRACE: Dance with me.

BUDDY: I don't dance.

GRACE: Your dad doesn't either.

BUDDY: Whatever.

GRACE: I touched a nerve.

BUDDY
BUDDY

GRACE: I touched a nerve. I can tell. When I said "you're back to celebrate your dad!" I touched a nerve.

BUDDY: It's all good.

BUDDY
BUDDY

GRACE: How about some eggs? It's no trouble for me to burn some eggs.

She starts cooking eggs.

GRACE: I wanted to have a party. Happy Homecoming! But when you didn't show yesterday Vet squashed it.

BUDDY: Whatever.

GRACE: The last time you were here. God. You were 10 years old. It was a horrible horrible day. Vet and your mom in here yelling. Yelling like they were trying to yell the house down. Both of them saying awful things. And you and me sat on the porch outside. And your shoelaces dragging.
(Rest.)
You were 10. I was twice that. Twice that plus some.

BUDDY: Yep.

GRACE: *(Rest.)* I'm sorry your mom died. And about your house too.
> *(Rest.)*

You and me on the porch. Me and Vet were newly married. You were 10. I was worried about you. And you didn't want to tie your shoes. You didn't want to tie your shoes and you didn't want me to tie them for you. You just wanted them to drag around in the dirt.

BUDDY: That's right.

GRACE: You want some cake? It's not the first time somebody got cake and eggs. Most people get steak and eggs though. What do you say?
> *(Rest.)*

Buddy?

BUDDY: It's hard being here. He hates me, I hate him.

GRACE: He doesn't hate you. And you don't hate him. Not deep down. Not deep deep deep deep deep deep deep deep down you don't.
> *(Rest.)*

Deep deep

GRACE: Deep deep deep deep   BUDDY: Deep deep deep deep

A moment of levity.

GRACE: When I saw you sleeping there, the first thing that came into my head was Camp David. You know, the place where the leaders of the world go to sort out their problems. I saw you sleeping there and I said to myself, I said, "Grace, Camp David begins at home."
> *(Rest.)*

"That's a stupid-dumb" idea, right? That's what Vet would say to that. You shoulda visited us over the years. We shoulda invited you. Better now than never, though. And whatever he says, he's giving it a go so I gotta hand it to him and here you are so I gotta hand it to you too.

She hands him the eggs. He just holds the plate.

GRACE: You should eat.

BUDDY: I'm not hungry.

BUDDY
GRACE

GRACE: "Camp David begins at home," I said to myself. And then I touched a nerve. But we can let that go, right? Put it behind us. Of course we can. Pretend like it never happened. Start fresh. Right? What do you say?

He steals a kiss. A quick peck on the cheek.

BUDDY: We made a baby just now.

GRACE: You used to say that when you were small.

BUDDY: Maybe it's true.

GRACE: You're silly.

BUDDY: Maybe we just did.

He reaches for her. She moves out of his range.

GRACE: You're really silly.

BUDDY: Sorry.

GRACE: Don't be sorry, just—don't—

BUDDY: I touched a nerve.

GRACE: —Not at all.
 (Rest.)

He starts eating.

GRACE: You know what I think, Mr. Silly? I think you and Vet ought to work together. Both of you, father and son, side by side, working Border Patrol.

BUDDY: It's not like I've got a job lined up anywhere else, so—

GRACE: So you'll stay. And work with Vet. Now we just gotta mention it to him. After he gets his medal he's going to be in a great mood. I say we bring it up then.

BUDDY: I already brought it up.

GRACE: Oh. OK. So, what'd he say?

BUDDY: He said something about showing me around tonight.

GRACE: He's taking you on a tour?

BUDDY: I might not go.

GRACE: You gotta go, Buddy. He took me on a tour. On our first date. You gotta go. He's opening the door for you. And you'll do your part and walk through it. If you two are going to make up you can't expect him to do all the work.

BUDDY: Kiss and make up.

GRACE: You don't got to kiss him, silly. Shake his hand. Look him in the eye. Stand up straight. Shoulders back. Show him that you're — that you're wonderful.

BUDDY: I'm not wonderful.

GRACE: Sure you are.

BUDDY: He wants me to get a haircut.

GRACE: So get a haircut.

BUDDY: We'll see.

GRACE: You two are just alike.

BUDDY: Is that a good thing?

GRACE
BUDDY

GRACE: You'll get the job and before you know it, you'll be walking around in the uniform. And then you'll get your own place. You'll meet a nice girl. You two will have a couple of kids and you'll be living in your own house right down the street.

BUDDY: And you won't send me any more letters.

GRACE: Sure I will.

BUDDY: Not if I'm right down the street.

GRACE: Neighbors send letters all the time. Happy Birthday! Merry Christmas! Get Well Soon! And if you need it, I'll tuck some money inside like I used to.
(Rest.)
I guess that little bit of money I was sending you and your mom didn't amount to squat. We would of sent more but things are tight.

BUDDY: Those stories you sent were better than the money.

GRACE: They were just newspaper clippings.

BUDDY: They were nice.

GRACE: At the diner, when I bus the tables I save the paper. Most people just leave it behind. At first I was trying to be, you know, "green." You know, thinking I'd recycle it. I had a whole big stack of newspapers from saving them. Then I had some—some time on my hands. And I started reading them. Clipping out things.

BUDDY: I liked the story about the dog.

GRACE: I thought you would.

BUDDY: A dog named Trouble. And the Disney World one.

GRACE: Disneyland. I get them mixed up too. I haven't been to either one of them. Disneyland's the one with the original Magic Castle. The second one's like, a copy.

BUDDY: Right. I like how it said when she saw that castle as a kid and it looked so big and then, how she went back when she was all grown up, and how it looked so small. How she could feel the whole passage of time right in that very moment. What'd she call it?

GRACE: The "luxury of perspective."

BUDDY: Right. I used to think this house was huge.

GRACE: Maybe cause of all the land around it. All the land we've got around it. And you were little. When you're little even a small house looks big.

BUDDY: Some things don't get smaller, though. Some things get bigger. Worse.

GRACE: And some things get better. "Look on the bright side for crying out loud it don't cost hardly nothing." That's what I tell Vet. More cake?

BUDDY: No thanks. Mom was sick. She got sicker. Bills for the house got bigger. And I was just—lost. Then I saw him on the TV. Out of the fucking blue. And as mad as I was at him, all I wanted was to get here, and sit with you on the porch. 'Cause as bad as it was, last time I was here, somehow you made it OK. You made it—nice.

GRACE: Thanks.

BUDDY: Too hot to sit outside now.

GRACE: Yeah.

BUDDY: You were sitting near me when I was sleeping. Doing what?
Watching me?

GRACE: Just sitting.

BUDDY: You were writing.

GRACE: Grocery list.

BUDDY: Right.
   (Rest.)
   "We the people … in order to form a more perfect union, establish
   justice, ensure domestic tranquility, provide for the common defense,
   promote the general welfare and secure the blessings of liberty to
   ourselves and our posterity do ordain and establish this Constitution."
   (Rest.)
   I got it all memorized, pretty much.

GRACE: Let's hear the rest.

BUDDY: Point is, we're establishing our Constitution. We're going to be
friends, right?

GRACE: Better than friends. We're family. By law anyway.

BUDDY: So tell me something about you. A secret. I feel like you know a
lot about me and I don't know anything about you. Go on. I won't tell.

GRACE: You first. Go.

BUDDY: I used to be scared of Vet. When I was a kid. Maybe I still am. Secret.

GRACE: I took a class once. I kept it secret from Vet. Algebra.

BUDDY: Algebra. Whoa. Algebra! So you can solve for X and stuff?

GRACE: Yes.

BUDDY: You pass?

GRACE: A couple of As on a couple of tests. Then Vet found out. He didn't
like me going.
   (Rest.)
   The teacher, he really liked me. Not in that way, but still, I had to quit.

> *(Rest.)*

Secret.

BUDDY: I don't have anymore.

GRACE: Yeah you do. Go.

BUDDY: You go.

GRACE: You go. Secret.

BUDDY: That hole in the yard. He dug it for you, right?

GRACE: He says it's a "deterrent."

BUDDY: He dug one for my mom.

GRACE: But he never used it.

BUDDY: No, he never used it. It just sat there. Where she could see it. Every day.

> *(Rest.)*

He used to hit my mom. He hit you?

GRACE
BUDDY

BUDDY: Yes, right?

GRACE
GRACE

> *BUDDY holds up two fingers. It's Strike Two.*

GRACE: Peace?

BUDDY: We'll see. Maybe. "Peace out." Maybe.

GRACE: Here's one you'll never guess. I'm writing a book.

BUDDY: That's what you were doing.

GRACE: Collecting my thoughts, yeah.

BUDDY: And then writing them down.

GRACE: And then rounding them up.

BUDDY: Show me.

She goes to the rug, pushing it aside. She removes a few pieces of loose flooring, pulling out several scribbled-on waitress pads, a few stray newspaper articles and, then, her red-marbled composition book, her Book of Grace.

BUDDY: What's it called?

GRACE: *The Book of Grace.*

BUDDY: Named her after yourself. What's it about?

GRACE: Kind of like—I dunno—the evidence of good things.

BUDDY: The evidence of good things.

GRACE: Yeah.
> (*Rest.*)
When I see a newspaper story that's nice, I cut it out and paste it in. The clippings I sent to you I copied down in here so we could both have them. I got a picture of the president in here somewhere. But it's not just clippings, sometimes, at the diner, someone'll tell me a story and I'll write it down, or sometimes I see something interesting and write it down. Some stuff I just make up. My thoughts. About—about things. I started it after I had to quit that math class. It's kind of like a self-help book.

BUDDY: I bet it'll be a bestseller.

GRACE: I dunno about all that, but, sometimes I pretend it's published. Dumb, right?

BUDDY: No

GRACE: Sometimes, you know, when those writers read, like at the library? Sometimes, when I read it out loud to myself, I set up chairs in here and pretend.
> (*Rest.*)
Stupid, right?

BUDDY: No.

> *Playfully, BUDDY snatches her Book, leafing through it.*

GRACE: Hey—

BUDDY: It's beautiful. You can draw too.

GRACE: Yeah. Gimmie.

BUDDY, reading from her Book:

BUDDY: "I like snakes. All kinds. Something deep within my nature, I guess … Most people don't like snakes, and so, I guess, me liking snakes sets me apart from most people."

GRACE: Give it back.

Instead of handing it over, he holds the Book close to his chest.

BUDDY: "The evidence of good things." How's it end?

GRACE: I'm not there yet.
    (Rest.)
"Stupid-dumb!" That's what Vet would say if he knew I was writing a book.
    (Rest.)
Gimmie.

But he continues to hold the Book close.

BUDDY
BUDDY
BUDDY
SNAKE
SNAKE
BUDDY

SNAKE
SNAKE
    (Rest.)

SNAKE: I just changed my name. Just right now. To Snake.

GRACE: Snake.

SNAKE: Yeah. It suits me better than "Buddy." It's cool, right?

GRACE: It might be.

SNAKE: You like snakes. And it suits me. "Evidence of good things!" You'll see.

GRACE: Footnote #3:

We see VET on the job. He pauses from his patrol work.

VET: My nickname used to be "Snake." Back in the day. But I'm on the good foot now.

SNAKE: Pop, he used to go by Snake.

GRACE: Yeah, I know.

SNAKE: You think I'm following in his footsteps?

GRACE: For you to know and for me to find out. Good thing I like snakes.

SNAKE: Yeah. It's a good thing. Secret.

GRACE: Your dad's really glad you're here.

SNAKE: That's a secret even from him.

GRACE: He's glad. You'll see.
>   *(Rest.)*
>   Secret.

SNAKE: What if I'm on the bad foot?

GRACE: What if that's just your mad-self talking?

SNAKE: If I was bad, could you turn me into something good?

GRACE: Footnote #4:

>   *Again, VET pauses from work.*

VET: And did I ever tell you about the time he put a firecracker in my car? That thing went bang and I just about wet myself. I'm laughing but it wasn't funny. That kid is bad news. Bad through and through.

GRACE: When you were little, sitting on the porch, you kept saying "I'm a bad boy. I'm a bad boy." I can see why you'd think that. But you were never really bad.

SNAKE: What if I was? What if I am?

GRACE: You're still that ten-year-old kid with his untied shoes trying to impress me.

SNAKE: And you're still good gracious Grace trying to make everything turn out all right.

GRACE
SNAKE

SNAKE: I'll go get that haircut.

Using his phone, he takes their selfie.

GRACE: And you'll let Vet show you around?

SNAKE: Looking on the bright side don't cost nothing.

GRACE: There you go.

He starts to leave.

GRACE: Snake. My Book.

SNAKE hands her back her Book. He goes on his way, leaving GRACE to her work.

CHAPTER 52

GRACE works, copying her notes into her red Book.

GRACE: Chapter 52: *The Book Of Grace.*

> *Day turns into evening. Evening turns into night.*
> *She takes a break from working, setting up chairs and reading from*
> *her Book to her imaginary audience.*

GRACE: Good evening. I'm going to read a little bit from *The Book of Grace.*
It's a work-in-progress. Today, just for fun, I'm gonna start from my
latest entry and then I'll read backwards all the way to the beginning.
And we'll see what that's like. OK. Here's something from today:
> *(Rest.)*

A friend of mine came home today. Not "home" but to his father's
house. Which, in this case, isn't the same thing. He also took his father's
name today. Snake. Funny how you can take someone's name. Junior
when you're born. I took, when I got married, I took my husband's
name: Smith. My husband's nickname used to be Snake. That would
make him Snake Smith. He's on the good foot now. And his son, now
Snake Smith Junior, he's following in his father's footsteps. So he must
be heading towards being on the good foot too. Except that snakes
don't have feet. Well.
> *(Rest.)*

My husband's son, he's all grown up. But he's still just as silly as he can be.
> *(Rest.)*

He changed his name because of something he read in my book. Maybe
this book is worth something after all.

> *She looks through her previously written pages, looking for something*
> *in particular. Finding it.*

GRACE: Evidence of Good Things: The Magic Castle. Here it is.

> *She shows us, then finds another interesting page.*

GRACE: More evidence of good: from Chapter 44: It snowed today. In the
middle of summer. It was like a miracle.
> *(Rest.)*

OK. From Chapter 43: More Evidence of Good: That baby who was
stolen from the hospital got reunited with her loving parents 23 years

later. There's a pig in China born without any back legs and the farmer didn't slaughter it, instead he keeps it as a pet and it hops around on its front legs and gets along just fine. And that lady, she got shot in the head. But she didn't die.*

(Rest.)

From Chapter 40: More Evidence of Good:

(Rest.)

Will, the cowboy, came in the diner today wanting grits and we were out of grits and he was about to pitch a fit and then he started laughing instead and we all laughed and he had white toast instead of grits.

(Rest.)

From Chapter 39: Today I got word from Buddy. He says he's coming to his father's Ceremony. How about that? Today I'm feeling like everything broken can mend. Today I'm feeling like a Gold Star.

(Rest.)

From Chapter 37: Charlotte's daughter Charlotte plays the tuba. She's in the marching band. The tuba is bigger than she is. She came in today and played her part of "Deep in the Heart of Texas." It didn't sound like much cause it was just the tuba part: bom-bom-bom-bom. But I clapped really hard when she was done cause it's important to encourage people. Especially when they're young. So they can get in the habit of hearing it.

(Rest.)

From Chapter 30: Today I was looking in the icebox for frozen broccoli and instead I found some old Halloween candy! How about that?

(Rest.)

From Chapter 23: Today I put my foot down and insisted that we invite Buddy to our house because he hasn't been here for many years.

(Rest.)

I wonder if forgiveness is possible? I think so. I hope so.

(Rest.)

What if we outsource forgiveness. Heck, we're outsourcing everything else. Then your forgiveness would come with a sticker that says "made in India" or "made in China" or "made in Farawayville."

(Rest.)

That makes me think of plastic bags. They say there's a big stretch of trash in the middle of the ocean. Like a land mass, but it's really just a

---

* Use these 3 stories or the production may insert their own 3 pieces of Evidence.

gob of trash. It's practically the size of Texas, that's how big they say it is. I use plastic bags. Do you? But it's not like I throw my bags into the ocean.

She hears the sound of a car. She scrambles to hide her Book. Then the sound turns to silence and the coast is clear. She goes back to reading.

GRACE: From Chapter 19:
> *(Rest.)*

Today I am thinking about the Rut. It's like, sometimes your life is a Rut, a Rut you've dug yourself. Sometimes your life-groove can become a Rut. Sometimes someone you're with, say your husband, or your wife, or your town, or your job, sometimes your repeated day-to-day can make a Rut or sometimes your S.O., aka, your Significant Other, sometimes they dig a Rut for you to live in and you don't notice cause the Rut looks like a groove, a thing with promise, but it's not a groove at all, it's a Rut. And by walking the Rut, by living in it, you only make it deeper.
> *(Rest.)*

Where do I begin? Where does "me" start? What is the past tense of "Us"? "Used." The past tense of "Us" is "Used." As in my "used-to-be."
> *(Rest.)*

That sounds stupid. Needs work. Stupid-dumb. S-h-i-t.
> *(Rest.)*

Sometimes I spell out bad words. 'Cause I read somewhere that we each have, inside of us, an "inner child." And I don't want mine hearing me say bad language. It's silly, but I think it improves me. Are there things you'd like to try that might improve you?
> *(Rest.)*

More Evidence of Good: Javier, our busboy is learning Japanese. When I ask him how come Japanese he just smiles.
> *(Rest.)*

From Chapter 10: My friend, Cowboy Will, he's got this story about a dog. A dog he had years ago. When he was a much younger man. That dog was pure trouble. And that was its name too: Trouble. How was that dog ever gonna do anything good with a name like that? One day Will gets so tired of the dog he puts him in his truck and drives 100 miles away and dumps him on the side of the road. End of story? No. Will says there's an end to it, but he won't tell me. He will not for the life of him tell me how that story ends. So I've made up some endings for myself:
> *(Rest.)*

I say there's a flash flood and a drowning man, and Trouble jumps in the river and saves the man and the man renames him Savior.

(Rest.)

Or I say Trouble's just walking along and some kids are going to the circus and he follows them and joins the circus and travels the world.

(Rest.)

Maybe you could make up your own ending to that story.
Try it. It's fun.

(Rest.)

(Rest.)

This is Trouble.

She shows a picture of the dog.

GRACE: From Chapter 6: More Basic Guidelines: Know your cowboys. For example: it has occurred to me that there are two kinds of cowboys: a cowboy with a horse and a cowboy without a horse. A cowboy with a horse is a real cowboy. A cowboy without a horse is just a guy that wears the clothes. Which one are you?

(Rest.)

Everything reminds you of something, after a while. Like when you move to a new town and nothing is familiar and then, after a few years, you look around and hear yourself saying to yourself: Here is where I met him, over there is the last time I saw her, that's the place where I stood with the chocolate double-dip cone and felt happy, there is where the bad thing happened, and there's the lake where we all jumped in.

(Rest.)

More Basic Guidelines: You can either spread the love or spread the shit. Your choice.

(Rest.)

From Chapter 3: Today, walking home from work, I saw a snake. And that got me to thinking. I like snakes. All kinds. Something deep within my nature, I guess … Me liking snakes sets me apart from most people. What do you like that sets you apart?

(Rest.)

From Chapter 2: On Hope: It's good to hope. Hopes can be large or small. One of my hopes involves a piece of clothing, specifically, a dress. It's very pretty. It's red. It's been hanging in the window of our local department store for a long time now. You could say I've put my name on it, even though I don't dare buy it. Still, it's mine.

(Rest.)

From Chapter 1:

(Rest.)

I like algebra and some day I would like to live in The House of Wisdom.

(Rest.)

Did you know that "The ancient science of algebra was invented by the revered Persian, Muhammad ibn Musa al-Khwarizmi. He wrote a book called *Algebra*. He was perhaps an orthodox Muslim. He was born around 780 and, in addition to being considered the father of algebra, he was also an accomplished astronomer, astrologer and geographer. He lived for many years in Baghdad, living and working in a place called The House of Wisdom."

(Rest.)

Here's more from Chapter 1, my first entry:

Today Vet got mad at me and he dug a hole in the yard. And he told me I had to quit my math class so I quit it. And when he went to work, I started this book. I'm calling it *The Book of Grace*.

(Rest.)

(Rest.)

That's all. Thank you.

> *Smiling to herself, she might take a little bow to her imaginary audience. Then she turns on the radio, resets the living room chairs and puts away her Book as the lights fade.*

INTERMISSION

CHAPTER 53

Much later. In the wee hours.

GRACE: *The Book of Grace*, Chapter 53: It's Bigger Than I Thought.

> *GRACE retires to the bedroom.*
> *The guys come home.*
> *SNAKE, with his fresh haircut, watching new video-playback on his phone.*
> *VET following behind.*

VET: You're quiet.

SNAKE: I'm thinking about it.

VET: Thumbs up or thumbs down. Does my speech work? Say something.

SNAKE: Gimmie a minute.

VET: I showed you the Fence. I extended you a privilege. I'm not some goddamn tour guide, but there I was, acting like some goddamn tour guide, telling you the history of it.

SNAKE: I'm taking it all in.

VET: You were taking pictures.

SNAKE: Video. Like you got. I liked it.

VET: You liked it?

SNAKE: The Fence. Yeah.

VET: Anything else?

SNAKE: It's bigger than I thought.

VET: Anything else?

SNAKE: You've got the one in China beat.

VET: We beat China? How so.

SNAKE: Yours is active.

VET: Damn right.

SNAKE: You beat Berlin 'cause yours is still standing. And you got the one in the Middle East beat 'cause yours is longer.

VET: Pretty much.

SNAKE: See, I'm thinking about the Fence.

VET: You—you thinking about anything else?

SNAKE: The Fence, it's kind of filling up my whole mind, you know?

VET: It grows on you.

SNAKE: Maybe I could work there.

VET: Let's wait on that.

SNAKE: Hurry up and wait.

VET: Don't get ahead of yourself, that's all.

SNAKE: But, it could happen. The guys seemed to like me. I fit socially. That's no small thing. Not everybody does, right?

VET: Right.

SNAKE fiddles with his phone, looking at his footage.

SNAKE: Mind if I share this footage with my friends?

VET: You've got friends?

SNAKE: I'm part of an online community.

VET: You didn't video anything that's classified, so go ahead. Sure.

SNAKE: Gr8.

VET: Goddamnit to hell, aren't you going to say anything about my speech?!

SNAKE: Like what?

VET: Like anything.

SNAKE: It's real interesting.

VET: "Real interesting"? You're smug cause you took some college classes.

SNAKE: I'm not smug.

VET: You've got the Constitution and the Declaration all memorized and you stood there spouting it off for the guys and what did I do? Did I tell you to shut up?

SNAKE: You let me talk.

VET: Damn right I let you talk. On and on and on. And I even led in the goddamned applause.

SNAKE: Ramirez clapped first.

VET: But I joined in, didn't I? And I whistled hooray. I even complimented your haircut. You're a show-off. You're a goddamned show-off!

SNAKE: I'm out of here.

SNAKE gets his footlocker. Starts to go.

VET: You're staying. What's it going to look like with you showing up and then leaving? They'd have a good time with that, I'm telling you. You're staying. You're staying.

GRACE comes out of the bedroom, wearing her bathrobe and slip.

GRACE: How'd it go?

VET: Complete waste of time.

SNAKE: I liked the Fence.

VET: I need some sleep.

SNAKE: And I liked your speech too, OK?

VET: You liked my speech?

GRACE: You did your speech for him?

VET: In the truck. On the way home.

GRACE: You haven't done it for me. Say it again.

VET: It's still pretty rough.

SNAKE: I liked it.
     (Rest.)
   I got some pointers, though. If you're interested.
GRACE
VET

SNAKE
GRACE

GRACE: I'll go back to bed.

> *She gives VET a kiss and goes back into the bedroom.*

SNAKE: You should say it out loud for Grace. See what she thinks.

VET: Thinks? Jesus. She thinks I should open up. She wants me to go bleeding all over them.

SNAKE: I'm thinking a 180 on that.

VET: Me too.

SNAKE: You need to give them something they can fix their minds to. Everything in your speech should be substantial. Like the meat and potatoes that they'll be chewing on, something that they'll be talking about long after you're done talking. Not rambling. Not vague. Not poetic. Not personal. Not revealing. Something solid and commanding.

VET: Something that'll stick in their minds long after I'm done running my mouth.

SNAKE: Exactly. So that, when they look at you from here on out, they'll be thinking of the words you said to them. You'll be just doing your day-to-day and they'll be running your words in their heads. And they'll stand a little straighter in your presence. Your words'll be like the Fence itself.

VET: Right.

SNAKE: And don't start off with "Aliens."

VET: It was just an idea.

SNAKE: Don't have "Aliens" anywhere in it.

VET: Right.

SNAKE: Makes you sound like a—a nut job.
> *(Rest.)*
> Run it one more time and let's see.

VET: Not right now. I need to keep my own counsel with it. Maybe later.

SNAKE: You'll be up there talking before you know it.

VET: Maybe later I said.

SNAKE: Suit yourself.

VET: You think you're Border Patrol material?

SNAKE: Sure.

VET: But it's not about what you think, is it?

SNAKE: I guess not.

VET: Let's see what you've got.

> *VET drops to the floor and starts doing push-ups. When SNAKE joins him, VET stands and talks.*

VET: Three Tonks armed to the teeth. You've been tracking them for days. Suddenly you find them. What do you do?

GRACE: Footnote #5:

> *GRACE, from the bedroom, eavesdropping, answering for herself.*

VET: What would you do?

GRACE: ((I would call for back up.))

SNAKE: Call for back up, right?

VET: Back up is a long time coming.

> *Now, jumping jacks.*

SNAKE: I would go in with guns blazing. Figuring my firepower will beat theirs.

VET: Or theirs would beat yours.

SNAKE: So I'd—die in the line of duty. Defending our Border. That'd be good, right? Right?

VET: That's "brave."

SNAKE: Brave is good, right?

> *Now, running in place.*

VET: You're on Patrol and you catch up with another one. This time, this one's really nice. Sneaked in all alone. Speaks good English. A sort of poetic soul. Read the stars to find his way north. All he wants is a better life for himself. He'll get an honest job and send his earnings back home. He's a good guy. But a Tonk. He's got a bag of money for you if you'd look the other way. What do you do?

GRACE: Footnote #6: ((I would take the money and let him slip in.))

SNAKE: I wouldn't take the money.

VET: Pesos or greenbacks?

> *Now, full up-down squats.*

GRACE: ((Pesos or greenbacks?))

SNAKE: Money is money is money. What difference does it make?

VET: Does he have pesos or greenbacks? Ask.

GRACE: ((Does he have pesos or greenbacks?))

SNAKE: Does he have pesos or greenbacks? Cause greenbacks'd be worth more.

VET: Bingo. Let's say he's got a big bag of greenbacks.

SNAKE: So I would want to take the money, but I don't take the money. Right?

GRACE: ((Right.))

> *VET switches to sit-ups. SNAKE follows suit. This time VET keeps talking as he drills.*

VET: Say he tries to strike a bargain. The greenbacks in exchange for him to be allowed to just sneak back home.

SNAKE: No way, José. I'd turn him in.

VET: And all those greenbacks he had would probably "disappear."

SNAKE: Sometimes that happens.

> *VET finishes his sit-ups.*
> *SNAKE continues with his.*

VET: Oh, does it?

SNAKE: Yeah. But it wouldn't happen with me. Not on my watch!

GRACE: ((Gold Star, Buddy.))

> *The pop quiz has concluded. GRACE goes back to bed.*

SNAKE: *(Rest.)* How am I doing? Did I pass?

VET walks to the refrigerator. SNAKE finishes his sit-ups and stands.

SNAKE: Did I pass?

VET, holding a beer, walks over to the rug. Pretending it's just an accident, he toes back the rug. SNAKE replaces the rug. VET notices that.

SNAKE: Did I pass, yes or no?

VET: I'll let you know, Buddy.

SNAKE: Snake.

VET: Right. Snake. Have a seat.

VET sits on the couch. SNAKE tentatively joins him.

VET: Unwind. We're just home from work. We've got a big day tomorrow. Now we unwind.

SNAKE: Right.

VET's relaxed. Drinking. SNAKE is tense.

VET: You nervous?

SNAKE: Not at all.

VET: I like to unwind with entertainment.

SNAKE: Watching the Fence?

VET: Better.

SNAKE: Like what.

VET goes to his footlocker.

VET: I got hot stuff in here.

VET unlocks his locker, showing piles of videotapes.

VET: Your pick.

SNAKE: What's on them?

VET: Girls.

SNAKE: Girls?

VET: Girls. Your pick.

SNAKE: The cases all look the same, no pictures or nothing. No names.

VET: More exciting that way. Like a game of chance. Pick.

> *SNAKE chooses a tape. VET puts it in the player, retakes his seat.*

SNAKE: You should upgrade your technology.

VET: The picture's fine. Pretty girls, right?

SNAKE: Yeah.

> *The girlie-porn video plays on the TV and the light plays on their faces. The sound is barely audible.*
>
> *Parts of the video are reflected on a window or a wall.*

VET: I like to just kinda sit here and let them do their thing. Kinda like background music. Kinda like ambiance. It unwinds my mind.

SNAKE: Right.

> *The two men sit there watching porn. They look like they're watching paint dry.*

VET: The Ceremony's going to be something. I'll stand at the Fence and give my speech. Standing there getting my medal. Icing on the gravy.
> *(Rest.)*
You telling them how you're "Snake" and how I used to be "Snake."
That went over all right.

SNAKE: Yeah, it did. They looked at you with respect.

VET: Yeah. They did.
> *(Rest.)*
Your mother didn't want to have anything to do with you. Came here trying to dump you on me. But I couldn't take you in. You were— troubled. And I was starting fresh. It wouldn't of been fair to Grace. You were like a whole can of worms and I was making a fresh start.

SNAKE: Is that an apology?

VET: No. I'm just telling you what was going on.
> *(Rest.)*
Maybe I could get you some help. Somebody to go talk to, you know, once a week like they do.

SNAKE: No thanks.
>   (Rest.)
>   Let's hear it again. Your speech.

VET: I'm working it out in my head. When I stand up there saying it, you'll hear it fresh.

SNAKE: Have you written it out?

VET: I've composed it. But I wouldn't write it down.

SNAKE: You should totally write a book. Veteran of the Border Patrol. That would really put you out in front.

VET: Only I don't think much of books. Books cause a weakening of the mind. You write something down you don't use your brain muscles to remember it. Take, for example, your Cro-Magnon man. Or your Neanderthal. Or your Australopithecus. He may have had a smaller brain than we do today, but he used it to the fullest. He had to remember where the game was and how to get home after he'd bagged it. And he didn't have a GPS. He didn't have advanced technology. Plus, when things are in your head, they're safe. Less chance of theft.

>   *He looks at SNAKE's footlocker.*

VET: For the job, there'll be a thorough background check. They'll look through all your personals.

>   *He examines his ring of keys, selecting one. Trying it. No luck. He tries another. He unlocks SNAKE's footlocker and is about to raise the lid before SNAKE stops him.*

SNAKE: You already searched it once. What are you scared of?

VET
SNAKE
>   (Rest.)

>   *VET backs off.*

VET: I'll be up there with the governor. I'll be getting my medal.

SNAKE: And I'll be wearing mine.

VET: You'll wear yours.

SNAKE: Sure.

VET: You should just wear the bar pin. You don't want to be too loud with it.

SNAKE: I lost that part so I'll have to wear the whole medal. Right on my lapel. It's not regulation but it'll be all right.

VET: You'll want everybody to see it.

SNAKE: Sure. Why not.

VET: You'll want to show it off.

SNAKE: I earned it. It's mine.

VET: You wanna steal my thunder.

SNAKE: Oh, come on, Pop.

VET: Too bad you can't get on the job in time for the governor's visit, right? Is that what you're thinking?

SNAKE: I'm OK to meet him as just a civilian.

VET: And flash your medal.

SNAKE: Sure. Plus, being your son.

VET: Following in my footsteps.

SNAKE: That's right.

VET: Legacy.

SNAKE: Yeah. That'll be something, right? Us both working Border Patrol. Side by side. I got the job, don't I? It's a go, right?

VET: It's a no. It wouldn't work. You wouldn't work. Not around me.

SNAKE: You gotta give me a hand. I'm good enough, right? I'm good enough. It's normal to give your kid a hand, Pop.

VET: You'll find your feet. Just not here. Somewhere else.

SNAKE: Come on, Pop.

VET: You'll find your feet. Just not with me, just not in my footsteps. It'll be better that way. For both of us.

SNAKE

VET

SNAKE

It's Strike Three. SNAKE flashes three fingers. Gently, defeated.

SNAKE: Three.

VET: Three what?

SNAKE: The three of us here. You, me and Grace. That's three.

VET: You understand about the job, right? There's plenty of jobs in the universe. You'll find one somewhere out there just not here, OK?

SNAKE: Sure. OK.

> *VET glances at the clock. Drinks. SNAKE watches the TV. Time passes.*
> *VET eventually falls asleep on the couch. SNAKE gets up, puts away the*
> *porn video, turns on the live feed and, alone, watches the Fence. After a*
> *beat, he fiddles with his phone. GRACE comes out of the bedroom. Men*
> *on couch. VET sleeping. SNAKE texting. Fence video going.*

GRACE: Hey.

SNAKE: Hey.

> *She lovingly helps VET up, helping him to bed.*
>
> *Then, coming out of the bedroom, she gets her Book from its hiding*
> *place under the floor.*

GRACE: Talking with your friends?

SNAKE: Texting.

GRACE: In a chatroom?

SNAKE: Yeah.

GRACE: Nice haircut.

SNAKE: Thanks.

> *She goes outside, sits on the porch, reading from her Book.*
> *SNAKE comes outside to watch her.*

SNAKE: It's not working out.

GRACE: I heard. When things are bad I read this and it helps me feel better.

SNAKE: It's not getting any better with him.

GRACE: Not right now, but it will. Plenty of bad things turn good in the fullness of time.

SNAKE: Sometimes bad things go from bad to worse.

GRACE: Not always.
>   *(Rest.)*
> It's bigger than I thought, the stuff between you two, right?

SNAKE: Yeah.
>   *(Rest.)*
> The things he did to me. When we were all living together. Me and him and Mom.

GRACE: Like what?

>   *VET, in the bedroom, sits on the bed. Awake but not listening.*

SNAKE: Unspeakable. Saying it was my fault, saying I was the bad one. And that he was just trying to keep me in line. That's what he had to do, you know? Keep the bad one in line.
>   *(Rest.)*
> I just went from bad to worse.

GRACE: But you were never bad.

SNAKE: I'm going to blow something up.
>   *(Rest.)*
> I'm going to blow something up. You heard me.

GRACE: That's just your mad-self talking.
>   *(Rest.)*
> Buddy?

SNAKE: Snake.
>   *(Rest.)*
> Can I read it?

GRACE: OK.

>   *Snake takes her Book, choosing pages at random, reading to himself. Then aloud.*

SNAKE: Disneyland.
>   *(Rest.)*
> The dog named Trouble.

(Rest.)
The House of Wisdom.

GRACE: No one's ever read it but you.
(Rest.)
What?

SNAKE: Nothing.

More pages read silently to himself. Then aloud.

SNAKE: "Red dress."

GRACE: Yeah. What?

SNAKE: Nothing.
(Rest.)
He closes the Book. Hands it back to her.

GRACE: Did it help?

SNAKE: Nope.

GRACE: You can read more—

SNAKE: No thanks.

GRACE: Maybe it takes time. To sink in. Here I am, little Miss-Wanna-Fix-It-All. Well, more like Mrs-Wanna-Fix-It-All now.

SNAKE: Leave me alone, all right?

GRACE: All right. Sure.

She scoots a distance away from him, then gets up, about to go.

SNAKE: You ever thought of leaving him?

GRACE: Yeah. But your troubles follow you.

SNAKE: Not if you do something about it.

GRACE: Maybe I should change my name.

SNAKE: Don't. Grace suits you.

GRACE
SNAKE
(Rest.)
With Book in hand she goes inside, putting it away, then heading to bed.

SNAKE on the porch alone.
He takes out his phone. Starts making a selfie-video.

SNAKE: *The Book of Snake*, Chapter One: "We hold these truths to be self-evident, that all men—" No—
  (Rest.)
The Book of Snake, Chapter One.*(Rest.)*
"When in the course of human events it becomes necessary for people—"
(Rest.)
For a people to what? *(Rest.)*
Hhhhhhh.

  He quits his selfie. Just sitting on the porch as the wee hours change to dawn. Then he exits.

CHAPTER 54

GRACE: Chapter 54: *The Book Of Snake.*

> *Morning. VET, ready for work, prepares his dress uniform for later.*
> *GRACE, ready for work, comes from the kitchen with coffee.*

GRACE: I made coffee.

VET: Where's the kid?

GRACE: Gone for a walk, I guess.
> *(Rest.)*
That gives us some time—

> *She hugs him romantically. He pulls away.*

VET: Don't. I've gotta go down there, make sure things are set up, and then come back here and get dressed. I can't be late today, huh? Hurry up if you want a ride in.

> *VET exits.*

GRACE: I'll leave the door open for him.

VET: Don't worry about him. Come on.

> *GRACE exits. Hours pass.*

> *Around noon, SNAKE enters, whistling a tune. He carries a nice*
> *shopping bag from his recent expedition.*
> *After making sure the coast is clear, he deposits the bag's contents in the*
> *bedroom. He returns to the living room.*
> *Taking his phone out of his pocket, he records himself as he speaks.*

SNAKE: *The Book of Snake,* Chapter One.

> *He stops recording. Deletes. Starts over.*

SNAKE: *The Book of Snake,* Chapter One.
> *(Rest.)*
The Book of Snake, as told to you by Snake himself, coming to you recorded from—from the grounds of my training compound. And to be broadcast throughout the world in the fullness of time. OK.
> *(Rest.)*
Three Strikes. He's got Three Strikes against him. Three Strikes and now

he's out.

(Rest.)

You're probably at a similar place in your life. That's why you're watching this. You're probably watching this and wondering what to do. Like me you've done good, or if not all good, then you've done as good as you could. As good as you could within the confines of his rules. Living, if you want to call it that, bowing, stooping, scraping, crawling, working, just to get by, just to make ends meet. Punching his clock. On his time. We gave him a chance, didn't we? We've been trying to work within his rules, haven't we? More or less, right? More or less.

(Rest.)

Trying to work within some rules made by a man. Made by, made by "The Man." His clock. His rules. His order of things. His system. And guess what: his system don't work for us.

(Rest.)

Evidence of good: None. Evidence of bad: Strike One. Strike One is a crime in his past. A crime that he will not even admit to. An unspeakable series of crimes made against our person. We have given him every opportunity to admit his crimes, but he has chosen to ignore said opportunities. And so he has earned Strike One.

(Rest.)

Evidence of bad: Strike Two. Strike Two happened in the past and continues happening in the present. Strike Two involves both the past and current female members of the family unit which he beat down in the past and now, even with this fairly new member, continues the beating down and doesn't see anything wrong with it. So Strike Two.

(Rest.)

The Man, he likes to promise you something better. I'm telling you you're a fool for wanting his better. Take his better like a trained dog, take his hand, take his handshake, live your life in the palm of his hand, and for what? So that when he makes a fist he can just crush you?

(Rest.)

His systems and his rules and his laws, they aren't for you. They're for him. And the day has come for us to start wiping them out.

(Rest.)

More evidence of bad things: Strike Three. He's not content to beat down your past, he's not content with beating down your present, that's right, he wants to beat down your future too, doesn't he? The Man was promising us something better, right? He was promising us some golden castle where we could, where we could eat ice cream every day, or whatever. You know what I'm talking about. You've heard his promises. All about what he's going to do for you. But he never does anything. He's got a carrot on a stick and he's just holding it out there in front of your face, just holding it out there, just holding it out there, he's a big man, promising you stuff, but one day you get it: he's not holding it out there for you, he's just holding out. And he's always going to be holding out on you. He doesn't got anything for you. He doesn't want you to succeed. He wants you to fail. And fail big. He wants to spin your good into bad. He wants to leave you with nothing, all broken and sad. He wants you to follow in his footsteps so he can feel big, but in the end, I'm telling you, he wants you jobless, homeless and hopeless; rejected, neglected and disrespected. You know what I'm talking about. So Strike Three.

He opens his footlocker, taking out a hand grenade.

SNAKE: Maybe you, like me, Served. Maybe you like me had a mother and a house. Maybe you lost it all. And when you cried out to The Man he turned a blind eye and a deaf ear. Blind and deaf to you. Not wanting to have shit to do with you. Figuring we'll just dry up and blow away. Come again another day. Go away and come back tomorrow. Well tomorrow is now. And we are not going to blow away. Instead, we are going to blow him away.

He hears GRACE coming home. Quickly locking up his trunk, he takes his phone and grenade, heading through the backdoor and into the backyard. GRACE, on the porch, looking through her most recent notes. Choosing what she'd like to add to her Book.

SNAKE: The Man likes keeping Us down. The Man has dug a hole for you, a hole in your yard with your name on it, and it's up to you to do something about that. Take some kind of action. He had his chances but he struck out. Strike One, Strike Two, Strike Three. 3-2-1-Boom.

Entering the house, GRACE checks to see that the coast is clear. She takes out her Book and transfers notes from her waitress pad. In the backyard, SNAKE is holding his grenade up to his phone. He continues recording.

SNAKE: Now we will strike. And when we strike against The Man, striking him at his Ceremony, we will be careful, we will be smart. And after we've struck him, and after we've wiped him out, we will escape. We will move on. To the next target. He's just the first of many. He's got it coming to him. He's got it coming. The push-back starts here. We gotta rise up. And I'm gonna lead the way. Snake. Snake. Snake will rise up and lead "We the people." Do not tread on me. 'Cause I will take you down.

    (Rest.)

    (Rest.)

The Book of Snake will continue. More later. Stay tuned.

CHAPTER X

From inside the house GRACE sees SNAKE in the distant backyard.
Waves to him.
He waves back.
She works on her Book.

GRACE: *The Book of Grace*, Chapter X: The House of Wisdom.

> *SNAKE comes in carrying his phone and his hidden grenade. He goes to*
> *his footlocker, replacing the grenade without GRACE noticing.*

GRACE: Vet's over there making sure everything's set up right. He'll be
home soon, then we'll have to go, OK?

SNAKE: You're going?

GRACE: Sure I'm going.

SNAKE: What if you don't?

GRACE: I'm looking forward to it. It'll be fun.

SNAKE: But what if you don't go.

GRACE: If I don't go I'll never hear the end of it. And if you don't go I'll
never hear the end of it. So we're going. I'll bet money that, once he
gets his medal, he'll change up about you working with him. You'll see.

SNAKE: I don't want to work with him.

GRACE: It's a good job.

SNAKE: I don't want a good job.

GRACE: Sure you do.
  (Rest.)
We should start getting ready. If you need to use the shower you should
get in there now.

> *Instead of heading to the shower, SNAKE goes to the radio, turning it*
> *on loud, enjoying the music.*

SNAKE: Dance with me.

GRACE: I gotta finish this.

SNAKE: Lots of "evidence of good things" today?

GRACE: People from out of town visiting for the Ceremony, they were packing the diner. They had some good stories.

SNAKE: We never had my party. Come dance.

GRACE: You're happy.

SNAKE: Yep.

GRACE: What about?

SNAKE: Secret.

> *He goes to the fridge. Takes out two beers. Opens both, handing one to GRACE, drinking his down as she watches.*

GRACE: Tell me.

SNAKE: Not yet.
> (Rest.)
Cheers.

> *He drinks. She doesn't. He gets another beer, opens it. Drinks.*

GRACE: Music's a little loud.

SNAKE: Sorry.

> *He turns the radio down some. Keeps dancing. Shoots a selfie-video, including GRACE in the shot.*

GRACE: You're making a movie.

SNAKE: It's a book.

GRACE: OK. Outside you were talking it out. I saw you. That's great. Good for you.

SNAKE: Cheers.

> *They toast and drink.*

GRACE: What's your book about?

SNAKE: Secret.
> (Rest.)
I got something for you.

GRACE: Tell me about your book.

SNAKE: It's hanging in your closet. Go look.
> *(Rest.)*

It's a present. Go on.

> *GRACE goes into the bedroom. SNAKE, still enjoying the music, takes a glance at her new writing.*
> *A scream—of joy. GRACE comes back into the room, holding a pretty red dress.*

GRACE: You got it for me.

SNAKE: I was the first one in the store this morning.

GRACE: Coming home from work I didn't see it in the window and I thought someone else had got it.

> *GRACE stands in front of the tv, holding up the dress and styling. Feeling pretty.*

GRACE: TV works pretty good as a mirror.

SNAKE: It looks great! I just wanted to thank you, for you know, for inviting me.

GRACE: And I want to thank you for accepting our invitation.
> *(Rest.)*

It'll work out. You'll see.

SNAKE: Let's see you in it. Try it on.

GRACE: I can't keep it.

SNAKE: Sure you can.

GRACE: No. Vet will—I can't keep it.
> *(Rest.)*

I'll put this on and Vet will see me in it. Then he'll get to thinking. He's always thinking I'm running around on him. Although I never did. But he's always thinking I did, or I do, or I will. But I never did.

> *She lays the dress aside, then starts putting away her Book and notes.*

SNAKE: You'll finish your book some day.

GRACE: Maybe.

SNAKE: You'll be on all the talk shows with it. They'll interview you in lots of magazines. And your Book, your Book, it'll be translated into all the languages.

GRACE: Maybe.

> *She continues stowing her Book and notes.*

GRACE: What's yours called? Your book?

SNAKE: *The Book of Snake.*

GRACE: You might want to call it *The Book of Buddy.*

SNAKE: It's *The Book of Snake.*

GRACE: Well. I'm proud of you.

SNAKE: Thanks.

SNAKE
GRACE
> (Rest.)

> *She finishes hiding her Book and notes. She holds the red dress, loving everything about it. Almost everything.*

GRACE: You'll return it?

SNAKE: I'll stow it away then return it tomorrow.

GRACE: OK.
> (Rest.)
I gotta get ready.

> *GRACE goes into the bathroom to take a shower.*
> *SNAKE turns up the radio, gets another beer, drinking it down.*
> *He takes the red dress. He looks toward his footlocker, then decides on a better hiding place. He tucks it underneath the floor with GRACE's Book, then replaces the floor and the rug.*
> *Sounds of GRACE in the shower.*
> *He takes up his phone, watching himself on playback.*

SNAKE *(On playback.)* "When we strike against The Man, striking him at his Ceremony, we will be careful, we will be smart. And after we've struck him, and after we've wiped him out, we will escape. We will move on. To the next target. He's just the first of many."

From the shower:

GRACE: Once Vet gets his award, he'll feel like he's really accomplished something. He'll be more into you working with him, I'm telling you.

SNAKE: And I'm telling you I don't want to work with him.

GRACE: Sure you do.

SNAKE: Sure I don't.

GRACE: After the Ceremony it's all going to be better. I promise. You'll see.

> *She comes out of the bedroom, wearing a bathrobe and slip, toweling her hair.*

SNAKE: Don't go.

GRACE: I'm going.
> *(Rest.)*
What's your book about?

SNAKE: Secret.

GRACE: Tell me.

SNAKE: Take a look.

> *SNAKE rewinds his video, finding a spot to show.*

SNAKE *(On playback.)* "The Man likes keeping Us down. The Man has dug a hole for you, a hole in your yard with your name on it, and it's up to you to do something about that. Take some kind of action."

> *He stops the video.*

GRACE: What kind of action?

SNAKE: Something big.

GRACE: Like what?

SNAKE: It's a secret. I've got it all figured out. He's got it coming to him. Strike One, Strike Two, Strike Three. 3-2-1—You should stay home.

GRACE: What are you going to do? Tell me.

SNAKE
SNAKE

GRACE: Tell me.

> *The sound of VET's truck in the driveway.*
> *SNAKE gets another beer, opening it, drinking.*

GRACE: Buddy.

SNAKE: I'm Snake.

> *VET comes in. He surveys the situation: empty beer cans scattered*
> *around, the radio music blaring, SNAKE drinking a beer, and GRACE,*
> *wearing a bathrobe and slip, her wet hair in a towel.*

VET
GRACE
SNAKE

GRACE: You're home. I'm almost ready. We were just celebrating.

SNAKE: We were celebrating you.

VET: Is that what you're wearing?

GRACE: Of course not. I'll get dressed.

VET: Not yet. Let's celebrate.

> *He gets a beer. Opens it. Drinks. GRACE gets a beer.*

SNAKE: To Pop.

GRACE: Cheers.

VET: You wearing that, kid?

GRACE: Maybe you could put on a clean shirt.

SNAKE: I've got a suit coat.

> *SNAKE goes to his footlocker, opening it. GRACE tries to see inside, if he's*
> *hidden her dress there. Can't see. He takes out a wrinkled suit jacket.*

GRACE: Vet, you called me twice at work. To make sure I remembered to
get off early. And I did.
> (Rest.)
That's seen better days. I'll press it for you.

VET: Let him do it.

> *SNAKE sets up the ironing board, readies the iron.*

GRACE: A car's coming to pick us up. That's wonderful. Vet, that's really great. They're sending a limousine.

VET: It'll just be a car.

GRACE: Still, we'll have a driver, right? That'll be something, right? And there's a dinner afterwards. It's going to be really nice.

SNAKE: What's on the menu?

VET: Steak. Potatoes.

SNAKE: Sounds great.

> *SNAKE's ironing his jacket. Doing a pretty good job.*

GRACE: You're not nervous. But I'd be nervous. Having to talk in front of all those people.

VET: You and him can follow behind in the truck. You'd like that better, right?

GRACE: We'd like to ride with you.

VET: You'll ride in the truck. With the kid. OK?

SNAKE: Truck sounds great.

> *VET puts his truck keys on the table.*

GRACE: I should get changed.

VET: Sit.

> *She sits.*
> *SNAKE continues to iron his suit coat.*
> *VET turns off the radio.*

VET

VET

GRACE

SNAKE

VET

VET

> *The sound of SNAKE working the iron. Otherwise pretty quiet.*

VET

GRACE

VET

VET
SNAKE
GRACE
VET

VET: Look at him. Working the iron like his old man.

VET
GRACE
SNAKE
VET

VET
SNAKE
GRACE
VET

> *SNAKE finishes and unplugs the iron. VET sits.*

SNAKE
VET
SNAKE

> *SNAKE goes to the fridge, getting another beer. Opening it. Drinking.*

VET
SNAKE
VET

SNAKE: You should call for the time, Pop. Make sure we're on schedule.

> *VET, raging, grabs the house phone and throws it on the floor, breaking it.*

GRACE: Oh, the diner was crazy today. All those people in town for you. They had me running back and forth like a rat.

VET: And when you came home you had to unwind.

GRACE: We were celebrating you.

VET: Celebrating? Right.

SNAKE: It's your big day, Pop   GRACE: It's your big day, hon.
                                            We were celebrating.

VET: That's the problem with letting things slide, Grace. I give you an inch and you slide a mile.

> *VET goes to GRACE's hiding place, pulling away the rug.*
> *SNAKE starts toward him, then stops.*

VET: What? She's got something under here?

SNAKE: Who knows?

VET: It took me a whole year to find out, but it took you just a day.

> *VET removes the floorboards, taking out GRACE's Book.*
> *Then he finds the red dress. He takes it out, holding it up.*

GRACE: I bought it for you. So I could stand by your side and be your pretty wife.

VET: So put it on.

> *She takes the dress, heading toward the bedroom to change.*

VET: Stay. And put it on here.

SNAKE: Leave her lone, Pop.

VET: Put it on right here. Go on.

GRACE
SNAKE

> *SNAKE turns his back, kindly giving her privacy and wishing he were anywhere but here.*
> *GRACE puts on the dress as VET speaks.*

VET: I work the Border Patrol it's a serious thing it's a daily struggle against the elements mind-melting heat blue-balling cold sunlight that'll blind you and darkness that'll make you want to lose your mind so you struggle daily against the elements and against the elements of your own nature your nature and mine that's what I'm talking about I am talking about Us and Them I am talking about keeping the bad ones in line because it all comes down to Us and Them you know what I'm talking about Us and Them it's very clear it's very cut and dry it's very simple this over here is ours and that over there is theirs over here I am an Us and over here they are a Them but if we cross over to their side suddenly we become a Them and they become an Us "why'd you have to come here" I'd ask them I'm here because I live here not like you the

Fence it makes everything so clear and if I had my way if I had my way hell we'd have more of them we'd have a Fence in every city in every town in every house because it makes things clear it tells me what I am and what I'm standing for my way of life my own existence and yours too because one slip could cause a downfall a downfall for all of us on the job and at home too you are who you are because I am who I am it's not that complicated to understand.

    (Rest.)

That's my speech.

    GRACE now wears the red dress.

GRACE: That's a nice speech, Vet. Do I look all right?

    VET examines her Book.

GRACE: There's nothing bad in there. Nothing bad about you or anybody. Let me keep it, Vet.

SNAKE: Leave her lone, Pop.

VET: You two were intimate. I can tell.

SNAKE: Leave her lone, Pop.

GRACE: We— Don't be silly, Vet. Don't be. Don't be—

    VET starts ripping up her Book. GRACE runs at him, and he shoves her away.

SNAKE: Leave her lone.

    SNAKE watching, like a child would watch.

SNAKE: Leave her lone, Pop.

    VET dismembers her Book.

GRACE: No! You keep me in a cage. Like I'm a dog. Or worse.

SNAKE: Leave her lone. Leave her lone. Leave her lone, Pop.

    She takes another run at VET, again he shoves her away.

GRACE: You don't let me do anything. You don't let me have anything. You don't let me be anything. Except what you want. Which is nothing. You want me to be just nothing. You dig a hole in the yard for me? For what? I never did anything bad.

Another run at VET, again he shoves her.

SNAKE: Leave her lone, Pop. Please leave her lone.

GRACE: I'm good but you treat me like I'm bad. And if I ever acted bad,
    it'd be cause you drove me to it. Oh! That's what you do. You drive
    everyone to bad. Look at me. Look at Buddy. You drove him to bad just
    like you're driving me.

VET continues ripping up her Book.

VET: Did I drive you to bad?

SNAKE: Maybe.

VET: How so?

GRACE: Because of what you did to him. Something unspeakable.

VET: Something unspeakable.

GRACE: Yes.

VET: Did I ever do anything "unspeakable" to you, Son?

SNAKE

SNAKE

SNAKE

> *The Injustice, by its very nature, has moved just beyond the reach of words.
> And so SNAKE tries to speak but does not. Cannot.*

VET: See, Grace, I never did anything "unspeakable" to him.

> *VET gathers the ripped pages, plops them in a bucket. He takes some
> lighter fluid and douses them with it.*

GRACE: No, Vet, please. Lemmie keep it.

> *GRACE takes another run at him, again he shoves her.*
> *He lights a match. The pages burn.*

SNAKE: I'm gonna wipe you out.

> *SNAKE runs at VET. VET takes up the iron, raising it toward SNAKE.*
> *GRACE intercedes.*

GRACE

VET

    (Rest.)

GRACE: Fuck you.

    With one swift stroke VET hits GRACE with the iron. She falls down
    dead.
    SNAKE goes to GRACE, stops before reaching her.
    VET douses the pages with water, stopping the fire and clearing away
    the smoke.

SNAKE: She's dead.

VET: She's not your mother.

SNAKE: I know.

    VET wipes off the iron. Regards GRACE's body.

VET: Help me.

    (Rest.)

  Help me.

    The two men carry/drag GRACE outside through the backdoor. SNAKE
    returns alone. He cries.
    Tears for himself, and for the whole world.

SNAKE

SNAKE

    As VET comes back inside, SNAKE pulls himself together.
    VET cleans himself up, quickly changing into his dress uniform,
    complete with gold braid. Holding his hat.
    SNAKE watches him.

VET

SNAKE

VET

SNAKE

VET: She provoked me. It's her fault. I shouldn't of done it, but it's done.
  It's in the past. And whatever's between us, father and son, we'll work
  it out, starting right now. We'll work it out together. You're in this as
  much as me. You're the one who's got the blemishes on his record.

You're the one they'll go after. But not to worry. I'll fix things so neither of us gets the blame.

VET's car for the Ceremony arrives. We hear it idling outside.

VET

(Rest.)

We're so much alike.

VET's finished dressing. Resplendent in his uniform. Ready to go.

SNAKE: I'm nothing like you.

VET: Then why'd you have to come here? Huh? I moved out here to get a fresh start. And me and Grace, we were doing all right. We were doing great. I had it organized. And it was working great. And then you come visiting our home and you act like I never did anything good for you. Like I never gave you anything worth having. I gave you your life.

SNAKE: My life.

VET: Yeah. That's something, right?

VET's car sounds its horn.

VET: You can wear your medal, it's OK. You can show it off. You'll be a big deal, OK?

SNAKE: Yes, sir.

VET: I can count on you?

SNAKE: Yes, sir.

VET: Come ride with me.

SNAKE: I'll take the truck.

SNAKE turns on the TV. Sounds of the marching band and local news reports of the Ceremony.

SNAKE: There they are getting ready for your Ceremony.

VET: I'll see you there? Right?

SNAKE: You have my word. I'll be there.

VET goes.

SNAKE takes out his phone and props it up. Turns it on self-video mode.
He goes to his footlocker. He takes out an empty grenade-carrier vest
and puts it on. He removes the grenades from the footlocker, putting
them in the pockets of his vest. He puts his medal in his pocket too,
then turns the TV off. He speaks into his phone, finishing his book.

SNAKE: *The Book of Snake*, New Chapter: A Change in Plan. Because I am
The Man. I'm a part of him, anyway.

(Rest.)

He gave me my life. OK. And so I'll take it away. OK. I'll take away his
and I'll take away mine, his and mine both together. I'll take it all away.
And you'll watch this here when I'm gone, and then you'll know.

(Rest.)

[[When in the course of human events it becomes necessary OK for
a people OK to dissolve the bands which have connected them with
another OK—

(Rest.)

We hold these truths to be self-evident, that all men are created equal,
that they are endowed by their Creator with certain unalienable rights,
that among these are Life, Liberty and the Pursuit of Happiness. OK.
Whatever.

(Rest.)

Whenever or whatever form becomes destructive to these ends, it is the
right of the people to alter or abolish it.

(Rest.)

When a long train of abuses is designed to reduce us, it is our right, it is
our duty, to throw off such.

(Rest.)

He has refused to Assent to Laws

(Rest.)

He has protected himself from punishment for any Murders

(Rest.)

He has excited Domestic Insurrections amongst us

(Rest.)

Our repeated petitions have been answered only by repeated injury.
I therefore pledge my life, my fortune and my sacred honor.]]

The backdoor opens. After a moment, GRACE comes inside. Walking
slowly. Dirt spills off her. From her face and hands and hair. From the
creases of her dress and body. The dirt leaves a trail into the house. She

*stumbles, catches herself, runs her fingers through her hair, touches her
face, coughs, stops. SNAKE watches her.*

SNAKE: I thought you were—

GRACE: Dead. No.

> *She looks at her Book, its pages mostly all burned. At last she notices
> SNAKE. Dressed in his bombs.*

SNAKE
GRACE
SNAKE
GRACE

> *(Rest.)*

> *She brushes absently at her clothing.*
> *She coughs. More and more coughing for an uncomfortable amount
> of time. She gets water, douses her Book.*
> *SNAKE watches.*
> *She gathers up her Book, torn and burned.*

GRACE
GRACE
GRACE

GRACE
SNAKE
GRACE
SNAKE

SNAKE: I'm going to the Fence.

GRACE: Don't.

SNAKE: You can call for help if you want.

> *He moves toward the door.*
> *GRACE takes a page, reading from it.*

GRACE: "The Magic Castle ... After all those years ..."

> *He stops.*
> *Another page, another fragment.*

GRACE: "One of my hopes involves … I work … I've put my name on it … it's mine …"

Another page, another fragment.

GRACE: "… made in India or made in China or made …"

More pages, more fragments.

GRACE: "Today I'm feeling like … Gold St—"
    (Rest.)
"The House of Wisdom …"
    (Rest.)
"Javier … Japanese."

More pages, more fragments.

GRACE: "Charlotte's daughter Charlotte … about as big as she is …"
    (Rest.)
"… The lake where we all jumped in …"

Another page. Another fragment.

GRACE: "And then that Trouble headed off …"
    (Rest.)
"He never told me … So I make it up."

Not reading now, just talking.

GRACE: Like, like, like, like maybe, one day, Will comes home. And the dog's there. Just sitting on the porch. After all those years.

SNAKE: Tell me that part again.

GRACE: What part.

SNAKE: The part you made up.

GRACE
SNAKE
GRACE

    She faces him and extends her hand.

    He takes a step toward her.

    Perhaps even another.

    Then he stops.

And they might just stay like that forever.

GRACE
SNAKE
GRACE

A bell, thumb-cymbal sounding, rings.

End of Play

THE EDGE OF OUR BODIES

Adam Rapp

Adam Rapp is an OBIE Award-winning playwright and director, as well as a novelist, filmmaker and musician. His play *The Edge Of Our Bodies* received its first major UK staging in September at the Gate Theatre. Adam's play *Red Light Winter*, which he also directed, received a Citation from the American Theatre Critics Association, a Lucille Lortel Nomination for Best New Play, two OBIE Awards, and was named a finalist for the 2006 Pulitzer Prize. He directed a sold-out run of the world premiere of his play, *The Metal Children*, at The Vineyard Theatre, starring Billy Crudup.

Adam's other plays include: *The Purple Lights Of Joppa Illinois*, *Finer Noble Gases*, *Through The Yellow Hour*, *The Hallway Trilogy*, *Nocturne*, *Ghosts In The Cottonwoods*, *Animals And Plants*, *Stone Cold Dead Serious*, *Faster*, *Gompers*, *Essential Self-Defense*, *American Slingo*, and *Kindness*.

Rapp currently serves as Executive Producer on a new HBO series for Martin Scorsese.

Introduction

I've known Adam Rapp forever, I'm not sure if that's actually true or not, but he's lodged himself into my consciousness in what feels like in my consciousness in it feels like it in the best of ways.

First it was the plays, then the fiction and then when I was working on the TV show *The L Word* and we needed more writers, I thought, lets get Adam, because what does a television show about lesbians need more than a deeply male writer? I loved being in the writers' room with him – a writers' room is like a cross between marathon group therapy and improvisation. Adam bravely embraced being the only guy in a room full of very intense women – I actually think he loved it.

What draws me to his work is his willingness to explore the contradiction and complexity of the human heart – the risks, the pain, the sometimes invisible lines between love-hate, compassion and violence.

In *The Edge of Our Bodies*, the story of sixteen year old Bernadette, an aspiring short story writer/boarding school run-away who hops a train to New York City, Rapp captures a young woman's simultaneous need to be seen/known and to be invisible/protected all at once. Rapp writes this story of a young woman struggling to find herself amid a world of messed up adults and missed connections with an old fashioned sense of style, tenderness and a deeply modern unsparing emotional truth. The result is what I call, "the good kind of melancholy", it reminds me of the best of J.D. Salinger or Richard Yates – excruciating in its accuracy. I admire Rapp for not just painting a pretty picture, but instead taking on social structures, failure, love and the twisted dynamics between men and women that make the DNA molecule look simple. And in this case, he does it through the eye of a fragile and heroic young woman – who knows too much and nothing at all – brilliantly rendering that complex late adolescent deeply female experience, imbued with judgment, romance, grief and hope and the barest hint of nostalgia that drifts over it all like the perfume of your favorite elementary school teacher. Rapp's talent is limitless – his output is astounding, playwright, novelist, movie director, professor. I consume everything he does holding my breath, always a little terrified and always filled with admiration.

AM Homes

Production history

World Premiere at Humana Festival of New American Plays on March 22, 2011 under the direction of Adam Rapp

Composers: Christian Frederickson & Ryan Rumery
Scenic Designer: Tom Tutino
Costume Designer: Kristopher Castle
Lighting Designer: Keith Parham
Properties Designer: Mark Walston
Production Stage Manager: CJ LaRoche
Dramaturg: Lila Neugebauer
Directing Assistant: John Rooney

THE EDGE OF OUR BODIES was developed for the Humana Festival of New American Plays by Actors Theatre of Louisville through a partnership with Louisiana State University

Presented by Actors Theatre of Louisville
Artistic Director, Marc Masterson; Managing Director, Jennifer Bielstein

Cast
BERNADETTE: Catherine Combs
MAN: Michael J. Burmester

Produced at the Gate Theatre, London, on September 29, 2014
under the direction of Christopher Haydon

Design: Lily Arnold
Lighting: Mark Howland
Sound Designer: George Dennis
Associate Director: Jennifer Tang
Stage Manager: Natasha Jenkins

Presented by the Gate Theatre, London
Artistic Director, Christopher Haydon; Executive Director, Clare Slater

Cast

BERNADETTE:	Shannon Tarbet
MAN:	Trevor Michael Georges

Characters

BERNADETTE

MAN

The Blackbox Theater at Whitney Academy, a prep school in the northeast. The set of Genet's The Maids. A small platform stage that appears to be floating in darkness. A rococo dressing table with small colorful containers of perfumes, a glass jar of mimosa, a nice comb, and hand mirror, a silver tea pot. A small, richly upholstered stool. Upstage of the stool and table, a bench containing a silver tea set, an old-fashioned, arched radio, a fancy telephone, a bouquet of gladioli. Downstage left, a pouf, a teacup and saucer centered on the pouf. Above the table, an ornate chandelier.

BERNADETTE, 16, sits on the upstage bench. She wears a tartan skirt, white shirt, a tie, white knee socks, proper shoes. She wears a gray wool trench coat. Her hair is tied back with ribbon. Her face looks freshly scrubbed, without makeup. She sits very still, clutching a black moleskin notebook.

The theater is empty.

After a long moment, she opens the notebook, begins reading.

I

The Train.

BERNADETTE: *(Reading from the notebook.)* I'm on the New Haven platform for the train to New York. There are three men who are taking turns staring at me. Though I repeatedly try and drift away from them we somehow enter the same car. They politely let me board first, as men who are pretending to be gentlemen will do. After I find a two-seater safely near the doors, whether they realize it or not, they wind up surrounding me. I feel like I've been thrown into the deep end of a public pool and they are treading water, waiting for me to resurface with tubes of sun block clenched between their teeth. Two of them wear dark business suits and I am paranoid that the one in front of me – the mono-browed Israeli – is going to whirl around and hit on me. Recently I have perfected the art of keeping to myself and I believe that I can make myself smaller; my face, my arms, yes even my breasts, though I can't afford to lose much in that area or I would be mistaken for a boy. At times I believe I can shrink down to the size of a rabbit.

When I'm feeling witchy, I even entertain the possibility of willing invisibility.

Only a few hours ago I was on the southbound Vermonter. I was supposed to board a connecting Amtrak train to Penn Station but I got nauseous and took too much time in the bathroom at New Haven and had to wait another twenty minutes for the Metro-North, which is always a sketchy prospect when it comes to a young woman traveling alone to New York City. It's been rumored that recently a man was murdered on the New Haven-bound train, just north of the Bridgeport stop.

It's late Friday afternoon and the light in my car is typically harsh and makes my three travel mates look green and middle-aged. I'm sure I don't look much better. I am desperately trying to seem older and with all the concealer covering my pimples I look more like a fledgling female news anchor than a junior running away from boarding school. The guy to my left – the one who isn't wearing a suit, but a large thick hooded sweatshirt with UCONN across the chest – has a face like lunch meat and he's staring out his window as if the years have suddenly tripled on him and he's just realized it. It's as if he's searching for a lost coat in the trees that are flying by. The third man is sitting a few seats behind me and within minutes he's fallen asleep on his shoulder. He's almost completely bald, a former redhead, and has a face like a fat sick baby. My roommate Briel always talks about how men just get sexier as they get older – she would know because she's having an affair with our field hockey coach, Mr. Katagas, whose dark, Mediterranean chest hair can always be seen creeping through the neckline of his V- neck T-shirts in simian tufts – but I'm at a loss, always searching for this mysterious older man magnetism on trains, at airport gates, and at the small café not far from campus where I eat two-dollar bowls of clam chowder and drink bad drip coffee. I mostly encounter men with jowly faces, potbellies, dyed, thinning hair, baggie, alcoholic eyes, arthritic limps, and an unfortunate phenomenon I've come to call middle-aged male asslessness.

It's early November and that troubling, pre-winter grayness that's capable of dulling even the most promising sunny morning has taken over. It's a week before Thanksgiving; that part of the late fall when the days seem to be cut in half and the nights are long and dank and fraught with the anticipation of a numbing winter. I'm on my way to New York to see Michael, who doesn't know I'm coming…or that I'm pregnant. Michael is nineteen and hasn't yet started at Brown because he's living with his dad, who is undergoing chemotherapy treatments for prostate cancer. When Michael and I kiss our teeth lightly clink together like champagne flutes and he never has bad breath and possesses a perfect, hairless chest. Michael can also quote Shakespeare and Pablo Neruda poems. In the past year he's turned me on to Truffaut films and Frederick Exley and The Beatles, though I resisted all of it at first, especially the Beatles, not wanting to get caught up in a band whose two remaining members are older than my grandfather. Michael works at a small Carroll Gardens coffee shop and I resist using my cell phone to text or call because I want the pleasant surprise to buffer any complications that might arise once the cat is out of the bag. We spoke last night and I wasn't able to tell him the news and I stayed up till dawn, tossing and turning and clawing at the backs of my hands.

We fell in love during the spring semester of his senior year while working on the third act of "Hamlet" for his senior thesis project. Of course, he played Hamlet and I was Ophelia and we went crazy for each other in about two days.

I spent most of this past summer in New York, taking an acting class at a private studio in the West Village. I've gotten pretty close with Michael's father, Wayne, a retired History Professor who taught at Brooklyn College. Their Carroll Gardens apartment smells like hemorrhoidal ointment and stale cigarettes and the recent disappearance of Michael's mother looms over everything like a dinner plate glued to the wall.

Michael came back to campus for homecoming weekend and that's when it happened. We don't like using condoms. Michael has somehow convinced himself that he's perfected a "natural contraceptive" technique, meaning that he pulls out at the last possible moment and comes on my breasts and stomach.

My sister Ellen had an abortion in the spring and never seemed to care much about it one way or the other. She lives with her boyfriend in Cambridge, Massachusetts, where she's in grad school at Harvard. I've thought of calling her but I'm afraid she'd tell our mother who has enough problems lately. She's convinced that my father is having an affair with an airline stewardess and spends most of her free time watching the Home Shopping Network and popping Xanax.

At this point the only person who knows is Briel, who found my over-the-counter test on the top of the toilet tank in our dorm room. Not a smart move on my part. I saw the little blue line and slid down the bathroom wall and sat there for what seemed like hours. I woke up in bed and Briel was standing over me, clutching the evidence. We hardly talked about it but I did manage to swear her to secrecy. For some reason I trust Briel. She's Jewish, after all, and the Jews seem to be the only trustworthy people at boarding school (my three fellow Unitarian students are perhaps the most conniving). Plus, I recently wrote an English paper for her comparing *The Bell Jar* to *Geek Love* of all things. Briel owes me.

Before New Haven, on the Vermonter train, there was a group of students from Loomis Chafee who were tripping on mushrooms. Three jock boys and a freshman girl with dyed black hair who kept climbing over the backs of seats and sitting in their laps. Things got strange when they all started making out with each other; even two of the jocks started going at it. At one point they offered me a stem but I said no thank you and opened the Edith Wharton novel that I'm supposed to be reading for my American Lit class. I'm not afraid of drugs. I've done my share of cocaine at Whitney – cocaine and Vivarin, mostly. Briel and I crush it up and snort it and play an old Talking Heads CD and take most of our clothes off and dance to "Once in A Lifetime." *Dun dun dun dun. Dun dun dun dun. Letting the days go by, let the water…* I have nothing against a good time; I'm just not into shrooming with the kind of strangers who travel with lacrosse sticks.

At the New Haven station, after getting sick and missing my train, I had about a twenty-minute wait for Metro-North. I got a coffee at the Dunkin Donuts and headed to the platform.

(Out.)
I should tell you that I've been drinking way too much coffee in recent weeks.

I should also tell you that I haven't slept in three days.

(Back to notebook.)
Outside my window the sky is like mop water and by the Milford stop it starts to rain. Even in the dim reflection I can see that my skin looks

terrible – I've been breaking out like crazy. I'm also starting to feel sick again. I've already thrown up twice today and the coffee isn't helping the nausea. The only relief is the trees, whose leaves are still colorful despite it being late fall. Growing up in northwest Connecticut, the site of the trees changing is the one thing I always look forward to.

At Stamford the train starts to fill up and an old man sits next to me. He wears soft, puffy clothes and a wool coat and carries a small suitcase. I pull out the Edith Wharton novel and start re-reading the section I couldn't get through on the Vermonter train.

The old man seems sad, lost even, and I worry that he's senile and has gotten on the wrong train. After a few minutes he catches my eye and points to my book. He asks if it's any good. He doesn't sound at all like I thought he might. I expected a thin, dry voice but he's loud and hard of hearing. I tell him parts of it *are* good. The truth is that the book is depressing and long and in my opinion Lily Bart is a fool. I have to admit that the man who loves her, Selden, is the first fictional character I have ever fantasized about and there are times when I wished Michael was more like him. Quieter. More polite. Less concerned with his perfect chest.

The old man says, "*The House of Mirth*. House of Happy, I guess."

He takes an apple out of his pocket, considers it and then puts it back. A few minutes later he tells me he's on his way to New York to visit his grandson who is going to meet him at Grand Central Station.

"We're gonna see the Knicks play Orlando," he says, "Amar'e Stoudemire."

His grandson's name is Paul and he's just moved to the city where he has a job on Wall Street.

The old man says, "Handsome kid. Movie star looks. Smarter than most…"

And then he asks me if I have a boyfriend.

I tell him I'm on my way to see him. He asks me his name and what he does and I tell him and that he's about to start at Brown, but has deferred a year.

He says, "Ivy Leaguer, huh?"

I nod.

The old man has a face like wet Kleenex, with little broken blood vessels on his nose.

He says, "Well, Michael's a lucky man. You're very pretty."

I tell him thanks and then he asks me how old I am. For some reason I tell him the truth.

"I'm sixteen," I say.

He says, "Do your parents know you're going into the city to meet a boy?"

"Of course," I lie.

Then he asks me what school I go to and I tell him Loomis Chaffee even though I'm at Whitney. I left Whitney without permission, so I am most likely returning to face probation or a suspension.

The old man says, "Sixteen's a great age. What do you want to be when you grow up?"

"I want to write short stories," I answer.

"What kind of stories?" he asks.

"The good kind," I say. "Sometimes I get in trouble for using too many similes."

He says, "You could write a story about a young girl who meets an old man on a train."

"I could," I say.

He says, "They could talk about things. Have a chat."

"What do you think they would talk about?" I ask.

"Oh, I don't know," he says. "The important stuff. Life. Football... Sandwiches. Just make sure it has a happy ending."

Then he asks me what my parents do and I tell him that my dad's a rocket scientist and my mom's a dwarf in the circus. This confuses him and I can't tell whether he's disappointed because he somehow knows that I've started lying or if he's working out the physics of a dwarf giving birth to a normal-sized girl.

He says, "She's little, huh?"

I nod.

Lying always makes me feel like my hair is falling out.

As far as I know my dad is still directing a bad TV show in Los Angeles and in addition to the Xanax my mom is mostly taking anti-depressants and trying to bait her South American massage therapist into having an affair with her.

Then the old man points to my raincoat and asks me if I'm going to be warm enough.

He says, "It's sposed to get pretty cold tonight. It might snow."

"Oh, good," I tell him. "I like the snow."

We're quiet for the rest of the trip. The three men who've been on the train since New Haven are all asleep now, their heads seemingly too heavy for their shoulders. They appear to have somehow aged in unison with our increased proximity to New York. By a Hundred and Twenty-fifth Street they are old withered men.

> *She turns the page. She sets the book on the bench, stands, starts to unbutton her trench coat when the radio snaps on. The chandelier lights goes out and she is in total darkness, save for the light coming through the radio. From the radio she hears her own voice. She quickly crosses to the radio, turns it off. The chandelier light snaps back on. She stares up at it, confused, looks to a vom.*

BERNADETTE: Hello?

> *No response.*

> *She eyes the chandelier suspiciously, looks up to the stage management booth, then carefully finishes removing her trench coat, places it on the bench, picks up her notebook, crosses stage right, staring up at the chandelier again, plants her feet, briefly looks at the radio, then begins from where she left off...*

II

Michael's House.

BERNADETTE: At Grand Central Station I say good-bye to Paul's grandfather and walk as fast as I can through the concourse. I'm feeling queasy again but I don't want to throw-up in a public bathroom or in my mouth for that matter, so I swallow hard and head for the subway.

I take the Four Train one stop uptown to Fifty-First Street and then transfer to the downtown F and arrive in Carroll Gardens at dusk. It seems like there are far fewer trees since the middle of August. Everything appears wan and withered. That mop water sky seems to have followed me from New Haven.

I walk over to Michael's coffee shop and nervously linger around the corner before going in. A guy with tattoos on his forearms and earrings the size of doorknobs tells me Michael isn't on the schedule and after buying a cappuccino I leave and spend several minutes entertaining the horrible possibility of him cheating on me; his beautiful chest poised over some Brooklyn girl, an Italian with olive skin and dark, smoldering eyes. I throw up most of my cappuccino on the street so I go to a deli and buy some gum and head over to Michael's dad's apartment on Third Place.

I am immediately buzzed in and Wayne, Michael's father, answers the door. Wayne is large and heavy like a football coach but much quieter and the cancer seems to have done more to his spirit than his body. He wears a light blue terrycloth robe, gray sweatpants, and a white T-shirt and slippers. His skin is waxy and he smells sickly sweet, of chemicals and perspiration.

He says Hello to me. His voice is dehydrated and one of his eyes seems like it's closing on its own.

He says, "What a surprise."

I ask him if Michael's around and he says he doesn't know where he is and asks me if I'd gone by the coffee shop. I tell him I just came from there and then he asks me to sit down, so we both sit at the kitchen table.

He pours me a ginger ale and sets the can next to my glass. He looks around confused for a moment and then tries to get up but something doesn't seem to be working – his knee or his hip maybe – so he remains seated.

I ask him if he's okay and he says, "I'm fine… Is it Friday?"

I tell him that it is and he points to a spool of coaxial cable in the corner. He says cable guy was there earlier and has to come back Monday to finish the job.

"Finally switching to broadband," he says. "After all these years."

He is holding the metal ice tray from which he has forgotten to remove ice cubes. I ask him if I can take that from him and he says, "Oh, sure. Ice."

As I'm placing ice cubes in my glass he says, "So it's Friday then."

"It is," I say. "Friday the twenty-first."

He says that this must mean Thanksgiving is right around the corner.

I tell him it's next Thursday and he asks me if I'm doing anything special.

I mention the usual dinner in Connecticut and that my sister and her boyfriend will be coming down from Cambridge and how we'll most likely wind up playing Scrabble and watching *Planes, Trains, and Automobiles* for the ninety-seventh time. And then my mom will pull out the old photo albums and start talking about how fat everyone's getting.

Then Wayne tells me I'm welcome to join him and Michael. He says that his brother Ed and his daughter Chrissy might be coming too.

He adds, "Someone's bound to cook something halfway decent. A celebratory fowl."

I say, "Thanks, Dr. Fitzgerald."

The truth is that Michael hasn't mentioned anything about Thanksgiving. I can feel my stomach again. Like I've swallowed potting soil.

I ask Wayne how he's feeling.

He says, "Oh, not so great. My hip's really bothering me. I have a cane but I keep losing it in the house."

He says that he's about had it with all the treatments. The headaches. The nausea. How everything tastes funny.

Then he says, "What about you, Bernie? How's school?"

I tell him school's good.

He says that Mike just told him that I might be doing a play.
I tell Wayne that I just auditioned for Genet's *The Maids* and that I'm waiting to hear.

He says, "Solange or Claire?"

"Claire," I say, and I do a little for him.

He laughs and says, "Susannah York played her in the film.
God was she beautiful. When they get it right it's a helluva play."

> *BERNADETTE touches the silver teapot on top of the dressing table, then sets it on the tea set on top of the bench.*

BERNADETTE: I tell him that I'm not getting my hopes up, that there are five girls vying for three parts.

He says, "Sixty percent. There are worse odds."

The kitchen light buzzes above us. I can see dead bugs in the fixture.

Wayne says, "Mike probably went into the city. You should give him a call."

I say, "I was sort of hoping to surprise him."

He says, "Well, surprises are always nice."

I tell Wayne how I'd just spoken to Michael the day before and how he'd told me he would be at work.

"They must have changed the schedule," Wayne offers.

I can hear the TV in the living room. It's CNN and someone is complaining about people who complain about the war.

Then Wayne asks me if I have any bags and I tell him I just have my purse.

He says, "What about a toothbrush? We got extras. Dozens of 'em. Never been taken out of the plastic. Mike's mother was always paranoid about losing the damn things. Her and her obsession with hygiene."

I tell him I have a toothbrush and then I ask him if he's heard from his wife.

"I'm afraid we haven't," he says.

I say, "I don't mean to pry, Dr. Fitzgerald."

He says, "You're not prying at all, Bernie. Hopefully Diana will show her face again at some point. Before the inevitable…"

The TV in the living room and the light buzzing above us seem to be enacting a conspiracy against peace of mind.

I ask Wayne when he'd last heard from his wife.

"Second week of September," he says. "Right smack dab in the middle of my last round of chemo."

I say, "She didn't leave a note?"

"No note," he says. "Not a single clue."

I say, "I'm so sorry, Dr. Fitzgerald."

He says, "Bernie, call me Wayne. My students don't even call me Dr. Fitzgerald."

"Wayne," I say.

After a pause during which I think I can feel my heart tightening, Wayne says, "Mike thinks she's in Central America. "

I ask him why she would go there and he says, "Who knows? Mike seems to believe she has this fascination with Costa Rica, though I've never heard a peep about it."

"That must be really hard," I hear myself say.

"Yeah, the not knowing," he replies.

Then I tell him I hope she comes back and he says Me too and then he looks at his hand…

(Looking at her hand.)
The front…the back. He looks at it for a long time.

"Is something wrong?" I ask.

He says, "Lately…"

"Lately what?" I say.

He says, "Lately I feel like I can get outside my body. Barely outside of it. Just beyond the edge of what we know. Where the skin... *contains us* I guess would be the best way to describe it. Just past that limit... I can get to that place and just sort of float there."

> *BERNADETTE breaks from looking at her hand. The lights shift and it is obvious that the audience has arrived. She speaks directly to us now, not needing the notebook.*

BERNADETTE: His face is suddenly gray and corpse-like. The last thing in the world I want is to cry in front of him. Their cat, Nelson, darts into the room and grazes my calf. He is black with white paws and more stuck up than most of the seniors at Whitney.

Wayne says, "Probably sounds like a bunch of cockamamie."

"Not at all," I say.

He says, "This is what happens when you spend too much time with yourself. You start getting all metaphysical and boring."

I tell him that it's not boring and then he asks me how my parents are.

He says, "Last time I saw your dad he was about to head back to L.A. He still working on that TV show?"

I tell him that he's directing half the season now and Wayne says, "Good for him. It's a good show."

And then he asks me if I watch it.

"No," I say, "I don't."

"Oh, you should watch it," he says. "It really is good."

And then he asks me how my mom is and I tell him she's fine and he asks me if she goes out to L.A. with my dad.

"She mostly stays at home," I tell him. "I think she and my dad hate each other."

He asks me why I would say that and I tell him because my Dad's fucking a stewardess.

I've never used this kind of language in front of Wayne. It just comes out of my mouth like water through your nose.

I say, "Her name is Candi. She has fake tits and lip implants and she's like six-two."

He tells me that he's sorry to hear about that and he hopes my parents will work things out.

I tell him that I doubt they will; that my dad hasn't been home in over a month.

Then Wayne tells me that these things happen; that the people we love the most are capable of unspeakable cruelties. He says it hurts more than anything else because of this profound love. He says that he still doesn't understand why his wife left; that they'd been married for twenty-three years.

I ask him if he thinks she's seeing someone else and then he looks at his hand again and asks if we can change the subject.

So we talk about my train ride: how I was on Amtrak but switched to Metro-North at New Haven. We talk about how uncomfortable the seats are and the strange smells.

Then he offers me something to eat. He says that there's sandwich meat in the fridge but I tell him that I haven't been feeling so well and pat my stomach.

He says, "There's plenty of Maalox on the premises."

I tell him I'm fine; that more than anything it's probably the result of a not-so-great week.

He asks me if it's anything I'd like to talk about and I tell him I'm late on an essay and I reference the Genet audition.

"Well, I'm sure everything will work out," he offers.

"I hope it does," I say.

He adds, "Stuff usually does when you're young…"

And then he suddenly goes blank. It's as if someone has flipped a switch. His body's machinery stalls for a moment. A terrible smell materializes. Something worse than human waste. I have to lean away and hold my breath. And then, just like that, he's back.

He says, "Well, I s'pose I should go rest. Feel free to stick around and wait for Mike if you'd like. You know you're always welcome here."

I tell him thanks and ask him if he needs anything and he gracefully declines my offer.

When he pushes away from the table, he almost falls. I move to help him but he holds up his hand to stop me. He then pushes off the table again and starts to exit toward his bedroom.

Just before he opens his door I call his name and ask him if Michael has said anything to him.

He says, "Said anything about what?"

"Our relationship," I say.

Wayne tells me that all Michael ever talks about is how madly in love he is. Bernie this, Bernie that. He says that if it'll put my mind at ease I can take comfort in the fact that I'm the subject of fervent hyperbole.

Bernie this, Bernie that.

Then I ask him if Mike has ever mentioned anyone else and Wayne tells me that as far as he can tell, the only competition I have for Mike's attention is Mike himself. He says that his son is a tenacious narcissist but that I probably already knew that. He says Mike takes after his mother in this regard.

And then he reaches into the pocket of his robe and produces a pocketknife.

He says, "Oh, by the way, you want this?"

I say, "Um. Sure."

And then he asks me if I have a penny.

I say, "I think I do. Why?"

He tells me that when someone gives you a knife, you're supposed to give them a penny in return. That it's good luck.

So I give him a penny and he gives me the pocketknife. It's much heavier than it looks. I slip it into my purse, and he says, "Those things always come in handy."

Then Wayne exits toward his bedroom, leaving the TV on in the living room.

After I put the ice tray back in the freezer I go into the living room and watch CNN. I think Wayne has gone to bed but he's stopped at the threshold of his room and he's just standing there, confused, his hand outstretched in front of him as if he's reaching toward a boyhood tree. He stays there for a long moment and then goes into his bedroom, leaving the door open.

On TV there is stuff about the war and stuff about the economy and stuff about women and men and how impossible everything is and I wind up falling asleep on the sofa.

I wake up a little after nine and turn the TV off.

I can hear Wayne snoring. It sounds like there's a stone lodged in his throat. I cross to his room and watch him sleep. His body reveals nothing more than it did when he was sitting with me in the kitchen. I figure that's what it's like with cancer: everything seems normal for a while and then there's one disastrous night when half of your mass digests itself or you wake up and all of your hair is lying next to you on your pillow. It's like a frost or a terrible lightning storm that destroys half a forest.

I close his door and go down the hall into Michael's room. He has recently bought a pair of circular mounts that are supposed to help you execute the perfect push-up, for the perfect chest. On his cluttered desk is a volume of plays by Edward Bond, half-opened to "Saved," about three dollars in loose change, and a fresh pack of Camel Lights. His bed is half-made and there are clothes strewn everywhere.

> *She sits at the dressing table. She opens a drawer, removes a silver cigarette case and a matching lighter.*

BERNADETTE: I remove a cigarette and light it with a Bic lighter that's sitting next to a take-away coffee cup. I remove my cell phone from my purse and dial Michael's number but hang up as soon as I hear his outgoing voicemail message.

His room smells like him – like his deodorant and his unwashed hair – and I'm almost sickened by its immediate effect on me. I open the window above his desk and the cold November air floods in. I look for any evidence of our relationship among his scattered things: a letter; a ticket stub; one of my hair elastics, but there is nothing.

I smoke in his chair and cry as quietly as I can while in the other room his father drifts somewhere outside the edge of his body.

> *She opens the cigarette case, removes a cigarette, lights it, smokes. After a moment, she stands, looks at the audience, and then slowly, teasingly, approaches the radio, turns it on. Some industrial punk music issues forth. She removes her school jacket, her tie, her hair ribbon, lets her hair down, rolls her sleeves up. The music gets louder and louder. She crosses to the pouf, grabs the teacup and saucer, ashes into it defiantly, turns, sets it on the dressing table, then sits on the corner of the dressing table, very much in control. The music ceases. She looks out at the audience, smiles, smokes, continues…*

III

Marc.

BERNADETTE: I leave Michael's father's house around ten o'clock and get back on the F Train and head into Manhattan. I get out at the West 4th stop and just walk for a while. The temperature has dropped considerably so I button my raincoat all the way to the top.

I call Michael again and get his voicemail. I leave a message asking him to please call me. I tell him I have something important to talk about. I don't tell him that I'm in New York.

I find a small dive bar on Greenwich Avenue where I figure I can get served and the bartender, an actress named Tanya, doesn't even card me. Tanya wears black jeans and no makeup. She has beautiful light green eyes and a smoker's voice and for a moment I wish I could have her life: a bartender-actress with pretty eyes who fears nothing.

The place is surprisingly empty for a Friday night. The jukebox plays Radiohead and Nina Simone and Otis Redding and a Hispanic bar back mouths the words to "Creep" while clearing booths.

Tanya tells me she likes my raincoat and asks if it's vintage. I tell her it is and she says something about how she can never find anything like it that fits her. I tell her about the vintage place I bought it from near Cape Cod and she asks me if that's where I'm from and I tell her that my family has a summer home there.

She eventually asks me what I'd like to drink and I order a Stella. She pours me a pint and lips a verse of some Van Morrison song in which he sounds like he's suffering on the toilet.

Part of me wishes I would see Michael pass by the window of the bar. I can feel myself willing his dark hair on the head of every young man who walks by. That summer, after the first time we made love, Michael laid his head on my stomach and I thought running my fingers through his thick dark hair represented the moment I had become a woman.

Tanya asks me if I'm new to the city and I tell her that I'm an NYU student. She asks me what I'm studying and I say Anthropology because I think it sounds good. She tells me she left SUNY Purchase after her sophomore year and that she came to the city to act and to sing in a chick band. To raise hell.

I ask her what her band is called and she says Tokyo Stunt Pussy. She says they mostly shout a lot and take their clothes off.

"Cool," I say. "That sounds cool."

Then Tanya pours herself a shot and says, "Here's to raising a little hell."

We clink glasses and drink and then Tanya moves away.

I am nursing my Stella when a man at the other end of the bar starts making eyes at me. He is barely handsome the way certain Southern U.S. Senators are barely alive.

He says, "I'm Marc."

I tell him my name is Diana and he comes and sits beside me. He tells me it's nice to meet me and that he's in town on business. Which probably means he has no business being in town.

Up close he's better looking, but just slightly, and I find that I like his teeth. They are chipped and one is a little discolored.

He buys me another Stella and himself a bourbon on the rocks. After Tanya slides us our drinks we talk about my adopted name.

He says, "Diana. Like the princess."

"Exactly," I reply.

He tells me his name is Marc with a C not with a K. I tell him that I'll keep this in mind. He tells me that that's good because people always get it wrong.

Then the music changes to Nina Simone and he asks me if I live in the city. I tell him I live in Brooklyn. He asks me what part and I tell him Carroll Gardens.

"That's nice," he says.

"It is," I say.

He says, "The fucking trees there."

And then he asks me if I'm originally from New York or if I'm a transplant. I tell him I'm from here and he says, "That's rare, you know. Practically everyone I meet is from somewhere else. Lots of Midwesterners. People from Kansas, Iowa, Ohio, Pennsylvania."

I tell him that Pennsylvania's not the Midwest.

He says, "Really? I thought it was."

Tanya comes over and tells him that I'm right; that she should know because she's from Pittsburgh.

Then she walks away and I ask him where he's from and he says New Jersey. The nice part of New Jersey, where they have steeplechases, shit like that.

I ask him what a steeplechase is and he tells me it's a horse race.

"They have to jump over hurdles," he says. "Hurdles and puddles."

Then he asks me if I like horses and I tell him I do.

He says, "Grace, power, speed. The ultimate animal."

After a silence Marc with a C looks at me and says, "Diana, can I tell you something?"

I say sure and he tells me that I'm the prettiest girl he's seen in a long time.

I say, "Oh, yeah? How long?"

He says, "Several months at least. Maybe even a year. And I travel."

His comment about traveling has not a shred of irony and I have an urge to tell him I have vaginal warts.

But instead I ask him if he ever travels to the Midwest.

He says, "Oh sure. The Midwest, the south, the west coast. Europe."

I say, "Europe. Wow."

Then he asks me what I do and Tanya swoops back in and tells him that I go to NYU and that I'm probably young enough to be his daughter.

To Tanya he says, "Hey, back off, Xena."

And then he asks me my major and I tell him Anthropology.

He says, "That's like human beings and shit."

"It is," I confirm for him.

He says, "And animals too, right?"

I say, "If you count humans as animals."

And he says, "Humans as animals? Definitely. I would definitely, definitely say that's true. I mean look at us. We're disgusting creatures. Animals all the way."

And then he sort of jiggles on his stool and says, "I'm thirty-four in case you were wondering."

I say, "Really?"

He says, "Yeah, why, you thought I was younger?"

I say, "Thirty-four's old, Marc."

He says, "*Old*. These days you're not old till your fifty. I'm still just a kid in his prime…"

He shifts a bit on his barstool again and says, "What does one do with a degree in anthropology, anyway?"

I say, "You learn how to read minds."

"Come on," he says.

I say, "No, you really can."

He says, "So you're saying you can read my mind?"

I say, "I can, yes."

He says, "What am I thinking, then -- don't answer that."

I ask him what he does and he tells me he's in Home Furnishings.

I say, "Is that like Interior Design?"

He says, "Sort of, yeah. Carpets. Countertops. Wall paper. All that pretty stuff that makes people feel better about their lives."

He watches me intensely for a moment. I feel like it's the first time someone's really looked at me in weeks.

He says, "So can I ask you a question, Diana?"

Before I can answer he asks me if I'm happy.

I say, "Happy meaning what?"

He says, "Happy meaning with your life."

I say, "Like on a scale from one to ten?" and he tells me it's a yes or no answer.

I say, "I'm happy," and he asks me if I'm sure about that.

"Yes," I say, "I'm sure."

He says, "Totally sure?"

I say, "Totally sure, yes."

He says, "Completely, like one hundred percent?"

I say, "I'm fucking happy, okay?"

And he says, "Then why are you crying?"

I feel my face and it's true. My cheeks are wet and I had no idea.

He says, "Rough day?"

I say, "Sort of," and he asks me if I want to tell him about it.

I tell him not especially and then he says, "That's some impressive thing you got going."

I say, "What thing?"

And he says, "Being pretty when you cry. That's not easy."

Then he says, "Come here," and I move to him and we hug.

Somehow the hug passes for the best thing that's happened to me in weeks. I collapse in his arms and it feels like all my bones have disappeared. His cologne smells peppery and somehow nauseatingly South American and I love it.

She moves off the dressing table, standing now.

BERNADETTE: We take a cab to the China Town Holiday Inn and Marc buys a scotch on the rocks from an Asian woman wearing a tuxedo and white gloves, tending a little bar near the front desk.

In the elevator we hardly speak and twenty minutes later we're in the room, simply staring at each other. He is lying in the queen-sized bed, on top of the covers, with his shirt off, still in his jeans, and I am sitting in a chair, still wearing my raincoat. He sips his scotch. We don't take our eyes off each other and I take strange comfort in this. I find his half-nudity somehow relaxing. Marc is at-once flabby and muscular, thick around the middle, doughy even, and I can see that he shaves part of his chest, which I imagine will leave red marks on my breasts.

From the bed he asks me if I'd like to try his scotch.

She crosses to the pouf, sits on it, her legs tucked under her knees.

BERNADETTE: I cross to him and take his glass and drink. Up close his cologne is overwhelming. I can almost feel it coating the back of my tongue. I tell him the scotch tastes like an old tweed coat. I tell him that my father drinks Dewars neat.

He says, "Dewars. That's like drinking Budweiser."

Then he stares at me and starts to sing a Bruce Springsteen song.

(Singing.)
Hey little girl is your daddy home? Did he go and leave you all alone? Um hm. I got a bad desire. Oh oh oh I'm on fire...

"Bruce," he says. "The Boss."

"The Boss," I say.

"He's the greatest," Marc with a C adds.

I hand the glass back to him and say, "So aren't you gonna try and fuck me?"

He says, "Diana, believe me, I would love to, but I can't."

I say, "Why not?"

He says, "Because of a slightly embarrassing situation that's not so easy to talk about."

I say, "What, you can't get it up?"

He tells me that that's far from the problem.

Then he drinks more scotch and tells me he has herpes.

I say, "Oh."

He tells me yeah, that it sucks pretty bad and that he takes medication for it, which makes everything basically normal, but that he's in the middle of an episode and he wouldn't want to pass it on.

I tell him that he's thoughtful.

He tells me he likes me.

"I like you," he says.

I ask him why he brought me to a hotel and he tells me because he enjoys my company.

"You're a beautiful girl, Diana. Plus you're nice. Most girls like you aren't nice."

Then I tell him my name's not Diana.

"It's not?" he says.

"No."

"Well, what is it?" he asks.

"Bernadette."

He says, "No shit? Bernadette? That's like French, right?"

"It is French, but I'm not French."

"What are you?" he asks.

"I'm just a little lost girl from the Northeast Seaboard," I reply.

Then he asks me if I would mind if he looked at me and *relieved* himself.

He says, "I'll totally understand if you say no."

"It's fine," I hear myself say.

He says, "Cool," and then he asks me if I wouldn't mind taking my shirt off.

So I remove my raincoat, and my sweater. I unbutton my blouse and undo my bra so I can show him my breasts.

He tells me I'm perfect. And then he reaches into his pants, pulls his cock out, and starts to masturbate. His penis is oddly dark. It looks poisonous and yet I find it comforting.

He tells me I have great tits. And that I'm so beautiful and that he wishes he could fuck me. He accidentally calls me Diana.

"It's Bernadette," I say.

He says, "I really wish I could fuck you, Bernadette."

I say, "You are fucking me, Marc."

He says, "Am I?"

I say, "You're fucking me so hard you're practically splitting me in half. Can't you feel it?"

He says, "Yes, yes, I can feel it."

I say, "And your cock is so big and hard."

He says, "I know. It's fucking huge, right?"

I say, "It is so huge. It's like a car."

He says, "It *is* like a car. It's like a Cadillac, right?"

I say, "It is a Cadillac."

He says, "It's the 2011 Escalade, right?"

I say, "It's the 2011 Escalade."

He says, "Black with smoked windows! Jesus, I'm gonna come!"

"Do it," I say. "Come *inside* me."

He tells me Holy shit, I'm coming.

He comes on his stomach in little grayish-white arcs. I can smell it from where I'm sitting. It smells gamey and chemical.

I hand him some tissues from the bedside stand. He wipes himself and hands them back. Like I'm a waitress. I cross to the bathroom and drop the tissues in the trash.

(Directly to someone in the audience.)
You hate me, don't you?

(Continuing on, after the question lingers a moment.)
When I come back out Marc has fallen asleep. His head has lolled back against the headboard, slightly tilted to the left. His mouth hangs open. It looks like he's been pulled from a car crash.

As I sit there watching him sleep I can feel myself outside of my own body, as if the thing that my skin was containing is now a slow, thick vapor drifting toward the small, inoperable window overlooking Lafayette Street. I'm not even aware of the sensation of breathing; I am simply vapor.

I am living someone else's life… the life of some stupid, desperate girl in a raincoat who likes to tease and lie to strangers.

I go into the bathroom and take a shower and wash my hair with the cheap shampoo sample and sit on the lid of the toilet and smoke another of Michael's cigarettes – the ones I had stolen from his bedroom. There's a silver handicap rail next to the sink and I briefly imagine myself with a broken leg, always lurching toward such things.

After I come out of the bathroom I take a twenty-dollar bill out of Marc's wallet. He does indeed have a New Jersey driver's license, but it says he is forty-four years old and that Marc with a C's name is actually Richard Romero. There's a small picture of a little girl, maybe six or seven, who I assume to be his daughter. She has his dark hair and big brown eyes. On the back of the photo it says "Angelface."

Before I leave I try to make myself cry again; I'm not sure why; maybe it's because I know Michael and I are over, or maybe it's because nothing really came of my little rendezvous with this strange man who is asleep in exactly the same position? Or maybe it's the simple fact that, at this late hour, my life isn't being witnessed by anyone; that this night hasn't ended in the disaster that part of me hoped it would.

It's the actress in me attempting to leave something behind; a few tears shed on the floor like rare coins to be found and cherished.

I even cross to the window and am nearly moved to feel something because of the sudden, surprising snow, but when I get right down to it there is nothing inside me so I let the drapes fall, pour the rest of his Scotch on the phone, and leave.

> *She rises off the pouf, paces, seething. She crosses to the desk and hurls all the objects off it. It makes a loud crash against the upstage wall.*
>
> *A MAINTENANCE MAN enters. The theater work lights snap on.*

MAN: You okay?

BERNADETTE: I'm fine.

MAN: You sure?

> *The MAINTENANCE MAN exits briefly, re-enters with a cart. From the cart he unloads a black, two-step stair unit. He sets it in front of the platform, on the upstage right side, uses it to join BERNADETTE on stage, where he begins to strike the set. He strikes the table, carefully steps down the stair unit, sets it on the cart, returns for the stool, strikes that as well, sets it on the cart, then returns again for the pouf. He lifts it, faces BERNADETTE.*

MAN: Is anybody else back there?

BERNADETTE: It's just me.

> *She rolls her sleeves down. He exits the stage with the pouf, sets it on the cart. He strikes the silver tea set, places it on the cart. He strikes the phone, starts to set it on the cart, stops.*

MAN: *(Picking up the receiver, playfully.)* Mission Control? Looks like we got a live one.

> *He hangs up the phone, sets it on the cart. He sets the radio on the cart. From the cart he produces a cardboard box, begins to pick the scattered objects up off the floor.*

BERNADETTE: Sorry.

MAN: Ain't no nothin', not at all. That's life, man.

> *He continues picking up the objects, whistling now. He picks up her notebook.*

BERNADETTE: That's mine.

He hands her the notebook.

MAN: *(Referring to the deck of the set, the chandelier, etc.)* All this is gonna be gone tomorrow.

He crosses to the cart, sets the box on it, starts to push it out of the theater, exits, returns moments later with a ghost light, sets it at the corner of the stage, unfurls the power cord, plugs it into the wall. The light is illuminated.

MAN: I gotta lock up soon.

She nods. He exits. Moments later, the work lights snap off.

BERNADETTE is left in darkness, the ghost light the only source of light now. She crosses to the light, sits under it, opens her notebook, begins reading...

IV

Home.

BERNADETTE: *(Reading from notebook.)* I catch a cab to Grand Central Station and board last train to Connecticut. The snow seems to thicken with every stop and by Stamford it's nearly a blizzard. I don't have enough money to go further than New Haven but my mom drives the ninety minutes south and picks me up at the train station. We barely speak in the car. I ask her if Michael has called but he hasn't. She seems bothered by something and it's obvious that we are both content with silence.

When I get home I finally sleep – nearly all weekend – and hide my morning sickness from her with a tenacity that I've not since mustered. My father's on set in Los Angeles and won't be coming home, so that makes things a little easier.

On Sunday morning I take a long walk down the two-lane road that runs in front of our house, treading through several inches of fresh snow in a pair of old rain boots, hoping that the trees will somehow make me feel better, but their leaves are all but gone now and they seem arthritic and withered.

That night my mother and I eat dinner in front of the fireplace. She makes a roast chicken with broccoli and we drink red wine because my parents allow that. Although I feel nauseous I force myself to eat my entire plate so as not to warrant any suspicion. I hadn't noticed it in the car a few days before but my mother has just dyed her hair a strange fiery auburn and I keep thinking she's wearing a wig.

After her first glass of wine she tells me that Dean Fessenden had called to tell her that I cut my afternoon classes on Friday without a permission slip. She asks me if it's true and I say, "Yeah. You gonna ground me?"

She doesn't answer.

I hadn't realized it but my mother has put on a Carpenters record. She loves to listen to the Carpenters and feel sorry for herself. She can spend entire weekends listening to the Carpenters and painting her dreary watercolors.

A few minutes later I take my dishes to the sink and come back with another bottle of wine and start to uncork it.

My mom tells me that my father wants a divorce.

"He emailed me last night," she says.

I ask her if it's because of the stewardess. She says that he didn't mention her in the email but that's her guess. My mom says that she thinks he cast her on the TV show.

I say, "So she's an actress?"

My mom says, "She is now."

I ask my mom if she's going to fight him and she says, "Tooth and nail."

And then she says, "Whatever you do, Bernie, don't let your ass get bad. A good ass will add years to your marriage."

While I'm drying dishes the phone rings. It's Michael. His voice sounds small and far away. When he says my name I feel myself turn to powder. I have to grip the countertop to keep my balance.

(Looking up now.)
He tells me that his dad has just killed himself; that he came home and he was hanging from a hook in the ceiling in the living room where a

light fixture used to be. He says Wayne had reinforced the hook with Gorilla Glue. Michael can't stop crying. He tells me his father used extra coaxial cable that the cable company had left when they came to install their high-speed Internet. I ask if he wants me to come to Brooklyn and he says No. I ask if there's anything I can do and he says No again. I ask if he still loves me and he says he has to go; that there are all these people in his apartment – cops and EMT professionals and his Uncle Ed and that he'll call me later. I wait for his call all night but it never comes.

*

BERNADETTE: *(Reading from the notebook again.)* That Monday, my mother drives me back to school and I get off with a warning from Dean Fessenden, whose recent dramatic weight loss makes me think of Michael's father. He possesses a long, unfortunate horsy face but beautiful hazel eyes.

At the end of the meeting I ask him if he is okay. He tells me he's fine. I tell him he looks thin and he says something about his new diet; how's he's been eating mostly oatmeal and presses his own juices. He tells me he still eats the occasional steak and smiles on the word *steak* in a way that almost makes it seem as if his face will get stuck that way.

As I'm about to leave he asks me what I want to do with my life.

He says, "What are your plans, Bernie?"

"I want to write short stories," I tell him.

"You *want* to or you're *going* to?" he asks.

"I'm going to," I answer.

"It takes great discipline to be a writer," he adds. "*Self*-discipline."

*

BERNADETTE: *(Looking up from notebook.)* Two weeks later I get an abortion at a small Planned Parenthood in Bennington, Vermont. Briel drives me there in her day-student-boyfriend's SAAB and waits for me while I take the mifepristone pill, which is large and white and tastes like a warm bitter spoon.

After speaking with the doctors about what to expect and how to deal with what's to come, Briel and I go eat pancakes at a diner near the Bennington campus. She tells me she's thinking about going to school here. We talk about the Donna Tartt novel in which all those college kids kill two of their classmates. She asks me where I want to go and I tell her I haven't really thought about it much. I tell her that my mom wants me to go to Mount Holyoke. Briel says that it's full of lesbians. I tell her she's confusing it with Smith and she says, "No, it's totally Mount Holyoke too. It's like the Lesbian Olympics there."

I can feel a new distance between us. It's as if I've acquired a permanent fishhook in my lip and there are those with fishhooks and those without.

Then Briel tells me that it's really fucked up about Michael's dad. She says he must have been in so much pain.

I tell her that I think he was.

She says that Michael must be so sad and asks me if we're officially over.

Then I reach into my pocket and give her the pocketknife.

She says, "What's that?"

I say, "A pocketknife."

She says, "What are you doing with it?"

I say, "I'm giving it to you."

She says, "Oh. Why?"

I tell her it's a token of my thanks for driving me up here.

She tells me that it's really no problem.

"So I skipped a few classes," she adds. "You'd do it for me, right?

"Of course," I say.

She says, "That's what friends are for."

Then I ask her if she has a penny. She asks why and I tell her that when someone gives you a knife you have to give them a penny; that it's good luck.

She asks me where I'd learned that and I tell her I'd read about it.

"Who gets the luck?" she asks.

I say, "We both do."

Briel reaches into her pocket and produces some change. She tells me all she has is a nickel. I tell her that that'll do and she pushes the nickel toward me and takes the pocketknife.

We drive back to Whitney in relative silence. The radio plays classic rock and Briel sings along to a rockblock of the Rolling Stones. At school I wind up getting cast as Claire in Jean Genet's *The Maids*, which is directed by my Drama Teacher, Mr. Chubb, who as a person is droopy and listless but occasionally seems delighted with my capacity to role-play with Solange at murdering Madame.

One day after rehearsal he tells me that I'm a natural talent and that I should seriously consider pursuing acting.

> *She rises, closing the notebook. She crosses to the other side of the stage. From here on, the notebook remains closed.*

*

BERNADETTE: After I take the follow-up pill, I wait for the miscarriage the way you wait for a mysterious package to arrive from the post office. When it finally happens it is more painful than the Planned Parenthood doctor said it would be and I have to leave a Great Books class feigning low blood sugar at the infirmary, where they give me vanilla wafers and let me take a nap.

I manage to get through the next few days by sheer will and as much pot as I can get my hands on.

A few weeks later *The Maids* is thought to be a great success by students and faculty alike.

> *BERNADETTE crosses to the upstage bench, opens it, removes a gold box, she sits, opens the box, removes emerald earrings, a hairclip, puts on the earrings, puts her hair up. She then sheds her skirt and white shirt, removing her shoes, her socks, only in Madame's white charmeuse slip now. She rises, crosses to the downstage corner. It is clear now that she is also wearing an emerald necklace.*

*

BERNADETTE: After the play opens, I try Michael every day for two weeks but he never calls back. With regard to his father dying I guess he's had a lot to deal with. Michael's way of breaking up with me was by becoming nothing, pollen, mist, perhaps something even finer.

It has been snowing a lot lately. The trees at Whitney are blanketed white and the occasional sound of a branch cracking can shatter even the most persistent campus silence.

Upstage of the platform, against the back wall of the theater, it starts to snow.

BERNADETTE: In my American Escapes class we read Jonathan Safran Foer's *Extremely Loud and Incredibly Close* and talk about how it relates to the endless war in the Middle East and all the problems in Egypt and our own small lives and I am mostly sad and bored.

> *She turns and faces the snow, crosses to her trench coat, puts it on over her slip, turns and faces the audience.*

BERNADETTE: Long walks through the snow at dusk are the one thing I look forward to.

The snow and the trees and the slow, unbearable silence of winter.

> *She exits the stage with her notebook, faces the back wall, crosses to the door in the wall of the theater, opens it, passes into the snow.*